EARLY LEA... RRICULUM

Ages 3-5 — Section 1

COLORS & SHAPES - PRESCHOOL

Preschoolers learn to recognize colors and identify shapes through these simple, fun and easy-to-understand lessons.

Ages 3-5 — Section 2

ALPHABET & LETTERS - PRESCHOOL

Preschoolers learn to recognize both capital and small letters and begin to print the alphabet through these simple, fun and easy-to-understand lessons.

Ages 3-5 — Section 3

NUMBERS & COUNTING - PRESCHOOL

Preschoolers learn to recognize numbers from one to ten, to understand counting concepts such as ... groups of objects, and how to order numbers ... essons.

Ages 5-6 — Section 4

BASIC S...

123-page basic ... field of education to teach the same ... ssons are carefully structured to tec... d citizenship.

Ages 6-7 — Section 5

BASIC S...

224-page basic ... field of education to teach the same ... carefully structured to teach basic skills ... comprehension, thinking skills, citizenship ...

Name: _____

Table of Contents

Name: _____

Bibliography

Enjoy these books about colors and shapes:

Color Zoo by Lois Ehlert (Lippincott, 1989).

White is the Moon by Valerie Greeley (Macmillan, 1990).

Of Colors and Things by Tana Hoban (Greenwillow, 1989).

Think About Shape by Henry Pluckrose (Franklin Watts, 1986).

Color by Christina Rossetti (HarperCollins, 1992).

Going Up! by Peter Sis (Greenwillow, 1989).

Seven Blind Mice by Ed Young (Philomel, 1992).

Colors (*Mouse Book*) by Monique Felix (Creative Education, 1992).

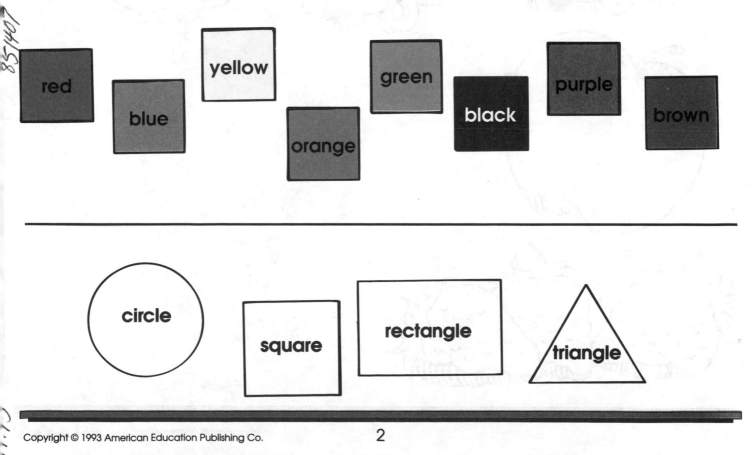

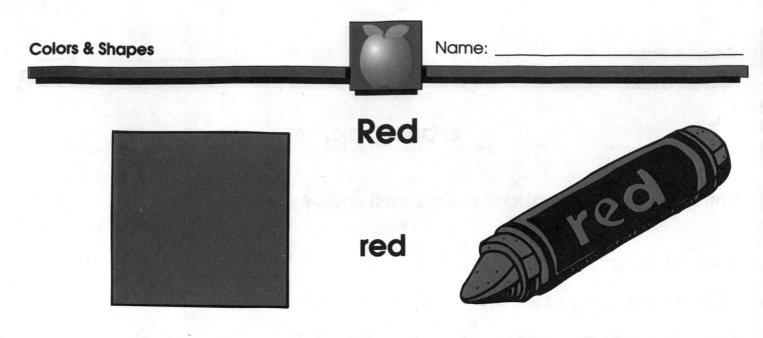

Name: _____

Red

red

Directions: Color each picture **red**.
Then draw a picture of something **red**.

Name: _____

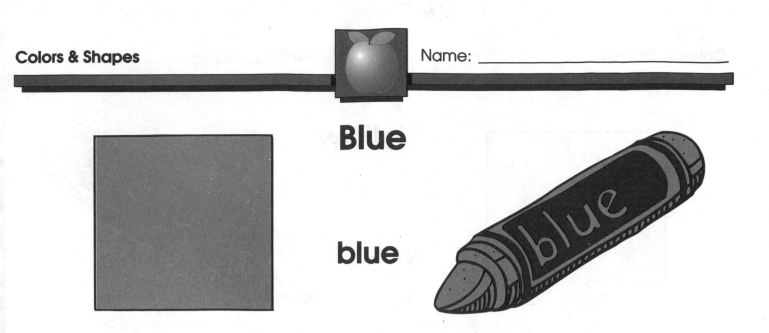

Blue

blue

Directions: Draw a circle around the **blue** picture in each row.

4

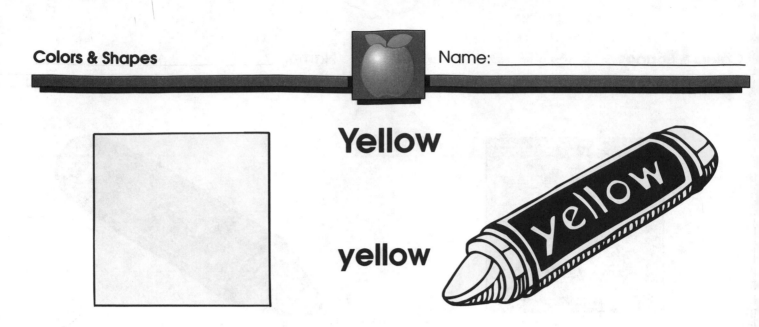

Name: _____

Yellow

yellow

Directions: Color each picture **yellow**.
Then draw a picture of something **yellow**.

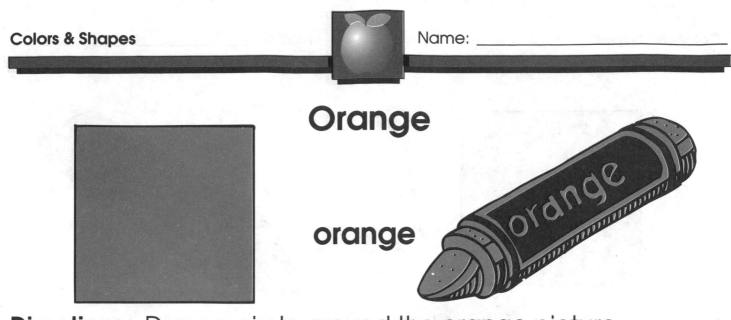

Name: _____

Orange

orange

Directions: Draw a circle around the **orange** picture in each row.

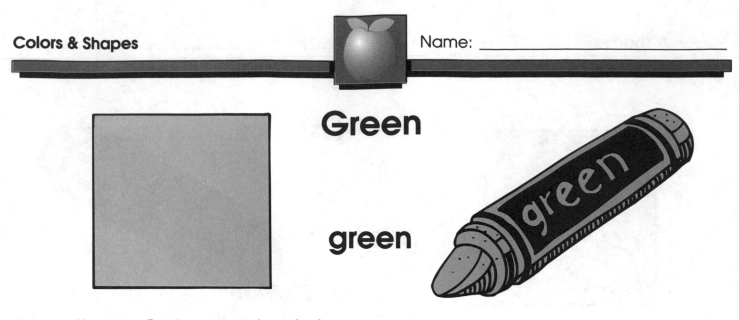

Name: _____

Green

green

Directions: Color each picture **green**.
Then draw a picture of something **green**.

Name: _____

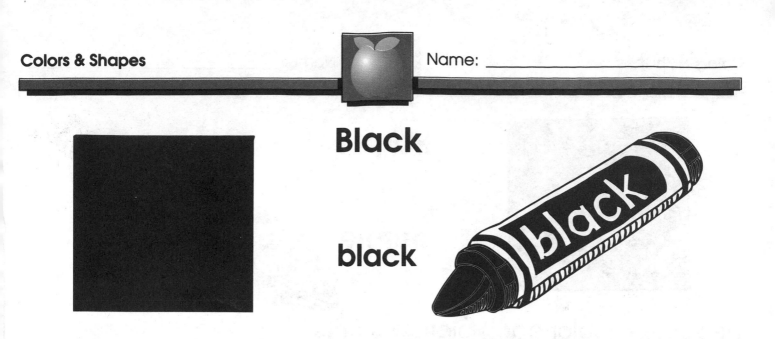

Black

black

Directions: Draw a circle around the **black** picture in each row.

Name: _____

Purple

purple

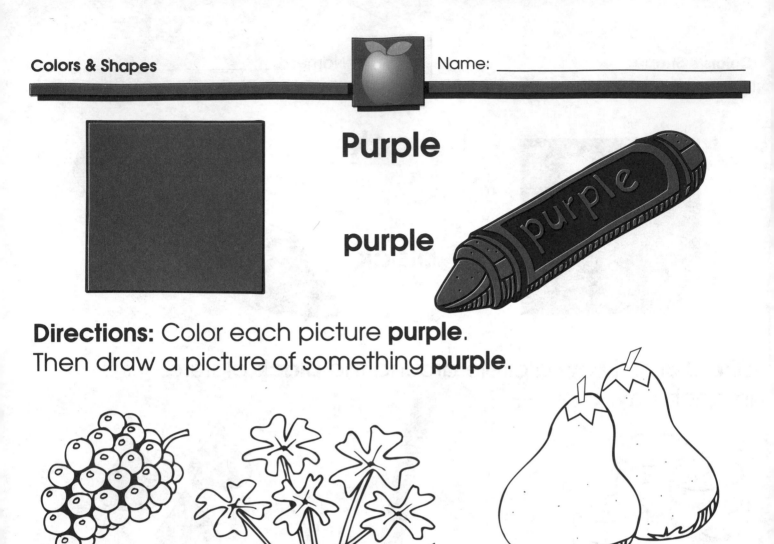

Directions: Color each picture **purple**.
Then draw a picture of something **purple**.

Name: _____

Brown

brown

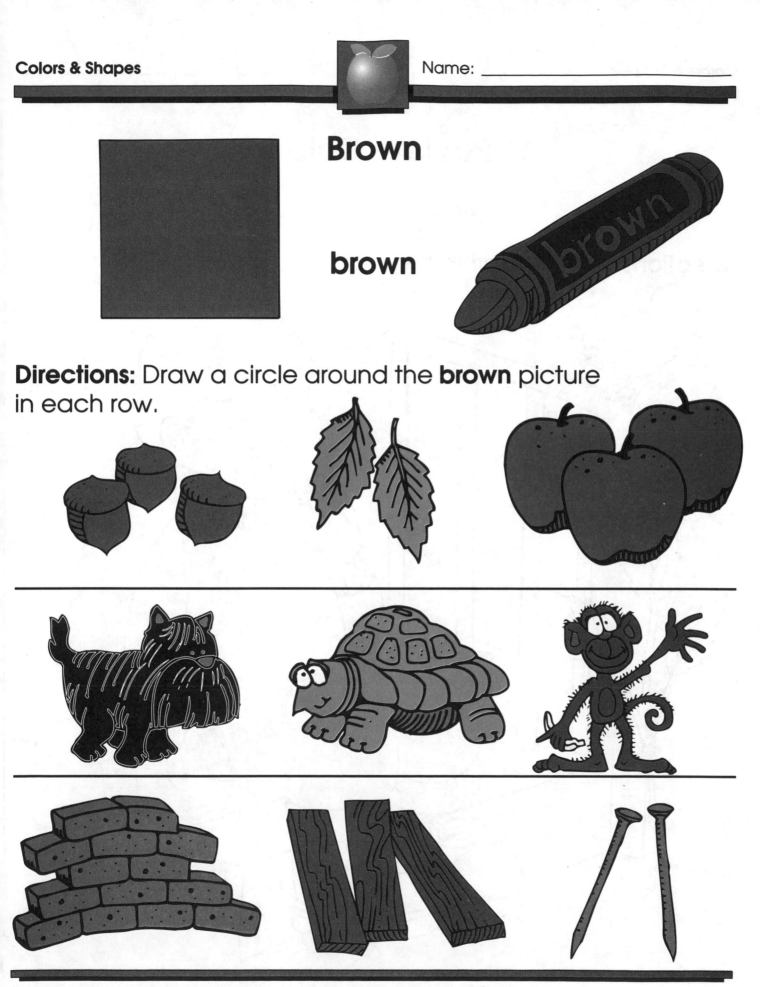

Directions: Draw a circle around the **brown** picture in each row.

Review Colors

Directions: Finish coloring the picture.

Name: _____

Review Colors

Directions: Color each picture the same color as the crayon above it.

ANSWER KEY

This Answer Key has been designed so that it may be easily removed if you so desire.

PRESCHOOL COLORS & SHAPES

Pull The Center Section From The Workbook

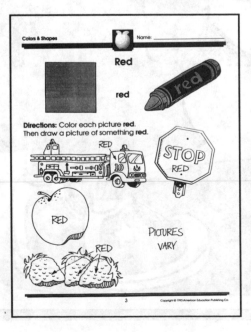

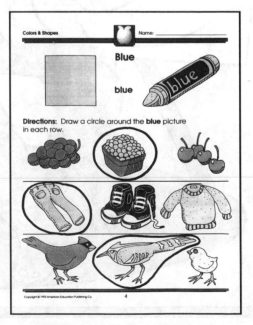

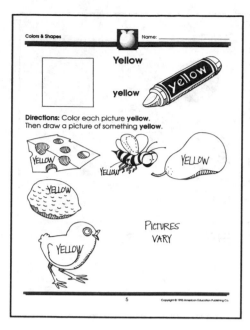

Yellow

yellow

Directions: Color each picture **yellow**.
Then draw a picture of something **yellow**.

YELLOW

YELLOW

YELLOW

YELLOW

YELLOW

PICTURES VARY

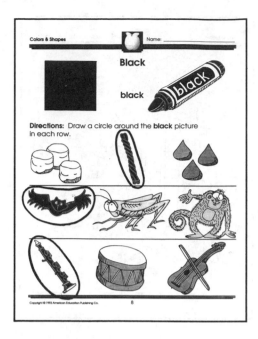

Black

black

Directions: Draw a circle around the **black** picture in each row.

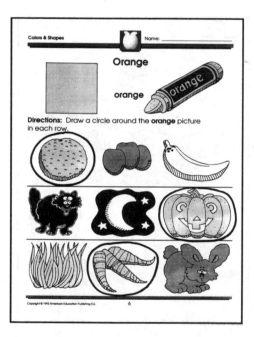

Orange

orange

Directions: Draw a circle around the **orange** picture in each row.

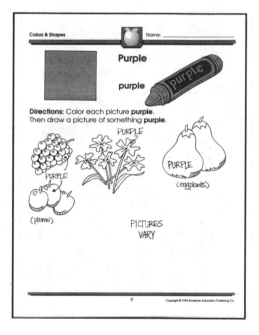

Purple

purple

Directions: Color each picture **purple**.
Then draw a picture of something **purple**.

PURPLE

PURPLE

PURPLE

(plums)

PURPLE

(eggplants)

PICTURES VARY

Green

green

Directions: Color each picture **green**.
Then draw a picture of something **green**.

GREEN

GREEN

PICTURES VARY

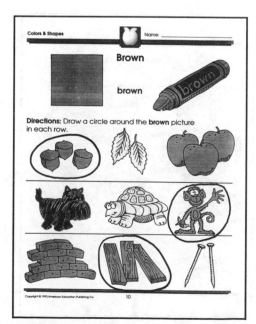

Brown

brown

Directions: Draw a circle around the **brown** picture in each row.

Name: _____

Review Colors

Directions: Finish coloring the picture.

GREEN

BROWN

RED

PICTURES VARY

BLUE

Name: _____

Circle

Directions: Trace the **circle**.

Directions: In each row, draw a line under the **circle**.

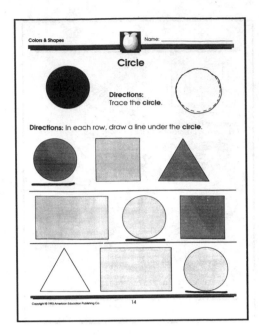

Name: _____

Review Colors

Directions: Color each picture the same color as the crayon above it.

YELLOW

BLACK

ORANGE

Name: _____

Circle

Directions: Put an **X** on the things that have the shape of a **circle**.

Name: _____

Review Colors

Directions: Color the fruits and vegetables.

YELLOW

ORANGE

PURPLE

GREEN

Name: _____

Rectangle

Directions: Trace each **rectangle**.

Directions: In each row, draw a line under the **rectangle**.

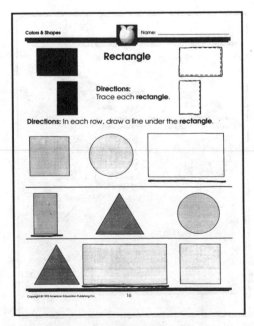

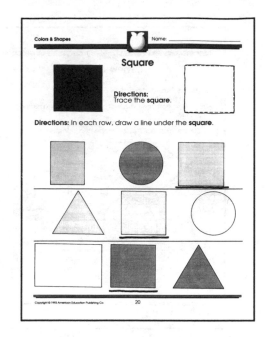

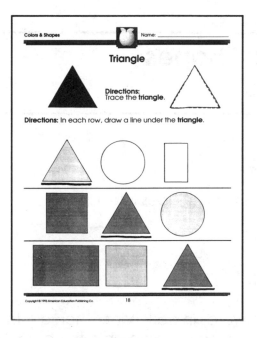

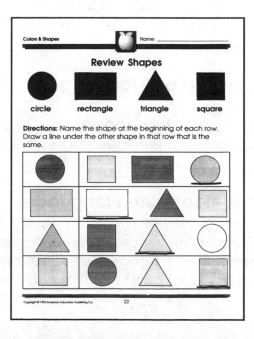

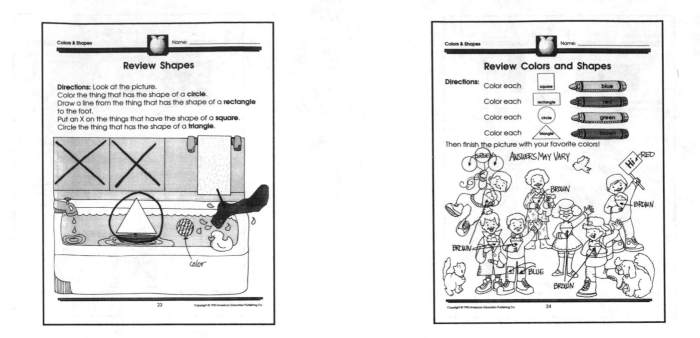

Preschool Colors and Shapes
SUGGESTIONS

Encourage enjoyment of reading.

Visit a library or bookstore to locate the books about colors and shapes listed in the bibliography on page 2. Enjoy the books together.

Develop concepts of how printed materials work.

Reuse workbook pages by asking children to point to the words in dark print. Then ask them to point to individual letters in the words. Some preschoolers may also be able to name the words and/or the letters they point out.

Develop oral language.

Reuse workbook pages 11, 12, 13, 15, 17, 19, 21, 23, and 24 by asking children to tell a story about what is happening in the picture. Ask them to predict what might happen next.

Develop written language.

On a chart, record some of the sentences children use in the stories about the pictures. Read the sentences aloud several times as you point to the words. Then ask children to read with you (choral reading) or after you (echo reading).

continued on next page...

SUGGESTIONS CONTINUED

Develop an awareness of classification.

Reuse workbook pages 4, 6, 8, and 10 by asking children to tell how the objects in each row are alike or go together. For example on page 6, the pictures in the first row are alike because oranges, plums, and bananas are fruits or things you eat, and in the last row the pictures go together because the bunny eats carrots and plays in the grass.

Review colors.

Reuse the bottom of workbook pages 14, 16, 18, and 20 by asking children to put an X on the two shapes that are the same color in each row. Then ask them to name the color of the shapes they put X's on.

Review colors and shapes.

Provide each child with a piece of paper on which you have written the word **red**. Ask children to use old catalogs and magazines to find pictures of red items. Invite them to use blunt scissors and paste to cut out and paste pictures of red items on both sides of their papers. Repeat this activity with the other color and shape words presented in this workbook. Compile their papers in color/shape workbooks of their own.

Develop an awareness of their environment.

Take children for a walk around the neighborhood. Ask them to name the colors and shapes they see along the way.

Reuse page 24 of this workbook and the neighborhood walk to lead children to conclude that people come in all colors and shapes.

Name: _____

Review Colors

Directions: Color the fruits and vegetables.

Name: _____

Circle

Directions:
Trace the **circle**.

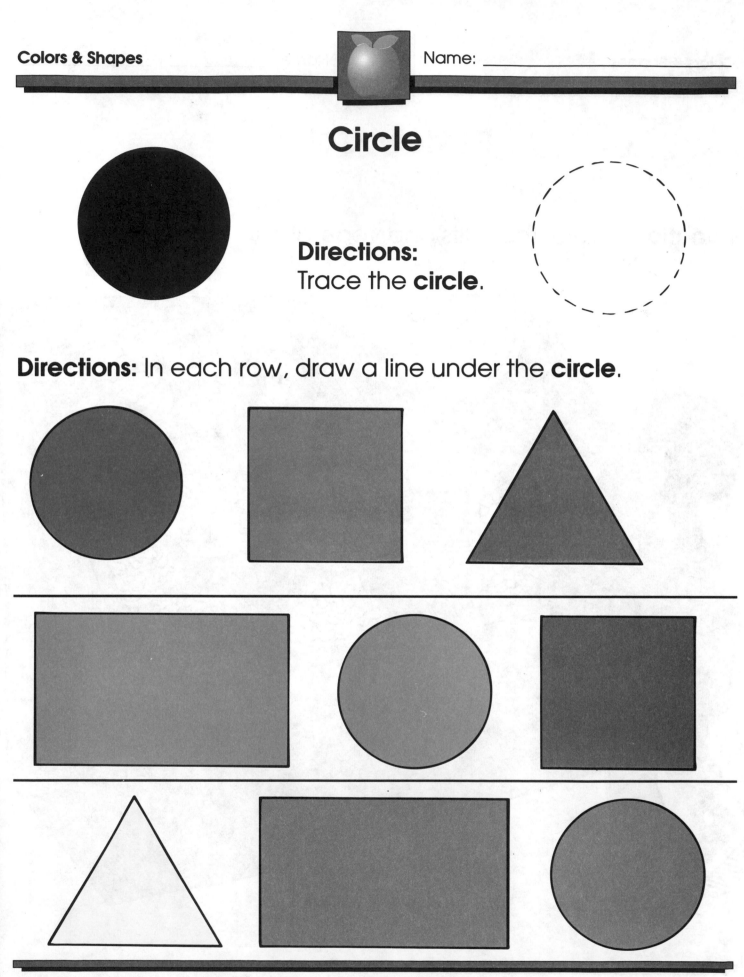

Directions: In each row, draw a line under the **circle**.

14

Name: _____

Circle

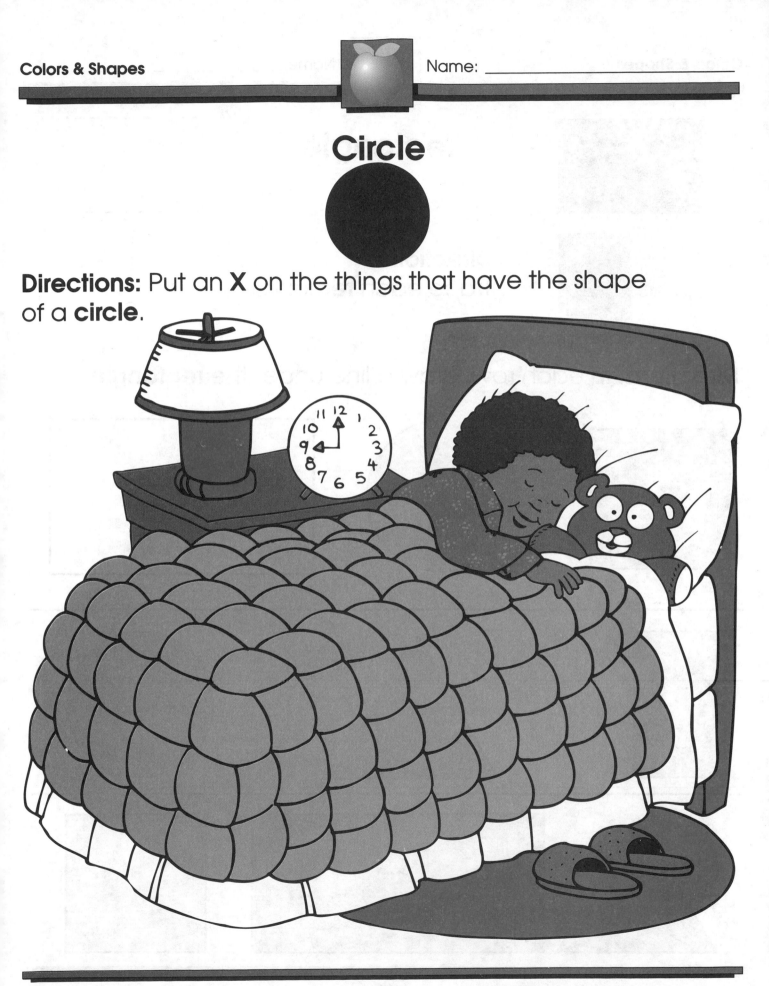

Directions: Put an **X** on the things that have the shape of a **circle**.

Name: _____

Rectangle

Directions:
Trace each **rectangle**.

Directions: In each row, draw a line under the **rectangle**.

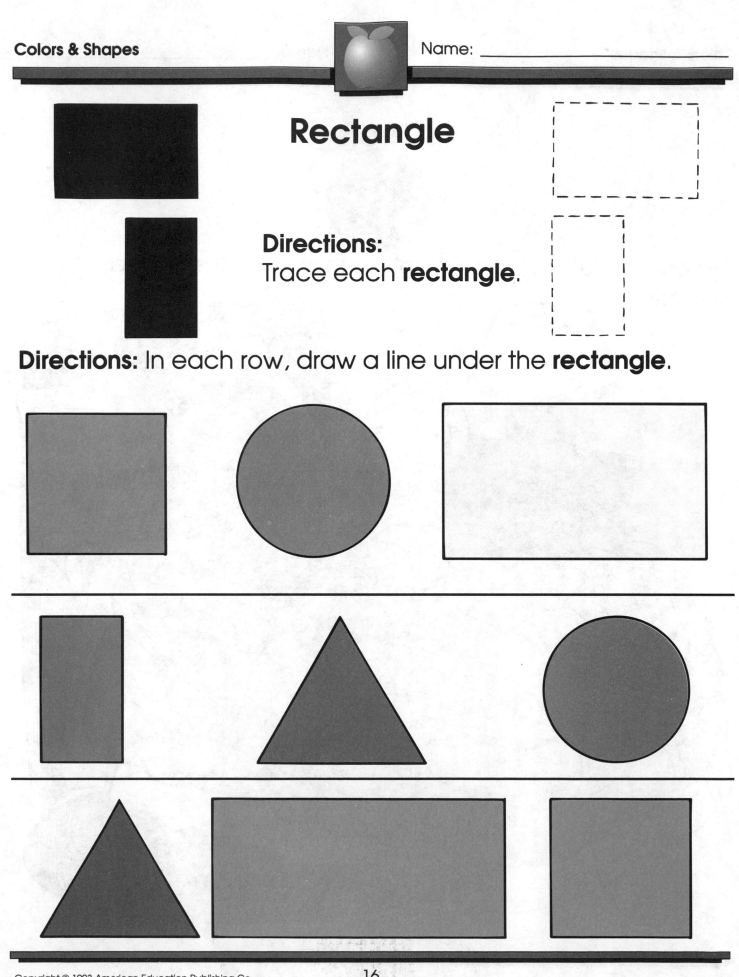

Name: _____

Rectangle

Directions: Put an **X** on the things that have the shape of a **rectangle**.

Name: _____

Triangle

Directions:
Trace the **triangle**.

Directions: In each row, draw a line under the **triangle**.

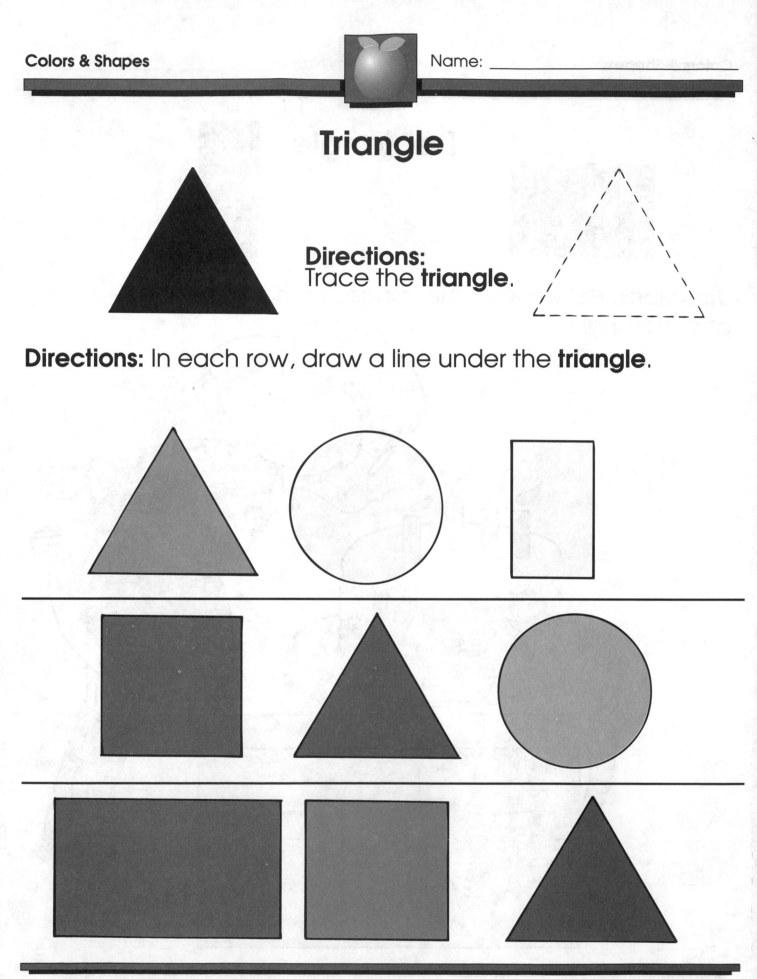

Name: _____

Triangle

Directions: Put an **X** on the things that have the shape of a **triangle**.

Name: _____

Square

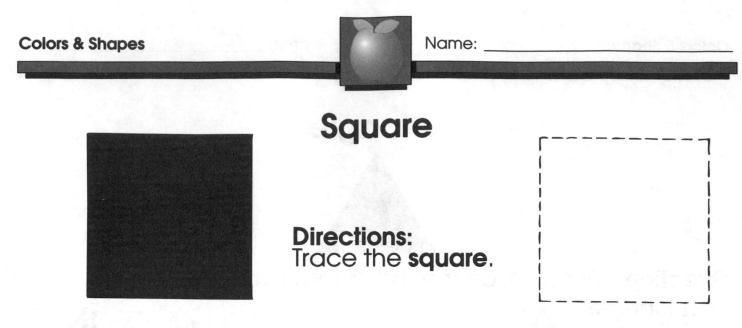

Directions:
Trace the **square**.

Directions: In each row, draw a line under the **square**.

Name: _____

Square

Directions: Put an **X** on the things that have the shape of a **square**.

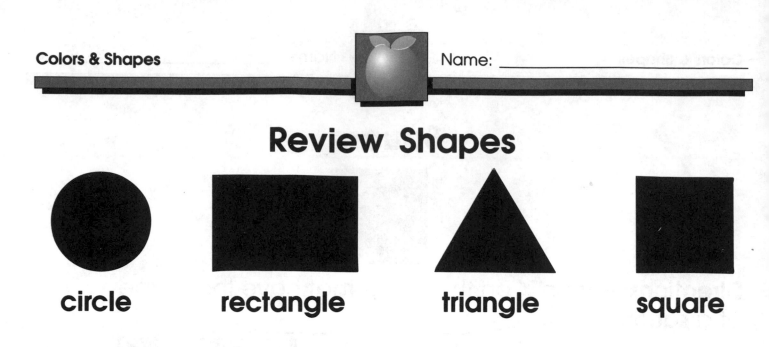

Name: _____

Review Shapes

circle   rectangle   triangle   square

Directions: Name the shape at the beginning of each row. Draw a line under the other shape in that row that is the same.

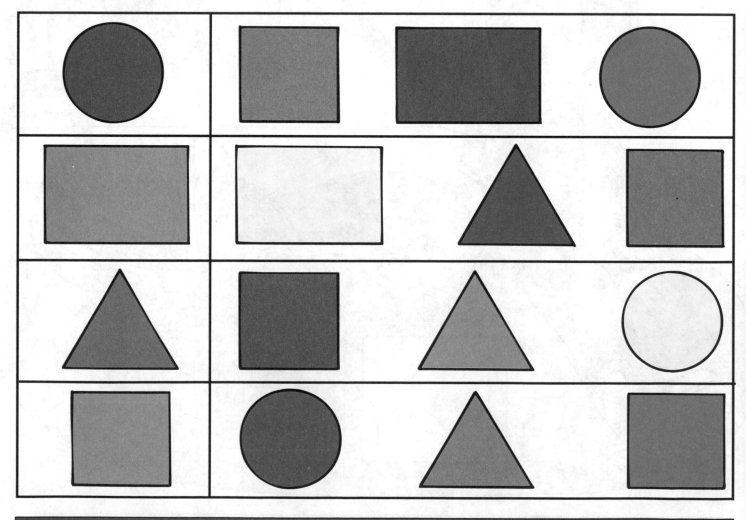

Name: _____

Review Shapes

Directions: Look at the picture.
Color the thing that has the shape of a **circle**.
Draw a line from the thing that has the shape of a **rectangle** to the foot.
Put an X on the things that have the shape of a **square**.
Circle the thing that has the shape of a **triangle**.

Name: _____

Review Colors and Shapes

Directions:

Color each [square] — [blue]

Color each [rectangle] — [red]

Color each [circle] — [green]

Color each [triangle] — [brown]

Then finish the picture with your favorite colors!

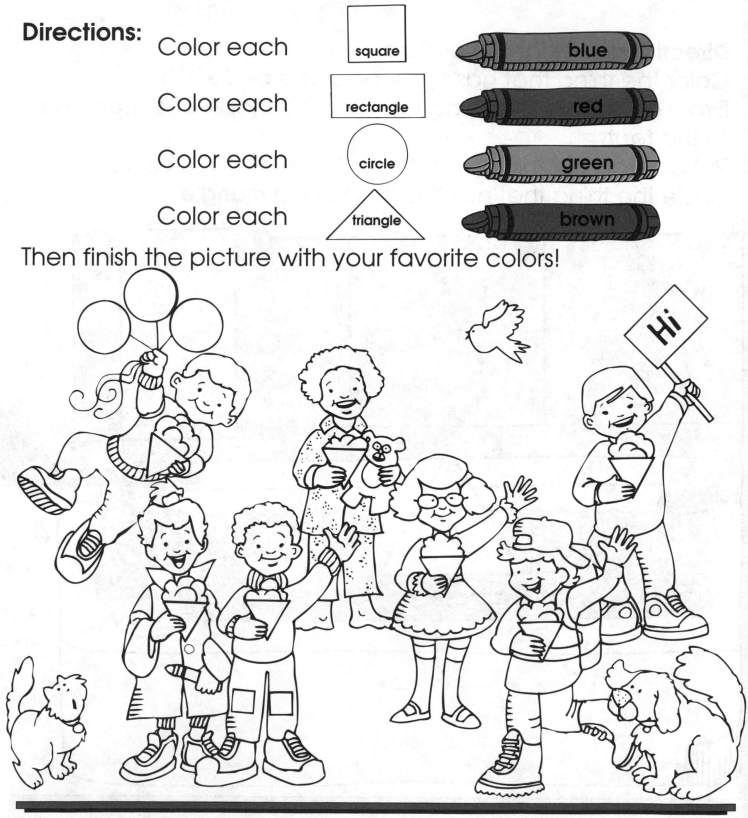

Name: _____

Table of Contents

Name: _____

Bibliography

Enjoy these books about letters:

Amazing Animal Alphabet Book by Roger and Mariko Chouinard (Doubleday, 1988).

Eating the Alphabet: Fruits and Vegetables from A-Z by Lois Ehlert
    (Harcourt Brace Jovanovich, 1989).

The Alphabet by Monique Felix (Creative Education, 1993).

Alison's Zinnia by Anita Lobel (Greenwillow, 1990).

Chicka Chicka Boom Boom by Bill Martin, Jr. and John Archambault
    (Simon and Schuster, 1989).

The Monster Book of A B C Sounds by Alan Snow (Dial, 1991).

Albert's Alphabet by Leslie Tryon (Atheneum, 1991).

These lines and arrows show how to print the letters.

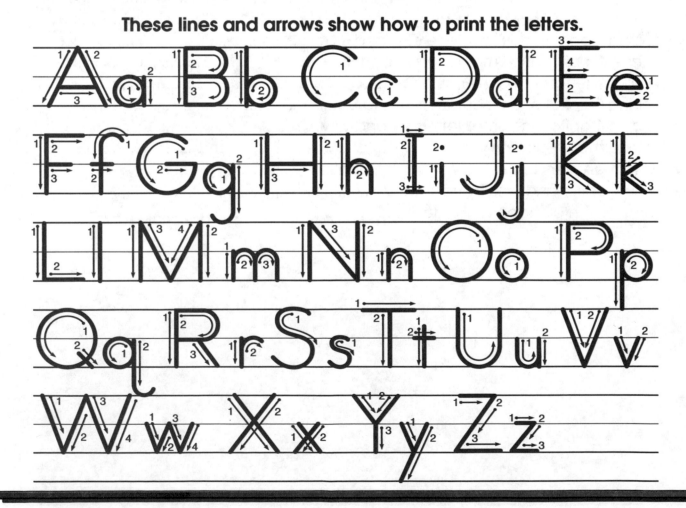

2

Name: _____

Recognizing Capital and Small Letters Aa

Directions: Name and trace the letters. Then help the hungry anteater find food by following the capital and small letter A's through the maze.

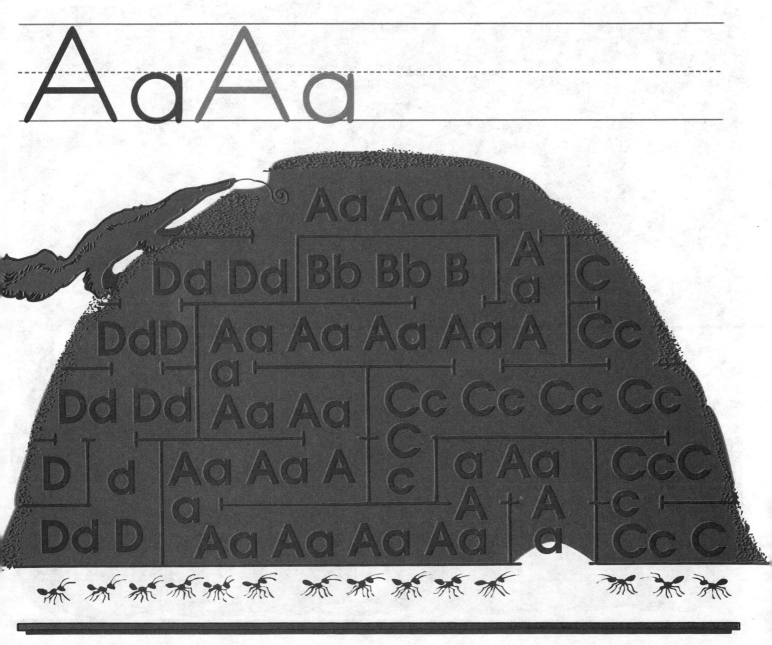

Name: _____

Recognizing Capital and Small Letters
Bb and Cc

Directions: Name and trace the letters. Use a red crayon to color each beet that has a capital B or a small b on it. Use an orange crayon to color each carrot that has a capital C or a small c on it.

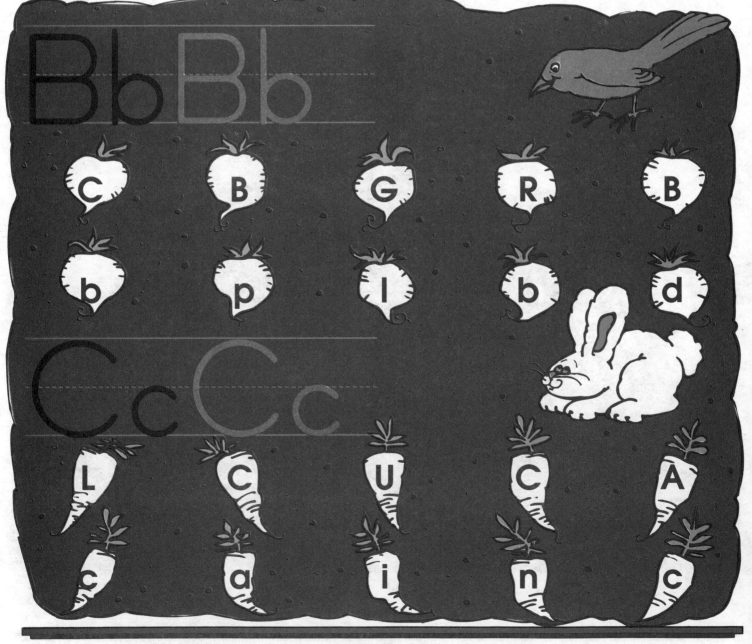

4

Name: _____

Reviewing the Letters Aa, Bb, and Cc

Directions: Look at the letter each person is holding. Circle the same letter each time you see it.

Name: _____

Recognizing Capital and Small Letters
Dd and Ee

Directions: Name and trace the letters. Draw lines to match the capital and small letters that go together.

Name: _____

Recognizing Capital and Small Letters
Ff and Gg

Yum! Good food!

Recycle bin

Paper

Cans

Directions: Name and trace the letters. Circle each capital F and small f. Do the same for each capital G and small g.

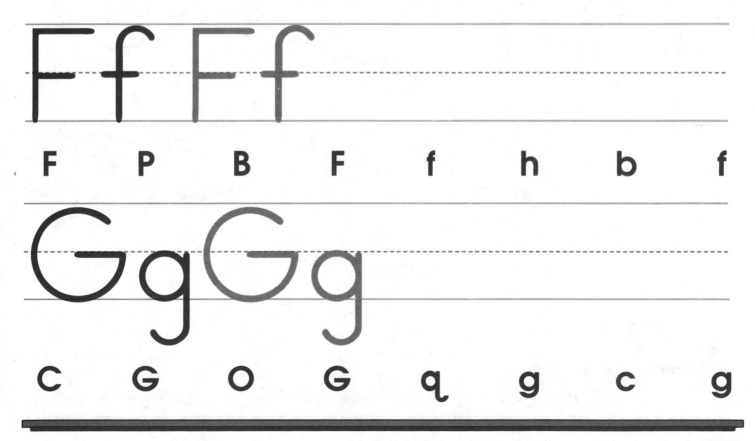

F f F f

F   P   B   F   f   h   b   f

G g G g

C   G   O   G   q   g   c   g

Name: _____

Reviewing the Letters Dd, Ee, Ff, and Gg

Directions: Look at the capital letter in each row. Color each picture that has the matching small letter.

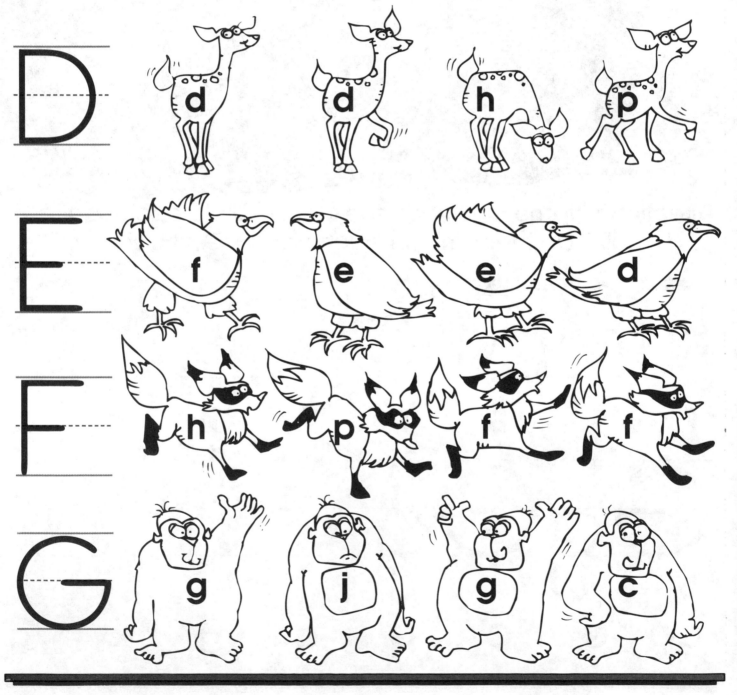

Name: _____

Recognizing Capital and Small Letters
Hh and Ii

Directions: Name and trace the letters. Color each hand that has a capital H or small h on it. Color each ice cream cone that has a capital I or a small i on it.

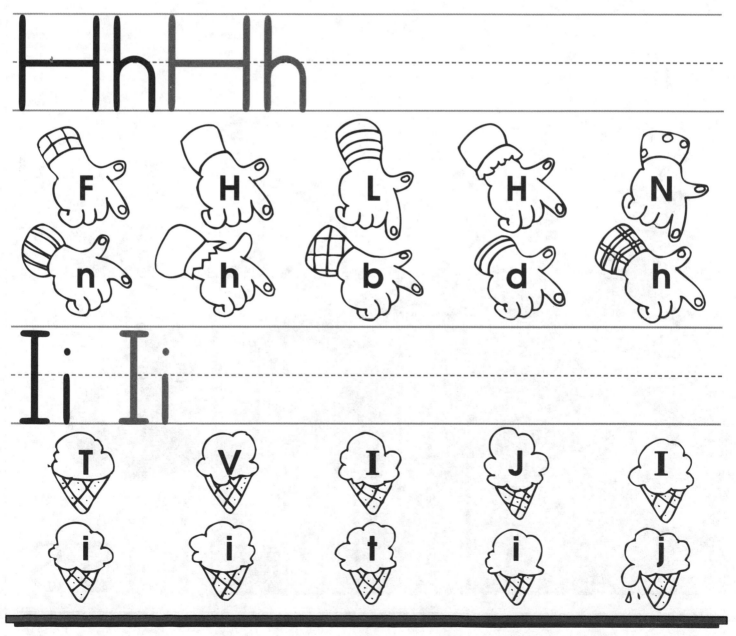

Name: _____

Recognizing Capital and Small Letters
Jj and Kk

Directions: Name and trace the letters. Help the joey, a baby kangaroo, find his mother by following the capital and small letter J's through the maze. Then write a small k to make a word that tells what mother and the joey do when they see each other.

Name: _____

Reviewing the Letters Hh, Ii, Jj, and Kk

Directions: Draw a string from the kite to the letter that matches. The first one shows you what to do.

Hh   Ii   Jj   Kk

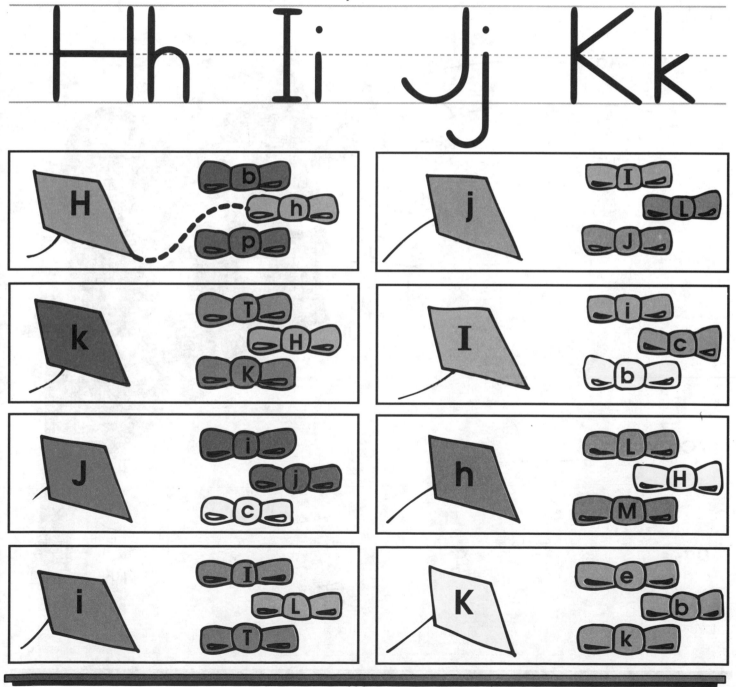

Name: _____

Reviewing A - K in Alphabetical Order
Aa Bb Cc Dd Ee Ff Gg Hh Ii Jj Kk

Directions: Find out what the elves are making. Draw a line to connect the dots in ABC order. Color the picture that you make.

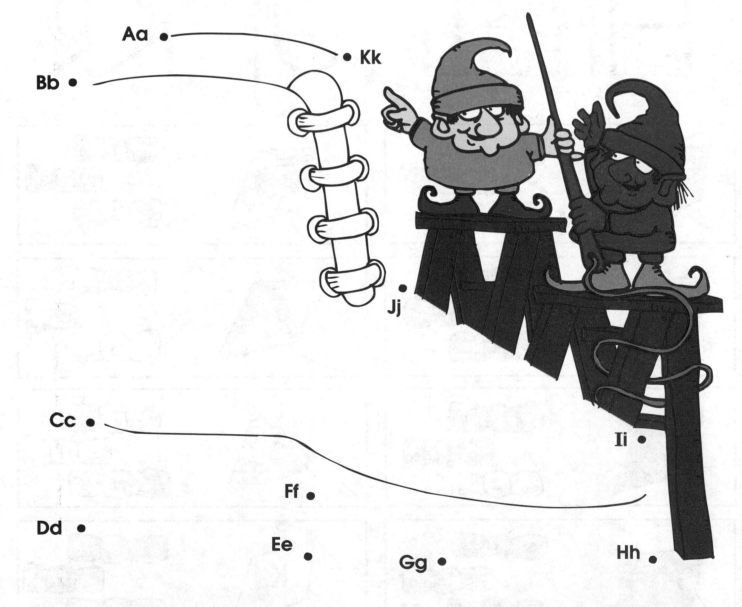

ANSWER KEY

*This Answer Key has been designed so that
it may be easily removed if you so desire.*

PRESCHOOL ALPHABET AND LETTERS

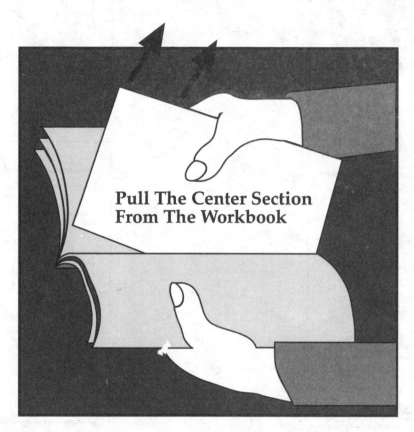

**Pull The Center Section
From The Workbook**

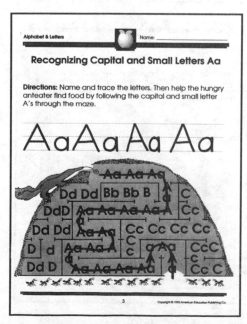

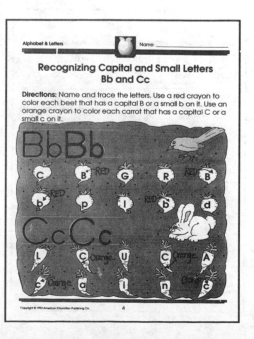

Reviewing the Letters Aa, Bb, and Cc

Directions: Look at the letter each person is holding. Circle the same letter each time you see it.

5

Reviewing the Letters Dd, Ee, Ff, and Gg

Directions: Look at the capital letter in each row. Color each picture that has the matching small letter.

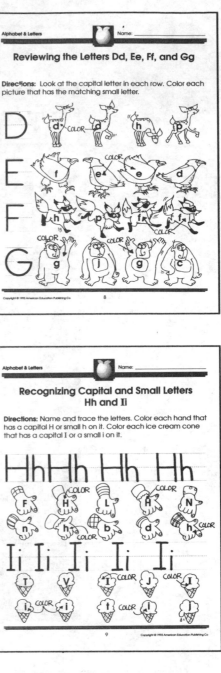

8

Recognizing Capital and Small Letters
Dd and Ee

Directions: Name and trace the letters. Draw lines to match the capital and small letters that go together.

DdDdDd

EeEeEe

6

Recognizing Capital and Small Letters
Hh and Ii

Directions: Name and trace the letters. Color each hand that has a capital H or small h on it. Color each ice cream cone that has a capital I or a small i on it.

Hh Hh Hh Hh

Ii Ii Ii Ii Ii

9   Copyright © 1993 American Education Publishing Co.

Recognizing Capital and Small Letters
Ff and Gg

Yum! Good food!

Directions: Name and trace the letters. Circle each capital F and small f. Do the same for each capital G and small g.

Ff Ff Ff Ff

F   P   B   F   f   h   b   f

Gg Gg Gg Gg

c   G   O   G   q   g   c   g

7

Recognizing Capital and Small Letters
Jj and Kk

Directions: Name and trace the letters. Help the joey, a baby kangaroo, find his mother by following the capital and small letter J's through the maze. Then write a small k to make a word that tells what mother and the joey do when they see each other.

Jj Jj Jj

KkKkK

kiss

10

Name: _____

Reviewing the Letters Hh, Ii, Jj, and Kk

Directions: Draw a string from the kite to the letter that matches. The first one shows you what to do.

Copyright © 1993 American Education Publishing Co.

Name: _____

Recognizing Capital and Small Letters Nn and Oo

Directions: Name and trace the letters. Circle the letters in each row that match the red letter.

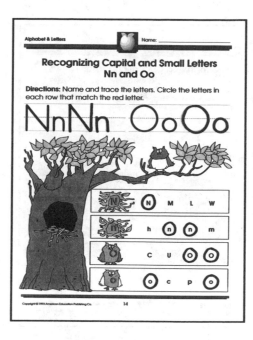

Name: _____

Reviewing A - K in Alphabetical Order
Aa Bb Cc Dd Ee Ff Gg Hh Ii Jj Kk

Directions: Find out what the elves are making. Draw a line to connect the dots in ABC order. Color the picture that you make.

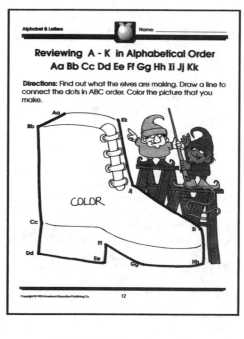

COLOR

Copyright © 1993 American Education Publishing Co.

Name: _____

Reviewing the Letters Ll, Mm, Nn, Oo

Directions: Draw a line from each capital letter to its matching small letter. Then color the mittens you matched the same color.

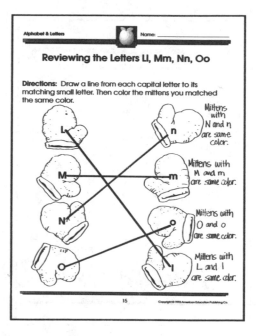

Mittens with N and n are same color.

Mittens with M and m are same color.

Mittens with O and o are same color.

Mittens with L and l are same color.

Copyright © 1993 American Education Publishing Co.

Name: _____

Recognizing Capital and Small Letters Ll and Mm

Directions: Name and trace the letters. Circle each capital L and small l. Do the same for each capital M and small m below.

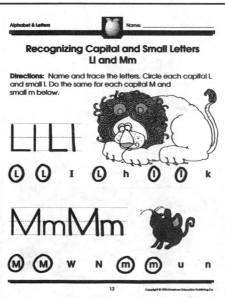

Copyright © 1993 American Education Publishing Co.

Name: _____

Recognizing Capital and Small Letters Pp and Qq

Directions: Name and trace the letters. Circle each capital P and small p. Do the same for each capital Q and small q.

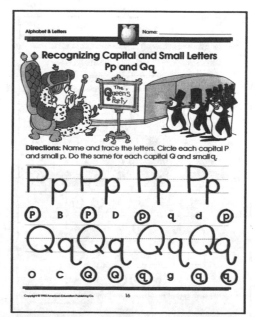

Copyright © 1993 American Education Publishing Co.

Recognizing Capital and Small Letters
Rr and Ss

Directions: Name and trace the letters. Draw lines to match the capital and small letters that go together.

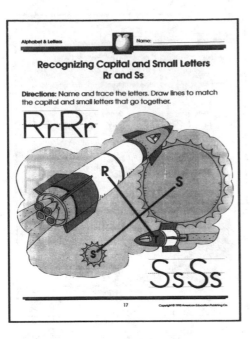

Recognizing Capital and Small Letters
Vv and Ww

Directions: Name and trace the letters. Use a red crayon to color each vest that has a capital V or a small v on it. Use a brown crayon to color each watch that has a capital W or a small w on it.

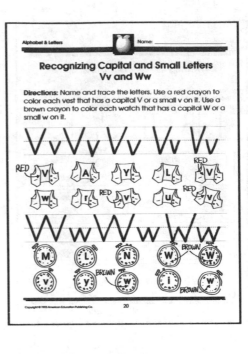

Reviewing the Letters Pp, Qq, Rr, and Ss

Directions: Color each toy racer that has a capital and small letter that go together. The first one shows you what to do.

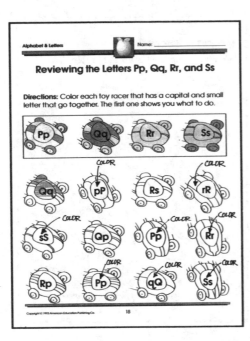

Recognizing Capital and Small Letters
Xx, Yy, and Zz

Directions: Name and trace the letters. Then put the toys back in the toy box. Use a red crayon to go from the X-ray in the play kit to the toy box by following the X's. Use a blue crayon to go from the yoyo to the toy box by following the Y's. Use an orange crayon to go from the zebra to the toy box by following the Z's.

Line is red.

Line is blue.

Line is orange.

Recognizing Capital and Small Letters
Tt and Uu

Directions: Name and trace the letters. Circle the letters in each row that match the red letter.

Reviewing the Letters
Tt, Uu, Vv, Ww, Xx, and Zz

Directions: Draw a line from each capital letter to its matching small letter.

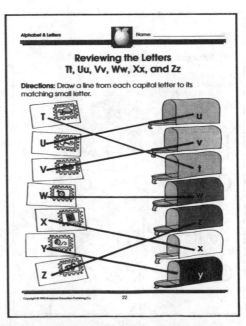

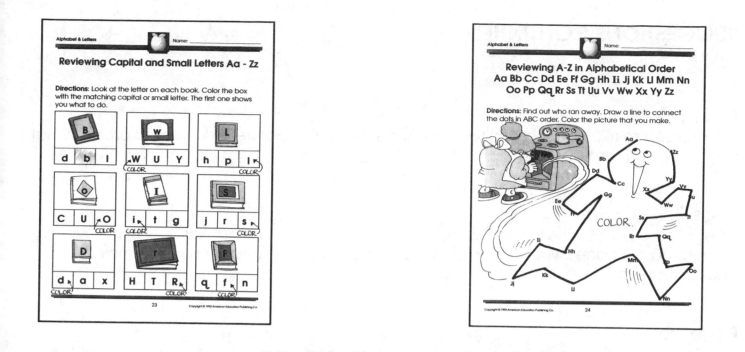

Preschool Alphabet and Letters
SUGGESTIONS

You may wish to use these additional suggestions
for the book pages below:

Page 3:
Talk about other animals and the foods they eat. Name other animals, such as bears, birds, and dogs, and ask children to name the foods they like to eat.

Page 4:
Encourage children to name other vegetables. Ask them to use drawing paper and crayons to create a picture of a big bowl of vegetable soup. If possible, have them make alphabet soup by gluing alphabet macaroni on their drawings.

Page 5:
Discuss the jobs of the people pictured on this page. Ask children to name jobs that they might like to do.

Page 6:
After completing the page, ask children to brainstorm for places where they have played or could play in water. (lake, bathtub, sprinkler, fire hydrant, puddles, ocean)

continued on next page...

SUGGESTIONS CONTINUED

Page 7:
Ask children to tell a story about what is happening in the picture. Ask them to predict what might happen next.

Page 8:
Point out the bald eagle in the second row. Tell children that it is our national bird. Invite them to name places where they have seen the bald eagle. (mail boxes and mail trucks, quarters, dollars, sports clothing)

Page 12:
After completing page 12, read a version or tell the traditional story of "The Elves and the Shoemaker."

Page 13:
Read a version of the fable "The Lion and the Mouse." This is the story of a lion who spares the life of a mouse. Later, much to the lion's surprise, the mouse gnaws the lion free from a rope trap.

Page 14:
You may want to read Caldecott Medal-winning book *Owl Moon* by Jane Yolen at this time.

Page 16:
Ask children to tell a story about what is happening in the picture. Ask them to predict what might happen next.

Page 23:
Invite children to talk about their favorite books.

Page 24:
After completing page 24, read a version or tell the story of "The Gingerbread Man."

Notes

Notes

Name: _____

Recognizing Capital and Small Letters
Ll and Mm

Directions: Name and trace the letters. Circle each capital L and small l. Do the same for each capital M and small m below.

L   L   L   I   L   h   l   l   k

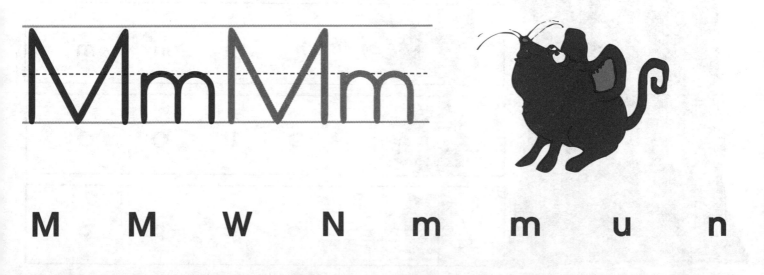

M   M   M   W   N   m   m   u   n

Name: _____

Recognizing Capital and Small Letters
Nn and Oo

Directions: Name and trace the letters. Circle the letters in each row that match the red letter.

NnNn OoOo

	N	M	L	W
	h	n	n	m
	c	U	O	O
	o	c	p	o

Name: _____

Reviewing the Letters Ll, Mm, Nn, Oo

Directions: Draw a line from each capital letter to its matching small letter. Then color the mittens you matched the same color.

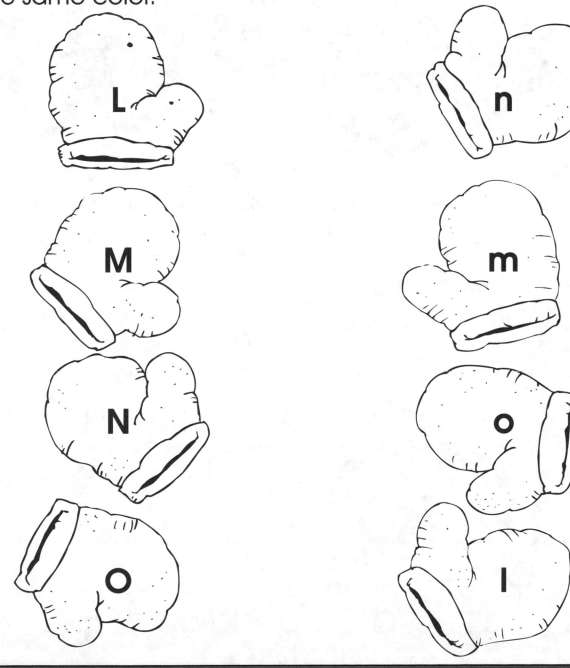

Name: _____

Recognizing Capital and Small Letters
Pp and Qq

Directions: Name and trace the letters. Circle each capital P and small p. Do the same for each capital Q and small q.

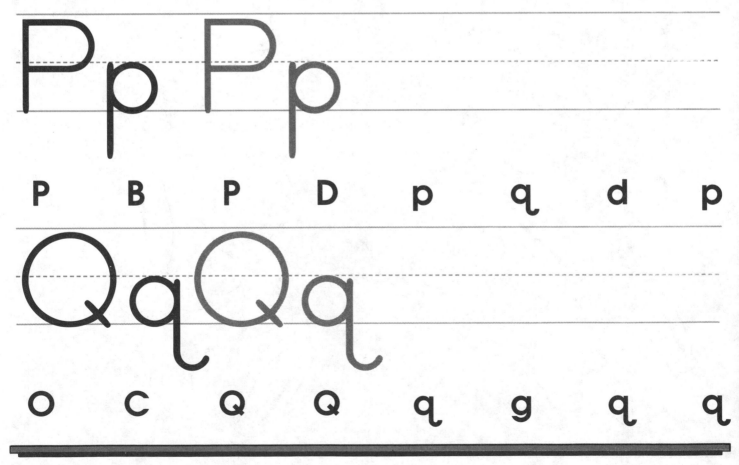

P   B   P   D   p   q   d   p

O   C   Q   Q   q   g   q   q

Name: _____

Recognizing Capital and Small Letters
Rr and Ss

Directions: Name and trace the letters. Draw lines to match the capital and small letters that go together.

Name: _____

Reviewing the Letters Pp, Qq, Rr, and Ss

Directions: Color each toy racer that has a capital and small letter that go together. The first one shows you what to do.

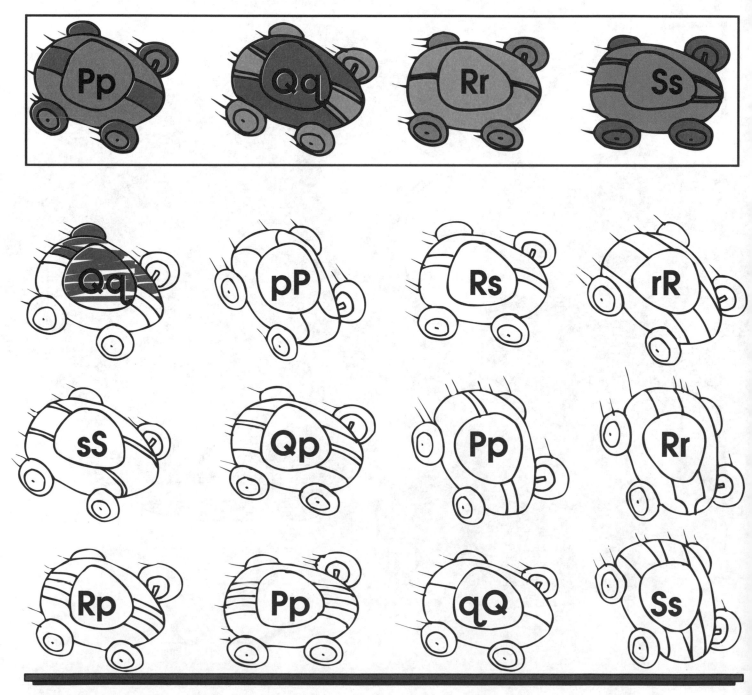

Name: _____

Recognizing Capital and Small Letters
Tt and Uu

Directions: Name and trace the letters. Circle the letters in each row that match the red letter.

	E	L	T	T
	t	h	l	d
	v	c	w	U
	u	u	n	v

Name: _____

Recognizing Capital and Small Letters
Vv and Ww

Directions: Name and trace the letters. Use a red crayon to color each vest that has a capital V or a small v on it. Use a brown crayon to color each watch that has a capital W or a small w on it.

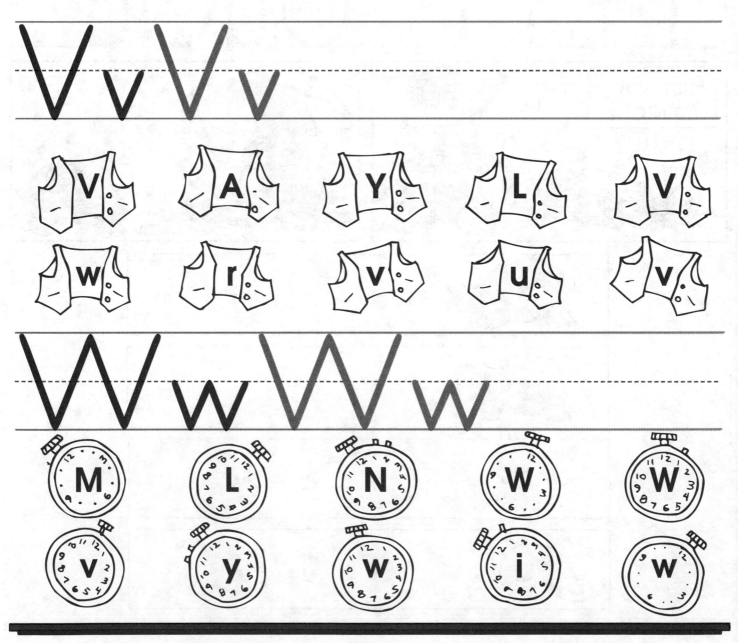

Name: _____

Recognizing Capital and Small Letters
Xx, Yy, and Zz

Directions: Name and trace the letters. Then put the toys back in the toy box. Use a red crayon to go from the X-ray in the play kit to the toy box by following the X's. Use a blue crayon to go from the yoyo to the toy box by following the Y's. Use an orange crayon to go from the zebra to the toy box by following the Z's.

Xx Xx Xx Xx Xx Xx Xx

Yy Yy Yy Yy Yy Yy Yy Yy Yy

Zz Zz Zz Zz Zz Zz Zz Zz

Name: _____

Reviewing the Letters
Tt, Uu, Vv, Ww, Xx, Yy and Zz

Directions: Draw a line from each capital letter to its matching small letter.

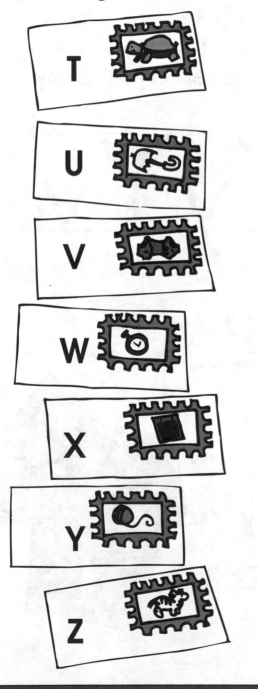

22

Name: _____

Reviewing Capital and Small Letters Aa - Zz

Directions: Look at the letter on each book. Color the box with the matching capital or small letter. The first one shows you what to do.

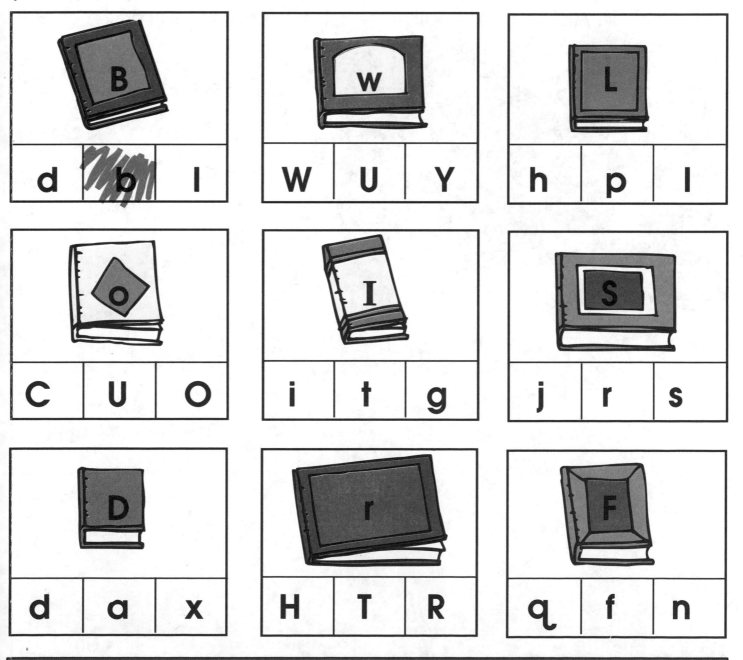

Name: _____

Reviewing A-Z in Alphabetical Order
Aa Bb Cc Dd Ee Ff Gg Hh Ii Jj Kk Ll Mm Nn
Oo Pp Qq Rr Ss Tt Uu Vv Ww Xx Yy Zz

Directions: Find out who ran away. Draw a line to connect the dots in ABC order. Color the picture that you make.

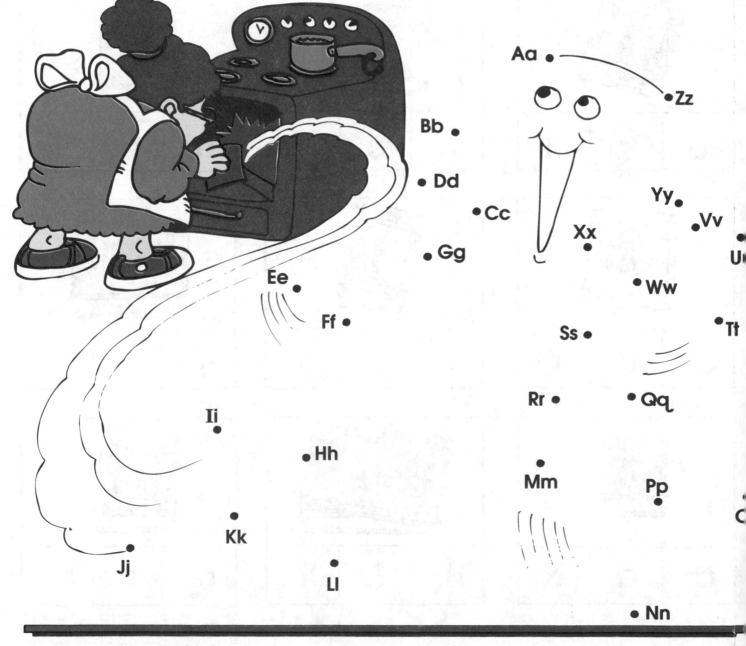

Table of Contents

Name: _____

Bibliography

Enjoy these books about numbers and counting.

Anno's Counting Book   by Mitsumasa Anno (Crowell, 1977).

Count-a-saurus   by Nancy Blumenthal (Macmillan, 1989).

Scott Gustafson's Animal Orchestra: A Counting Book   by Scott Gustafson
      (Contemporary Books, Inc., 1988).

Count and See   by Tana Hoban (Macmillan, 1972).

Knowabout Counting   by Henry Pluckrose (Franklin Watts, 1988).

Peter Rabbit's 1 2 3   with new reproductions from the original
      illustrations by Beatrix Potter (F. Warne & Co., 1987).

My First Look at Counting   (Random House, 1991).

Animal Babies 1 2 3   by Eve Spencer (Raintree, 1990).

Numbers at Play: A Counting Book   by Charles Sullivan
      (Rizzoli International Publications, Inc., 1992).

Numbers   by Monique Felix (Creative Editions, 1993)

These lines and arrows show how to print the numbers.

Name: _____

Matching Objects One-to-One

Directions: Draw lines to show the same number.

Name: _____

Identifying Groups That Have The Same Number of Objects

Directions: Color the groups in the rows that have the same number of objects.

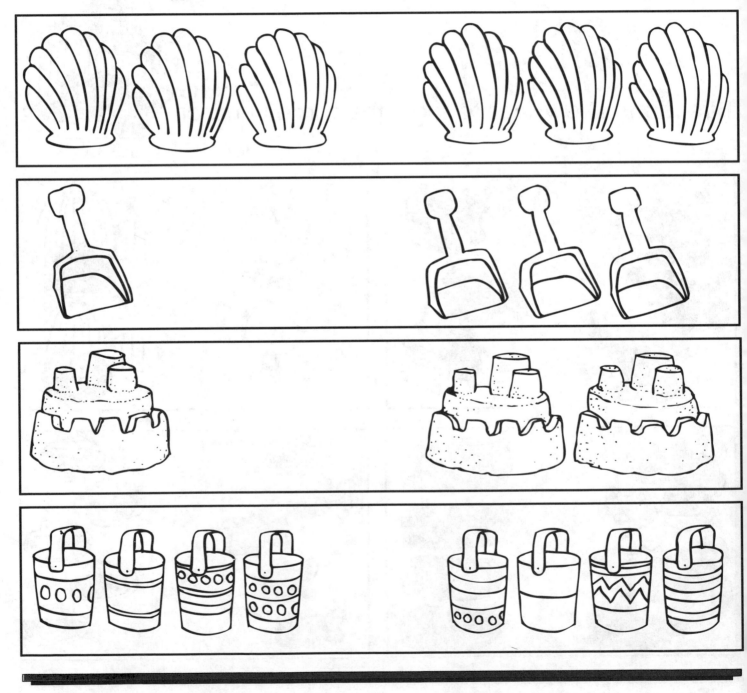

4

Name: _____

Comparing Two Groups to Determine Which Has More

Directions: Match the pictures. Circle the group that has more.

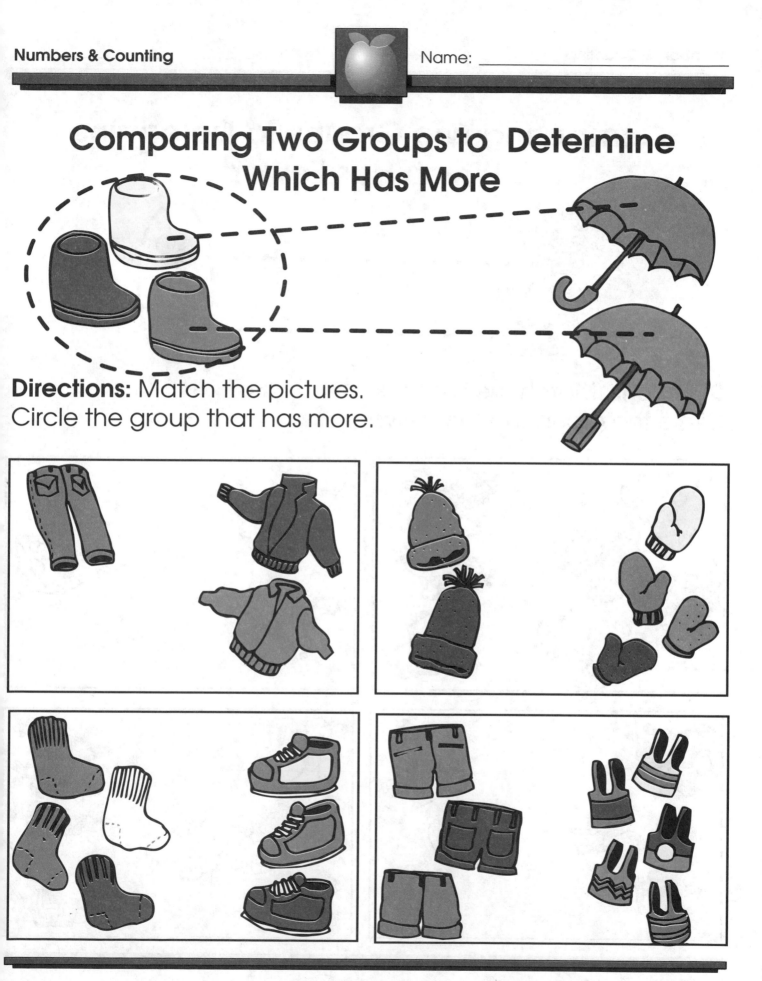

Name: _____

Comparing Two Groups To Determine Which Has Fewer

 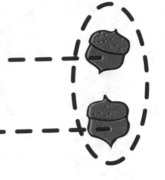

Directions: Match the pictures.
Circle the group that has fewer.

6

Name: _____

Identifying Groups of 1 and 2 Objects

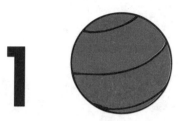 

Directions: Circle the groups of 1. Color groups of 2.

Name: _____

Identifying Groups of 1 and 2 Objects; Writing the Numbers 1 and 2

Directions: Write the numbers 1 and 2.

Directions: Draw balls on the nose of each seal to show the number in each box.

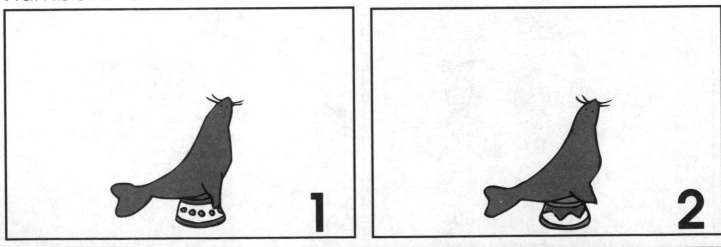

Name: _____

Identifying Groups of 3 and 4 Objects

Directions: Circle the groups of 3. Color the groups of 4.

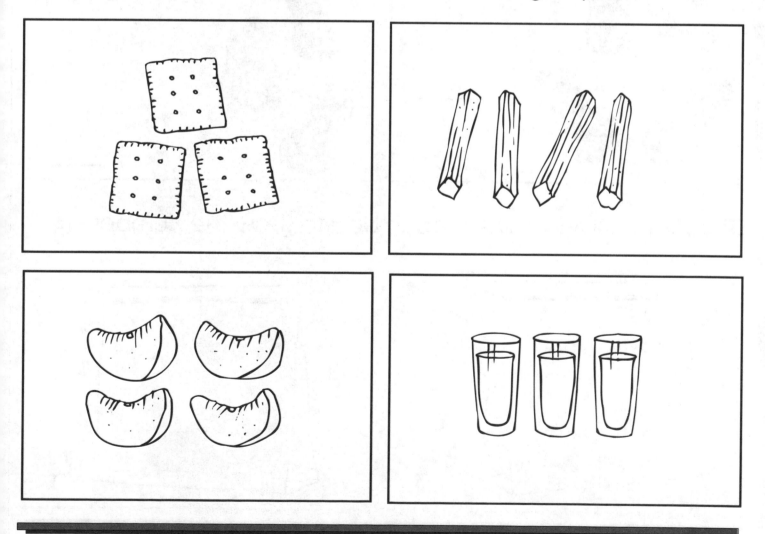

Name: _____

Identifying Groups of 3 and 4 Objects; Writing the Numbers 3 and 4

Directions: Write the numbers 3 and 4.

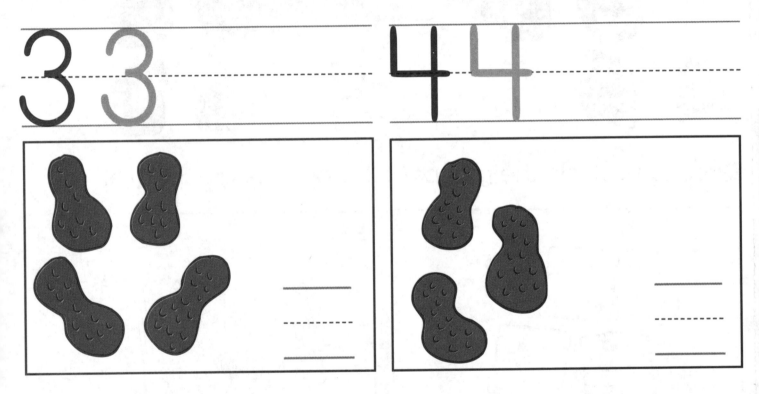

Directions: Draw raisins in each bag to show the number in each box.

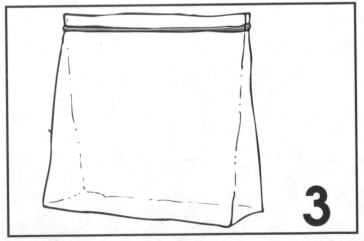

Name: _____

Identifying Groups of 5 and 6 Objects

5

6

Directions: Circle the groups of 6.

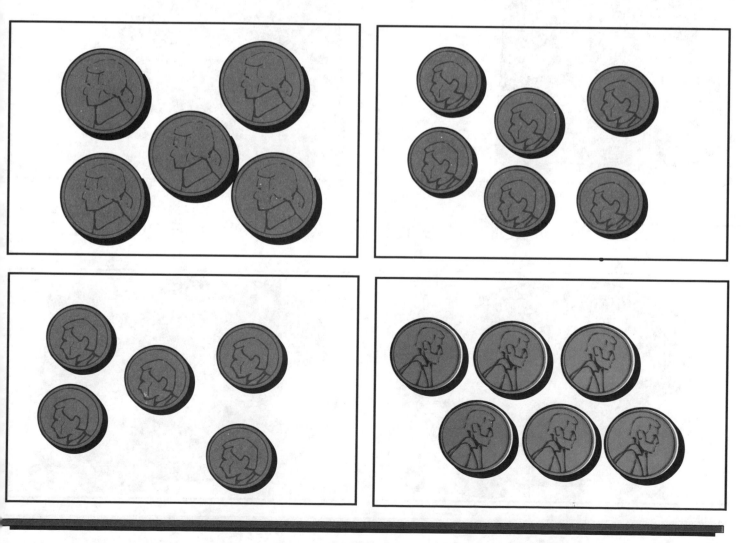

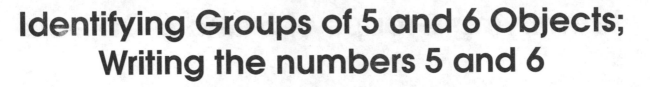

Name: _____

Identifying Groups of 5 and 6 Objects;
Writing the numbers 5 and 6

Directions: Write the numbers 5 and 6.

Directions: Draw coins in each bank to show the number in each box.

ANSWER KEY

This Answer Key has been designed so that it may be easily removed if you so desire.

PRESCHOOL NUMBERS & COUNTING

Pull The Center Section From The Workbook

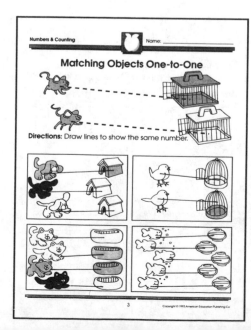

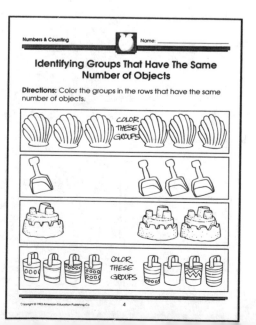

Name: _____

Comparing Two Groups to Determine Which Has More

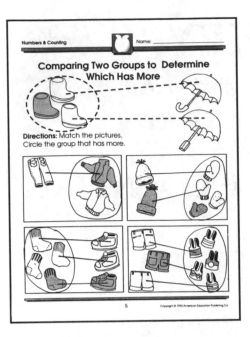

Directions: Match the pictures. Circle the group that has more.

Name: _____

Identifying Groups of 1 and 2 Objects; Writing the Numbers 1 and 2

Directions: Write the numbers 1 and 2.

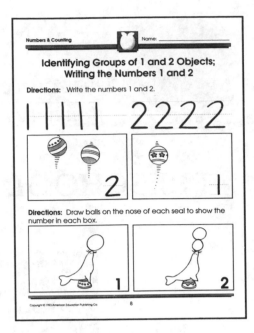

Directions: Draw balls on the nose of each seal to show the number in each box.

Name: _____

Comparing Two Groups To Determine Which Has Fewer

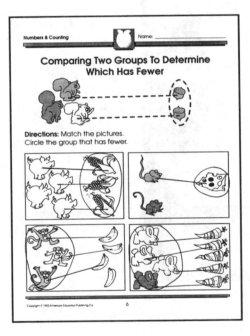

Directions: Match the pictures. Circle the group that has fewer.

Name: _____

Identifying Groups of 3 and 4 Objects

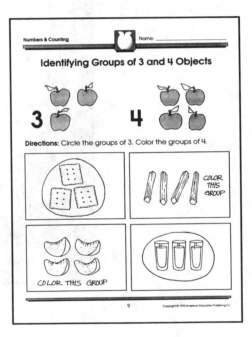

Directions: Circle the groups of 3. Color the groups of 4.

COLOR THIS GROUP

Name: _____

Identifying Groups of 1 and 2 Objects

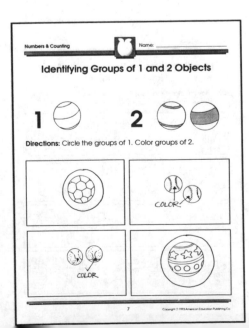

Directions: Circle the groups of 1. Color groups of 2.

COLOR!

COLOR

Name: _____

Identifying Groups of 3 and 4 Objects; Writing the Numbers 3 and 4

Directions: Write the numbers 3 and 4.

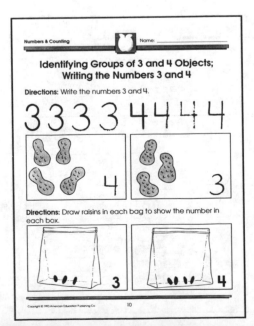

Directions: Draw raisins in each bag to show the number in each box.

Identifying Groups of 5 and 6 Objects

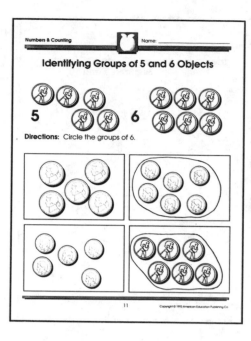

5   6

Directions: Circle the groups of 6.

Solving Problems Using Pictures

Directions: Circle the number that tells how many.

Identifying Groups of 5 and 6 Objects; Writing the numbers 5 and 6

Directions: Write the numbers 5 and 6.

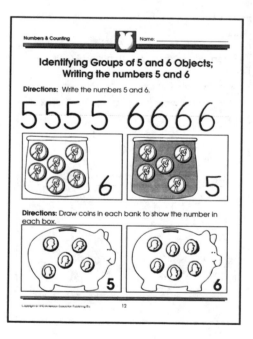

Directions: Draw coins in each bank to show the number in each box.

Counting Forward Through 6

Directions: Count each group of blocks. Trace each number.

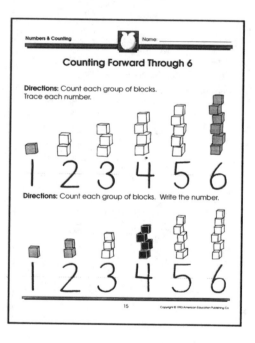

Directions: Count each group of blocks. Write the number.

Identifying Groups of 1 Through 6 Objects

Directions: Draw a circle around the correct number in each box.

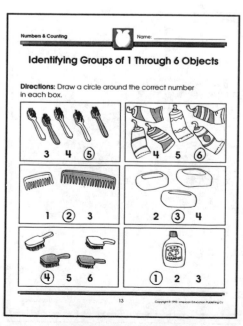

Ordering Numbers 1 Through 6

Where Is Snowball?

Directions: Beginning with 1, join the dots in order.

Name: _____

Identifying Groups of 7 and 8 Objects

Directions: Circle the groups of 7. Color the groups of 8.

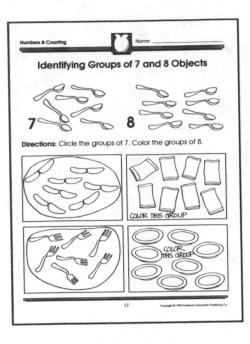

7   8

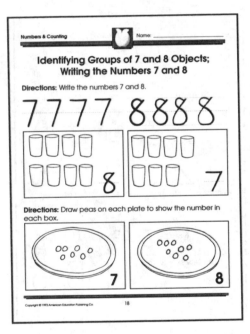

COLOR THIS GROUP

COLOR THIS GROUP

Name: _____

Identifying Groups of 7 and 8 Objects;
Writing the Numbers 7 and 8

Directions: Write the numbers 7 and 8.

7777   8888

8

7

Directions: Draw peas on each plate to show the number in each box.

7

8

Name: _____

Identifying Groups of 9 and 10 Objects

9   10

Directions: Circle the groups of 9. Color the Groups of 10.

COLOR THIS GROUP

COLOR THIS GROUP

Name: _____

Identifying Groups of 9 and 10 Objects;
Writing the Numbers 9 and 10

Directions: Write the numbers 9 and 10.

9999   101010

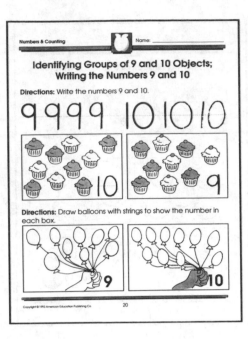

10

9

Directions: Draw balloons with strings to show the number in each box.

9

10

Name: _____

Identifying Groups of 7 Through 10 Objects

Directions: Draw a circle around the correct number of each group.

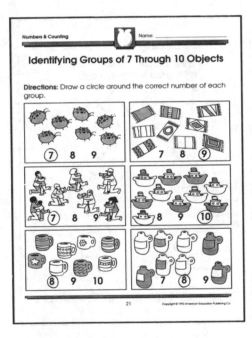

7 8 9   7 8 9

7 8 9   8 9 10

8 9 10   7 8 9

Name: _____

Solving Problems Using Pictures

Directions: Look at the picture. Draw a line to match each picture with the correct number.

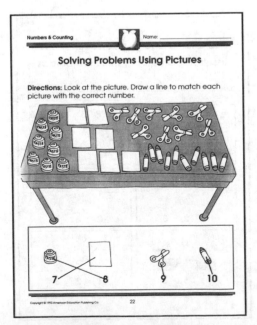

7   8   9   10

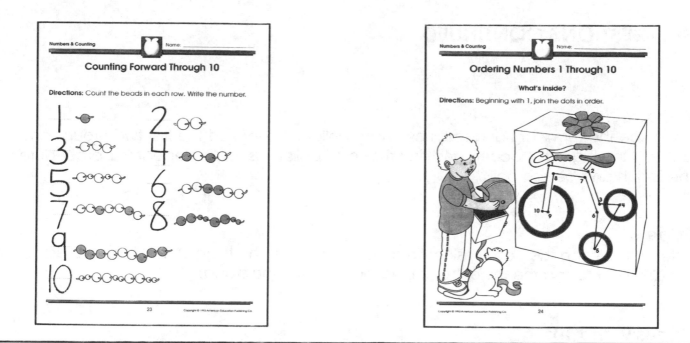

Preschool Numbers and Counting
SUGGESTIONS

You may wish to use these additional suggestions for each of the book pages:

Page 3:
Ask: How do the things on this page go together? (They are pets and their homes.) What might be good names for the pets on this page? Encourage children to talk about and draw their pets or pets they would like to have.

Page 4:
Ask: Where would you see the things on this page? (at the seashore) What other pictures might be on this page about the seashore? (sand dollars, strainers, sand molds, seaweed, waves, fish)

Reinforce the concept of "between" by asking children to look at the first row and ring the sea shell that is between the other shells in each group.

Page 5:
Discuss types of weather. Ask children to identify the clothes pictured that would be appropriate for rainy, snowy, chilly and sunny weather.

Page 6:
Ask: How do the pictures on this page go together? (They are animals and what they eat.) Name other animals, such as bears, birds, dogs, goats and ask children to name the foods they like to eat.

continued on next page...

SUGGESTIONS CONTINUED

Page 7:
Reinforce the terms big and small by asking children to look at the first two groups and put an X on the big ball (soccer) and ring the small balls (baseball). Repeat this procedure with the tennis and beach balls.

Page 8:
After completing this page, ask children to put an X on the thing(s) that is above each seal (ball(s)) and to ring the thing that is below each seal (the stand).

Pages 9 and 10:
Encourage children to discuss nutritious snacks they like to eat. If possible, have children place raisins or peanuts in their mouths as they count 1-4.

Pages 11 and 12:
Name each coin on the page, and give children opportunities to identify and name the coins. If possible have pennies, nickels, and dimes available for children to manipulate.

Page 13:
Ask children to ring the short comb and put an X on the long comb.

Page 14:
Talk about the importance of trees to our environment (homes for animals, food, shade, clean air). You may want to read the Caldecott Medal-winning book *A Tree is Nice* by Janet May Udry at this time.

Page 15:
Use this page to review colors and the shape of a square.

Page 16:
Before children complete the dot-to-dot, ask them to predict where Snowball is hiding. Afterwards, ask: What do you think will happen next?

Pages 17 and 18:
Encourage children to discuss how they help at home. Ask them to conclude how learning how to count can help in setting the table.

continued on next page...

SUGGESTIONS CONTINUED

Pages 19 and 20:
Ask: How old are you? How many candles were on your birthday cake? How many candles will be on your cake next year?

Page 21:
Point to each rhyming word, and ask children to repeat it after you. Present rhyming couplets:

> *"Give me a huge hug,"*
> *Said big Mama bug.*
>
> *Oh, no no! I dropped my mug!*
> *That's okay, it's on the rug!*
>
> *We watched as the little tugs,*
> *Pulled boats loaded with brown jugs.*

Page 22:
Ask: What would you make with the things in this picture? If possible, make art items pictured available for children to use in creating things they named.

Page 23:
Challenge children to identify the pattern in each row, and then tell what the next color or size bead should be.

Page 24:
Ask children to identify the small box and the big box.
Then ask them to predict what will be in the big box. You may
want to discuss bike safety at this time.

Notes

Name: _____

Identifying Groups of 1 Through 6 Objects

Directions: Draw a circle around the correct number in each box.

Name: _____

Solving Problems Using Pictures

Directions: Circle the number that tells how many.

🪹	1	2	3	🐿️	2	3	4
🦋	4	5	6	🐞	4	5	6
🐦	2	3	4	🍎	4	5	6

Name: _____

Counting Forward Through 6

Directions: Count each group of blocks.
Trace each number.

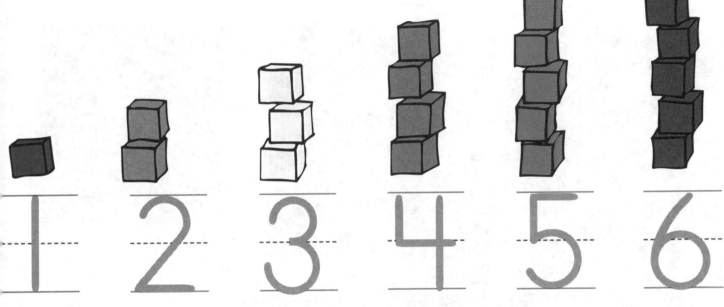

1   2   3   4   5   6

Directions: Count each group of blocks. Write the number.

    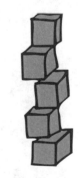

_____ _____ _____ _____ _____ _____

- - - - - -   - - - - - -   - - - - - -   - - - - - -   - - - - - -   - - - - - -

Name: _____

Ordering Numbers 1 Through 6

Where Is Snowball?

Directions: Beginning with 1, join the dots in order.

16

Name: _____

Identifying Groups of 7 and 8 Objects

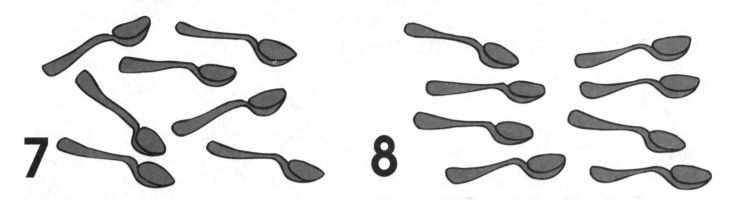

Directions: Circle the groups of 7. Color the groups of 8.

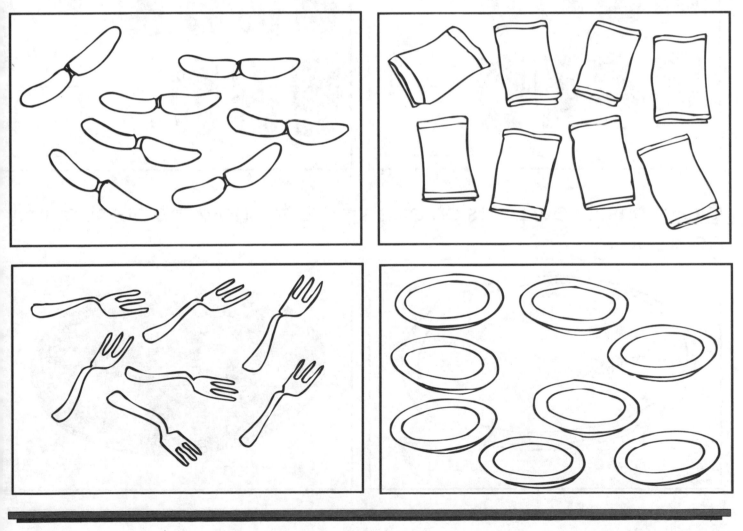

Name: _____

Identifying Groups of 7 and 8 Objects; Writing the Numbers 7 and 8

Directions: Write the numbers 7 and 8.

Directions: Draw peas on each plate to show the number in each box.

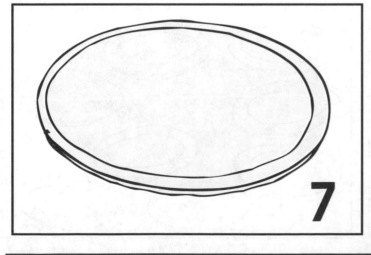

7

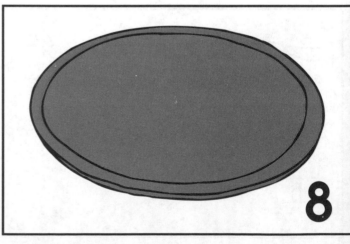

8

Name: _____

Identifying Groups of 9 and 10 Objects

Directions: Circle the groups of 9. Color the Groups of 10.

Name: _____

Identifying Groups of 9 and 10 Objects; Writing the Numbers 9 and 10

Directions: Write the numbers 9 and 10.

Directions: Draw balloons with strings to show the number in each box.

Name: _____

Identifying Groups of 7 Through 10 Objects

Directions: Draw a circle around the correct number of each group.

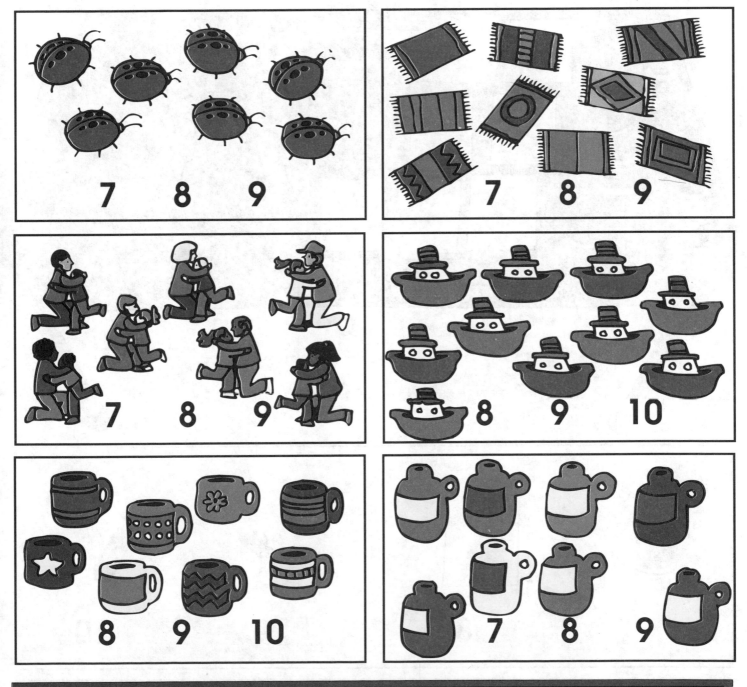

Name: _____

Solving Problems Using Pictures

Directions: Look at the picture. Draw a line to match each picture with the correct number.

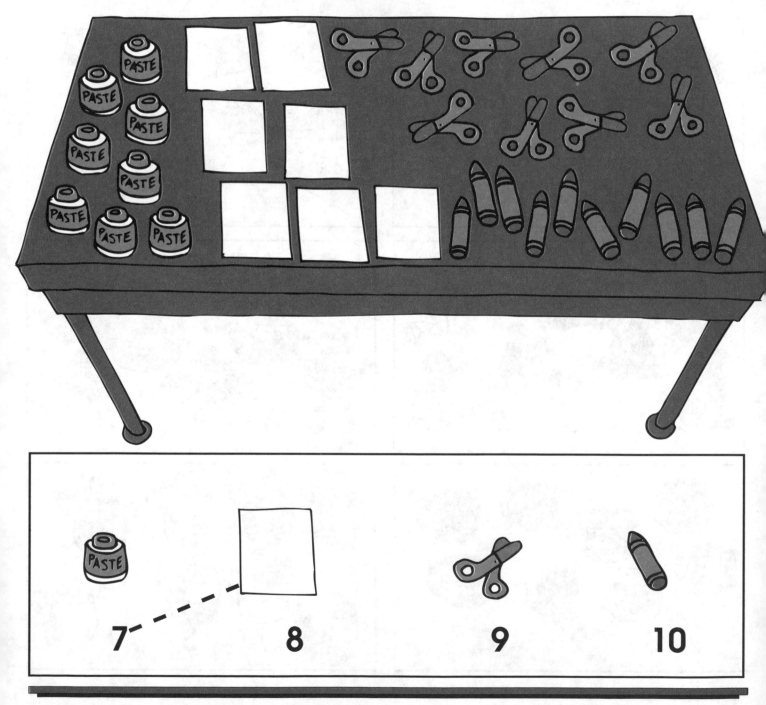

Name: _____

Counting Forward Through 10

Directions: Count the beads in each row. Write the number.

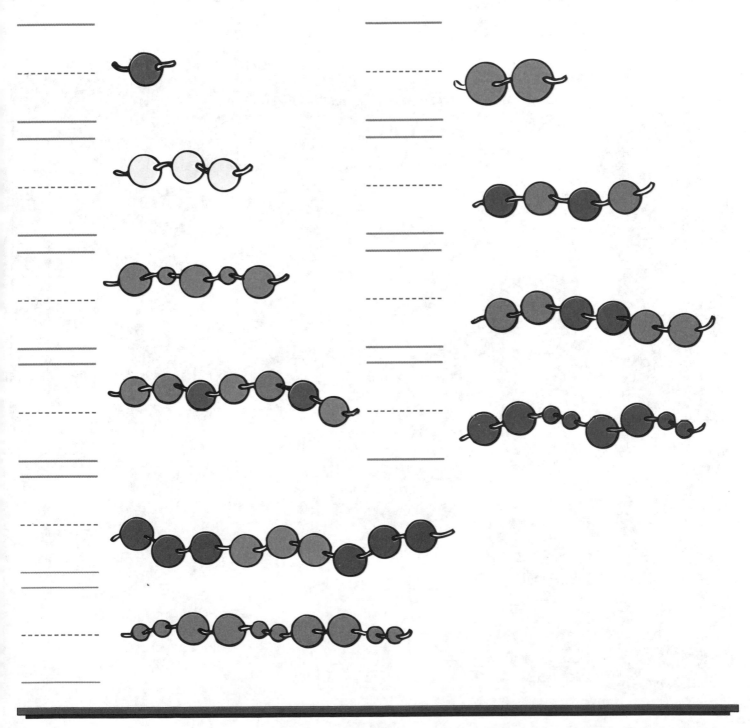

Name: _____

Ordering Numbers 1 Through 10

What's inside?

Directions: Beginning with 1, join the dots in order.

Table of Contents

continued on next page

Glossary and Answer Key are located in the back of the book.

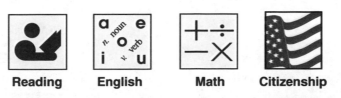

Reading   **English**   **Math**   **Citizenship**

These symbols are located at the top of every lesson and represent the subject area for each lesson.

Which Are Opposites?

Directions: Draw a line between the opposites.

boy

over

in

happy

under

sad

girl

out

Name: _____

Above Or Below ?

Directions: Color the objects above the clouds first. Then color the objects below the clouds.

above

below

Draw some other things you might find below the clouds.

Name: _____

ABC Order

Directions: Draw a line to connect the dots. Follow the letters in ABC order.

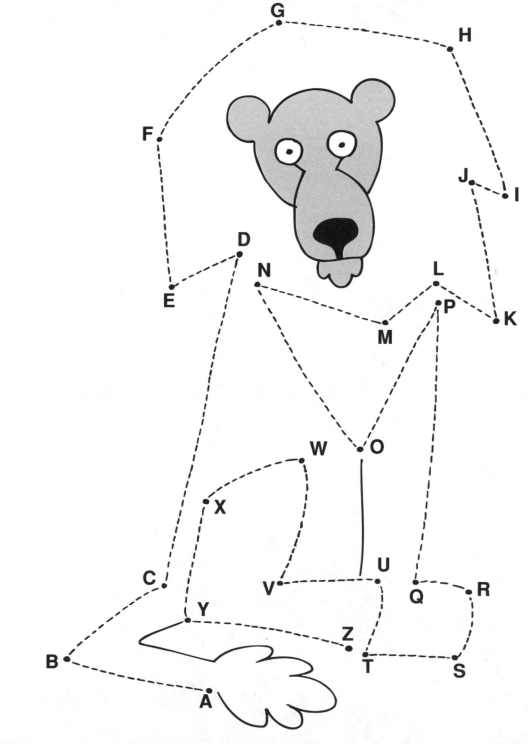

Name: _____

What Belongs?

Directions: Color the pictures in each row that belong together. Draw an **X** through the one that does not belong.

snowman	sled	skates	ball
dog	jar	rabbit	cat
book	shoe	sock	boot
helicopter	plane	tree	balloon

Name: _____

Between

Directions: Draw and color the cat between the other cats. Color each shape that is between the other shapes.

Example:

This bike is between two bikes.

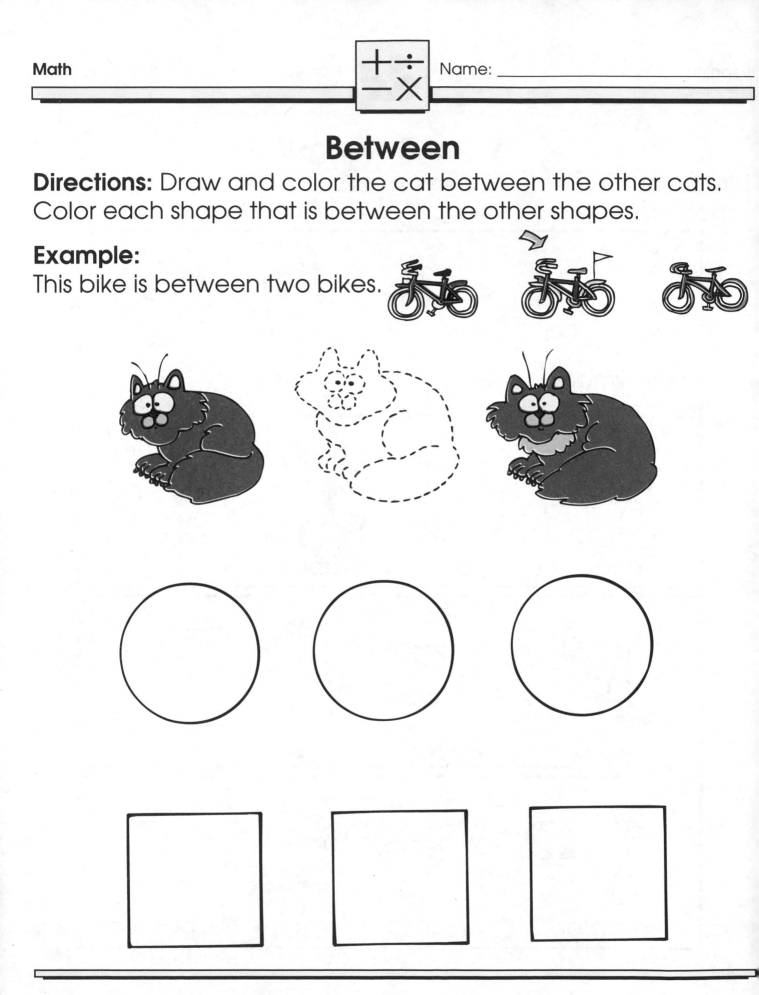

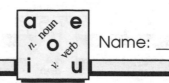

Name: _____

abc Order

Directions: Draw a line to connect the dots. Follow the letters in abc order.

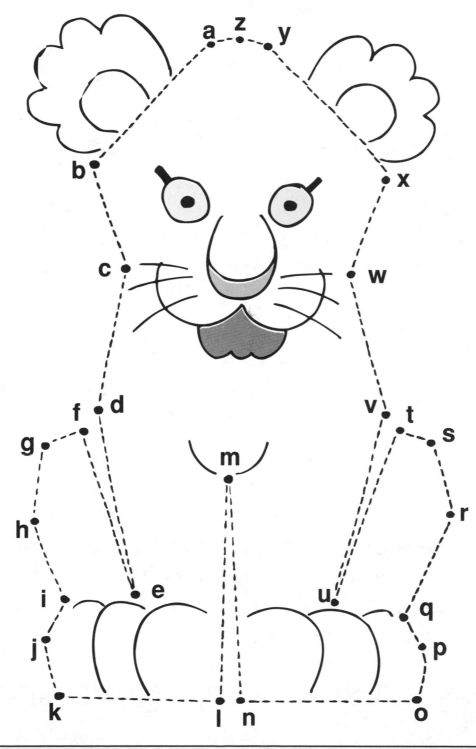

Name: _____

LESSON 1

Citizens Now

Your country is called the United States of America.

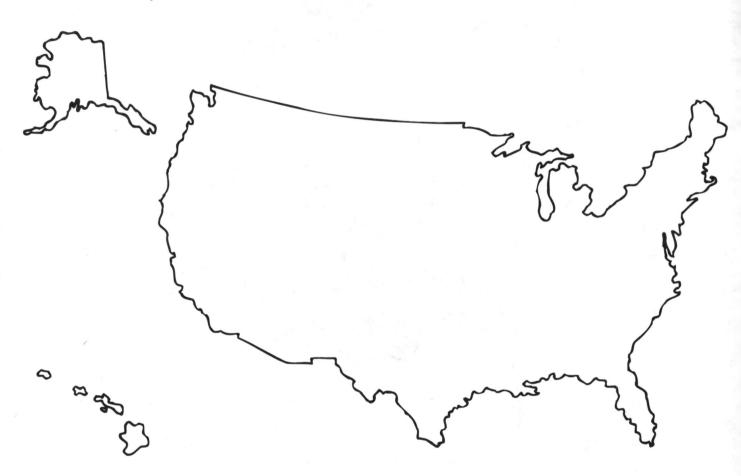

People who are members of our country are called citizens. You don't have to wait until you are a grown-up to become a citizen of our country. You already are a citizen of the United States. You are a **citizen now**!

What can you do to show that you are a good citizen of the United States?

Name: _____

ACTIVITY 1

Citizens Now

Directions: Look at the United States citizen doll. It could be anyone in the United States, but it is you. Make the doll look like you do now. Next, cut it out and paste one of its hands to a hand on a friend's doll. Then put more dolls together. Soon you will have a long chain that shows you are all **Citizens Now**!

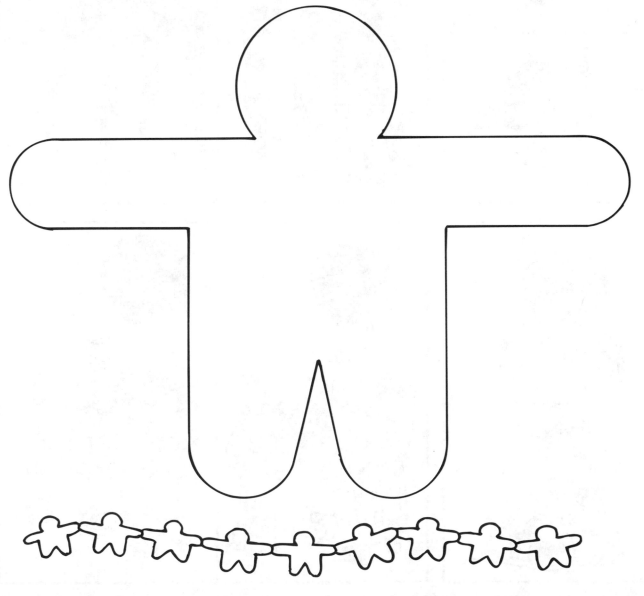

Name: _____

What Comes Before?

Directions: Draw a circle around the small picture that shows what happened right before the pictures in the big boxes.

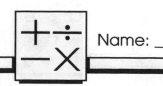 Name: _____

Longer Or Shorter?

Directions: Use your red crayon. Color each pencil that is longer than Jane's. Use your blue crayon. Color each pencil that is shorter than Jane's.

Example:

Jane's pencil

longer than Jane's pencil

shorter than Jane's pencil

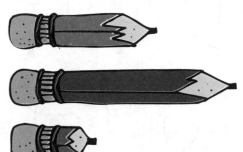

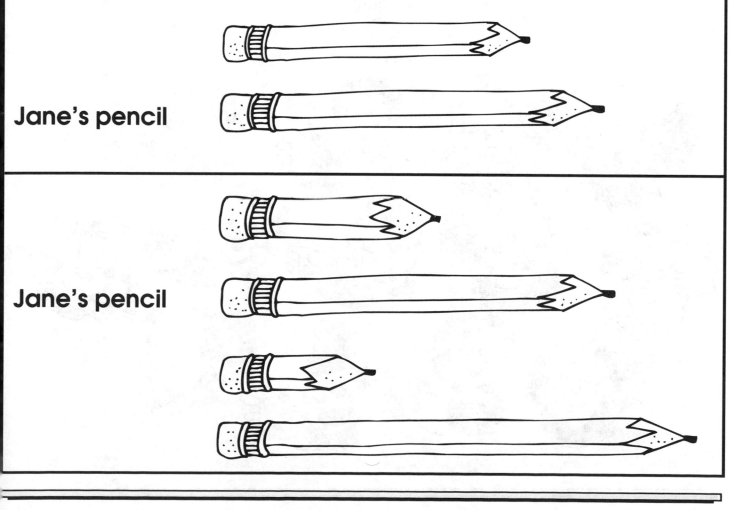

Jane's pencil

Jane's pencil

Matching Upper And Lower Case Letters

Directions: Draw a line from each upper case letter to its matching lower case letter.

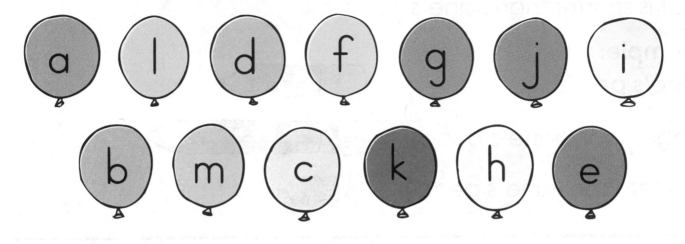

Name: _____

What Comes After?

Directions: Look at the large pictures. Draw a circle around the small picture that shows what would happen next.

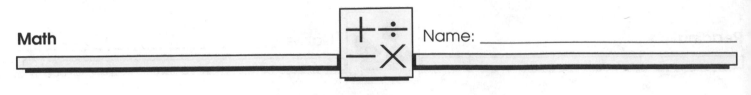

Name: _____

One For Each

Directions: There is one shoe that is right for each person's job. Draw a line to match each person to the right kind of shoe.

Matching Upper And Lower Case Letters

Directions: Draw a line from each upper case letter to its matching lower case letters.

Name: _____

LESSON 2

Barbara Bush

In 1989, George Bush became President of the United States. His wife, Barbara Bush, became the First Lady. She thought that every citizen should know how to read, so Barbara Bush made reading her special project. Mrs. Bush visits schools and shares books with students.

Barbara Bush wants children to know that reading is important.

If Mrs. Bush visited your class, what book would you ask her to read?

Name: _____

ACTIVITY 2

Barbara Bush

Directions: Think about your favorite book. What is the title? Who are the main characters? Where does it happen? Draw a book cover that will make others want to read your favorite book too.

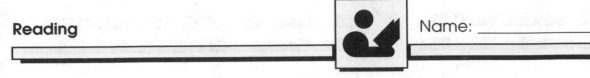

Name: _____

Story Order

Directions: Find the four pictures that tell a story. Color them.
Write numbers in the boxes to show the order they belong in.

Name: _____

One And Two

Directions: Follow the instructions.

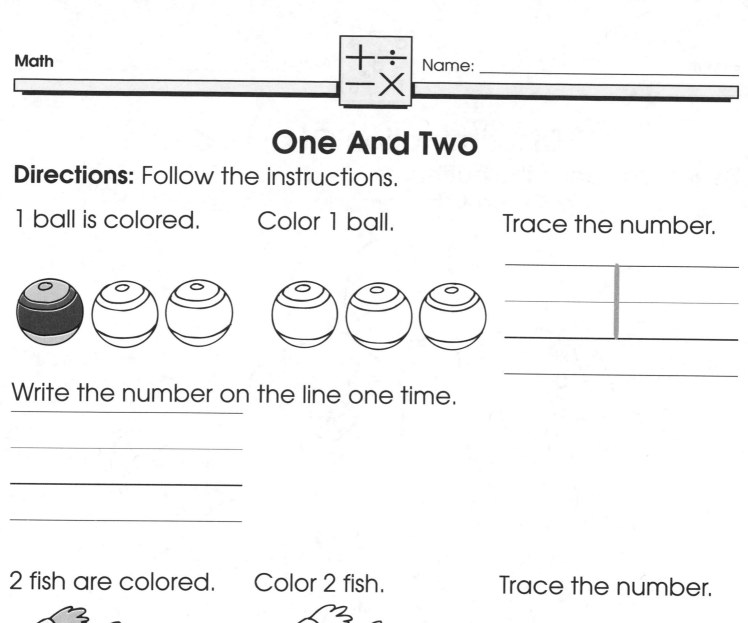

1 ball is colored.

Color 1 ball.

Trace the number.

Write the number on the line one time.

2 fish are colored.

Color 2 fish.

Trace the number.

Write the number on the lines two times.

Name: _____

Discrimination Of a, b, d

Directions: Color the butterflies.

a = yellow, b = orange, d = purple

Name: _____

Story Sense

Directions: Look at the large pictures. Draw a circle around the small box that shows what is more likely to happen next.

Name: _____

Three And Four

Directions: Follow the instructions.

3 birds are colored.   Color 3 birds.   Trace the number.

Write the number on the lines three times.

4 cats are colored.   Color 4 cats.   Trace the number.

Write the number on the lines four times.

Name: _____

Writing Upper Case Letters

Directions: Trace each letter. Write each letter again next to the letter you traced.

LESSON 3

The White House

The White House is where the President of the United States lives and works.

The President spends many hours reading in his beautiful office called the Oval Office. He must know what is happening in the United States and in other countries. The President must keep up with the news. Reading lets him know what is going on in the world. Reading helps the President decide what is best for our country.

What other things besides reading might the President do in the White House?

Name: _____

ACTIVITY 3

The White House

Directions: Look at the picture of the inside of the White House. The President has just finished eating breakfast. Now he is ready to work. Walk to the Oval Office with him by following the maze.

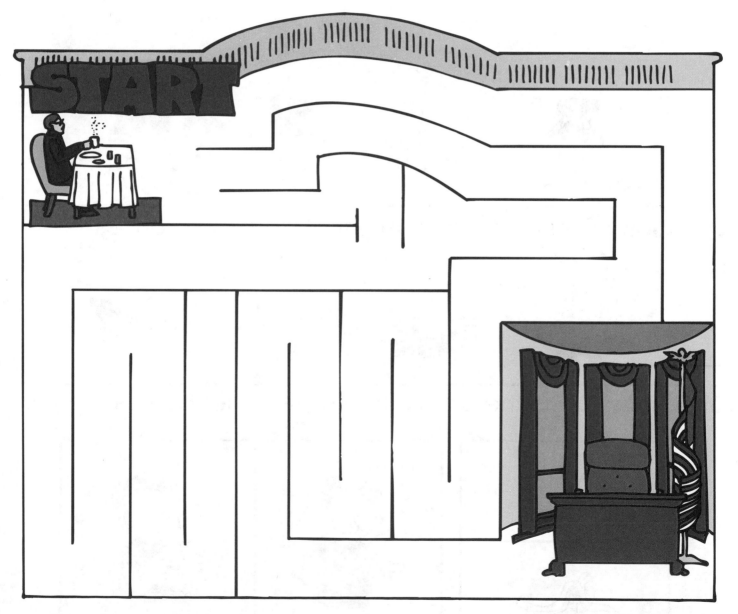

Review

Directions: Draw lines to match the opposites.

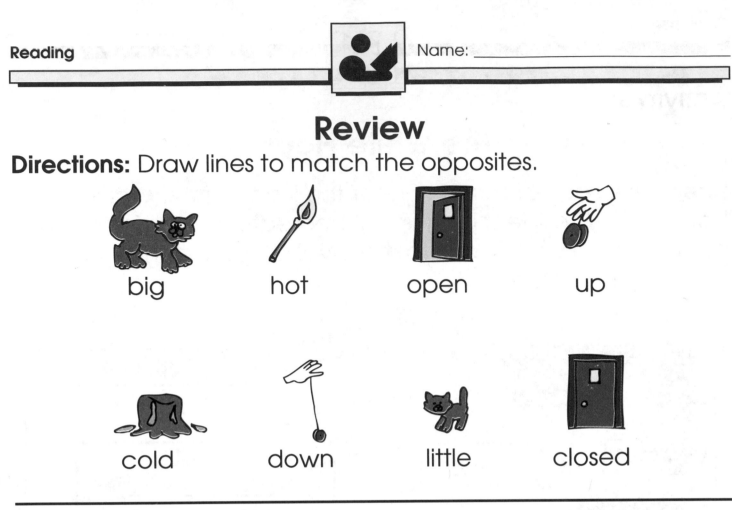

big   hot   open   up

cold   down   little   closed

Directions: Cross out the picture that doesn't belong.

Directions: Circle the picture that shows what comes before.

Name: _____

Five

Directions: Follow the instructions.

5 dogs are colored.

Color 5 dogs.

Trace the number. Write it on the lines five times.

5

Writing Lower Case Letters

Directions: Trace each letter. Write each letter again next to the letter you traced.

Name: _____

Review

Directions: Circle the picture that shows what comes after.

Directions: Write numbers in the boxes to show what order they belong in.

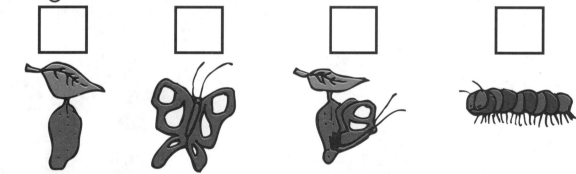

Directions: Circle the picture that shows what is likely to happen next.

Name: _____

Review

Directions: Follow the instructions.

1. Circle the pencil that is the shortest.

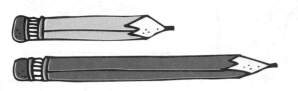

2. Draw a line from the number to the group that matches.

1

2

3

4

5

Review

Directions: Fill in the missing upper and lower case letters to complete the alphabet.

Name: _____

LESSON 4

The Declaration of Independence

On July 4, 1776, American leaders approved the Declaration of Independence. This important paper said Americans would no longer follow England's rules. It declared that a new country called the United States of America had been formed.

All citizens should know about the Declaration. The Declaration of Independence reminds us that we are free.

What does being free mean to you?

Name: _____

The Declaration of Independence

Directions: Pretend you were one of the people who approved the Declaration of Independence. What name would you have given to the new country? Write the nation's name on the line.

_____

_____

_____

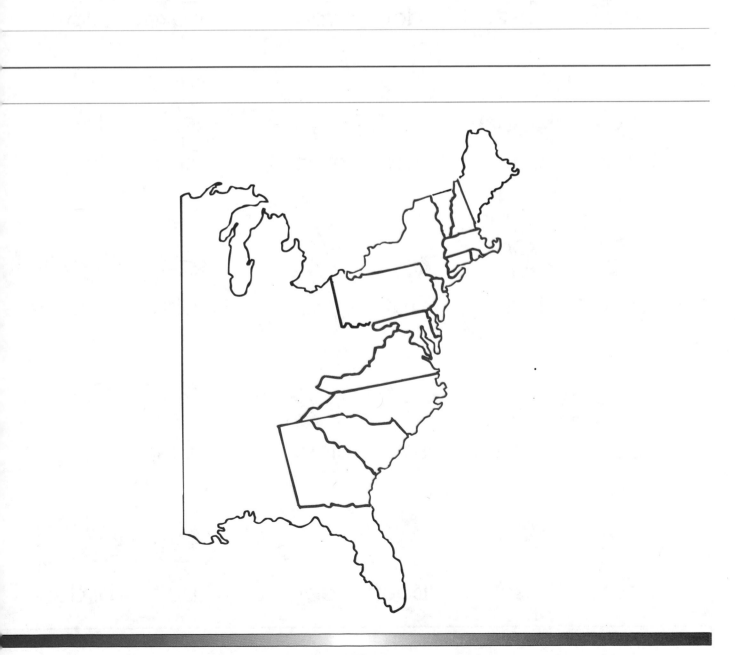

Name: _____

Rhyming Pairs

Directions: Circle the pairs that rhyme.
(Words with the same ending sounds.)

box   fox

map   nest

dog   frog

cake   cap

hat   bat

kite   mop

star   jar

can   fan

rat   pig

dish   fish

book   bottle

sock   clock

sun   leaf

nose   hose

beet   feet

ball   bird

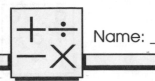

Name: _____

Numbers In Order

Directions: Look at each number. Count the balloons. Color the right number of balloons in each row.

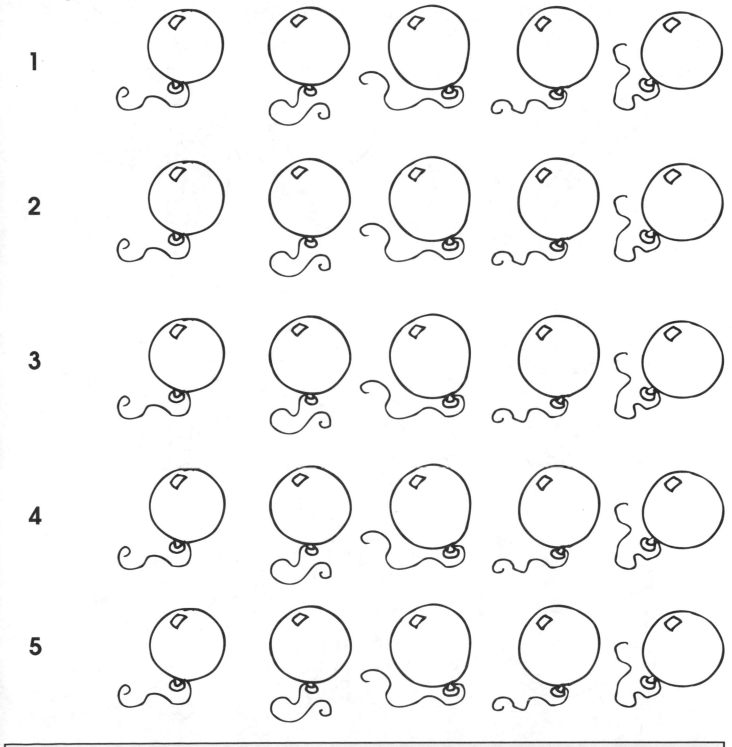

1

2

3

4

5

Beginning Consonant Sounds Bb, Cc, Dd

Directions: Say the sound that the letters Bb, Cc, Dd make. (Bb = buh, Cc = kuh, Dd = duh). Then say the name of each picture. If the first sound matches the letter, color it blue.

Name: _____

Rhyming Game

Directions: Think of a word that rhymes with the word given.
Draw a picture. Write the word.

cat

_____
_____
_____

pan

_____
_____

bug

_____
_____
_____

Name: _____

Numbers

Directions: Follow the instructions.

1. Write each number.

6   7   8   9   10

2. Write each number twice.

6   7   8   9   10

Beginning Consonant Sounds Ff, Gg, Hh

Directions: Say the sounds for the letters Ff, Gg, Hh. (Ff = fuh, Gg = guh, Hh = huh). Draw a circle around the picture if it begins with the letter in the column.

Name: _____

Christopher Columbus

In 1492, Christopher Columbus bravely set sail across the Atlantic Ocean from Europe. The places where Columbus landed had people, plants, and animals that Columbus and his sailors had never seen before.

Columbus's voyage opened up a whole new area of the world. It changed the way people lived.

How do you think the people on the islands felt when they saw Christopher Columbus, his men, and the three ships?

ACTIVITY 5

Christopher Columbus

Directions: Pretend you are a sailor. Think about what it would be like to leave on a long trip for an unknown land. Would you be excited? scared? happy? sad? Draw yourself leaving on one of Columbus's ships. Then color the three ships.

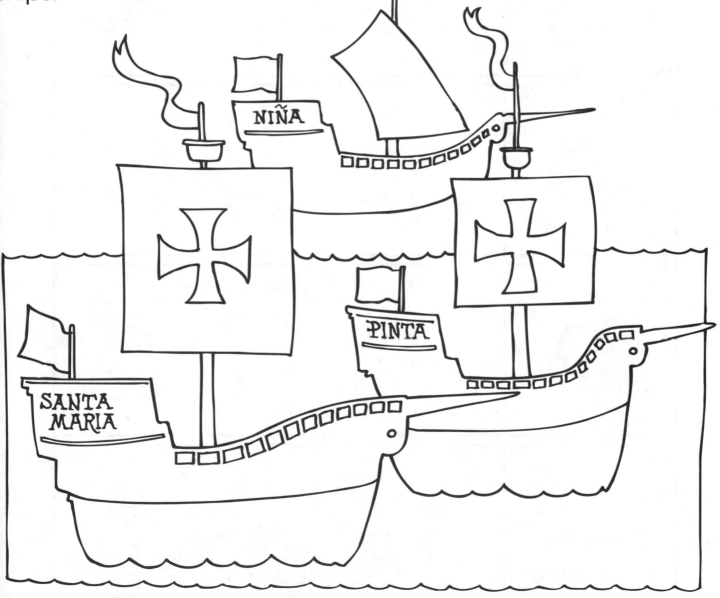

Beginning Sounds

Directions: Look at the picture in each box. Say its name. Color the pictures in that row beginning with the same sound.

Name: _____

Same

Directions: Follow the instructions.

1. Color the same number of ducks in the pond.

2. Draw kites so that Sue will have the same number as Billy.

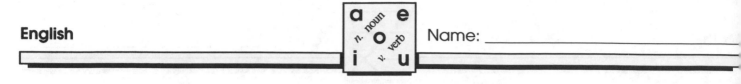

Name: _____

Beginning Sounds Jj, Kk, Ll

Directions: Draw a line from each picture to its beginning letter sound.

Name: _____

Words That Start With L

Directions: Color the picture in each box that starts like **lamb**.

Name: _____

More And Less

Directions: Follow the instructions.

Example:

more   **less**

1. Color the group that has more.

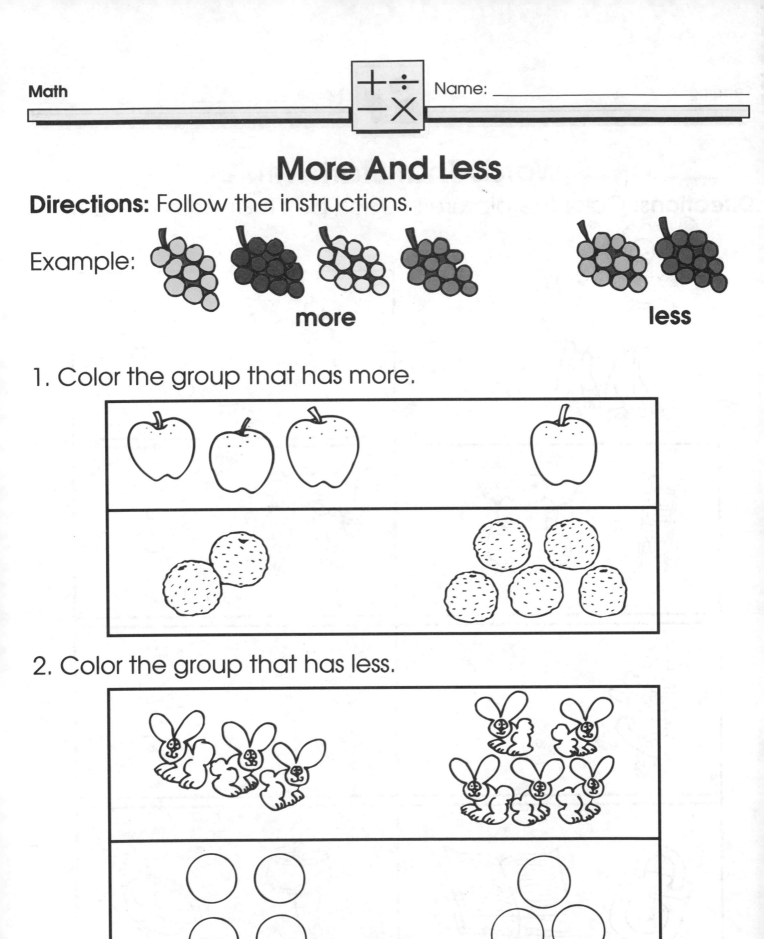

2. Color the group that has less.

Name: _____

Beginning Consonant Sounds Mm, Nn, Pp

Directions: Say the sound the letters Mm, Nn, and Pp make. (Mm = muh, Nn = nuh, Pp = puh). Color the picture if its beginning sound matches the letter.

LESSON 6

Thanksgiving Day

Long ago people called Pilgrims left England and came to America for freedom. Their first winter in New England was long and hard. Many Pilgrims died. But the next year, the Native Americans helped the Pilgrims learn to live in their new land. To celebrate a good harvest, the Pilgrims and the Native Americans shared a special feast of Thanksgiving.

Do you think that all the Native Americans were glad to help the Pilgrims?

ACTIVITY 6

Thanksgiving Day

Directions: Color the pictures of foods the Native Americans and Pilgrims ate at the First Thanksgiving. Then cut out the food and paste it on a paper plate. Enjoy the feast with other "Pilgrims" and "Native Americans."

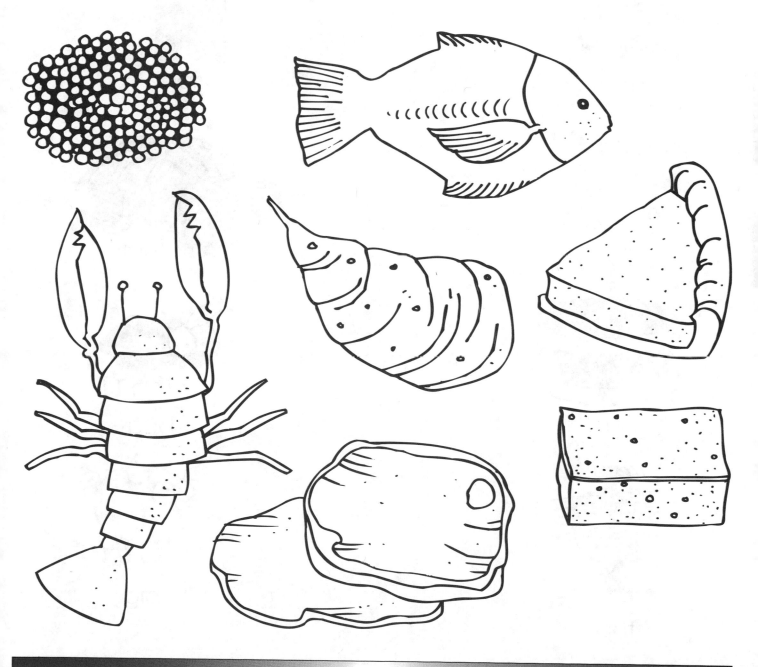

Name: _____

More Beginning Sounds

Directions: Look at the pictures. Say their names. Draw a line between pictures beginning with the same sound.

bee

door

pillow

turtle

drum

bug

top

pig

Name: _____

Counting

Directions: Study the picture. Read the questions. Draw a circle around the right number.

Count the s.   How many s in all?   **1   2   3**

Count the s.   How many s in all?   **1   2   3**

Count the s.   How many s in all?   **2   3   4**

Beginning Consonant Sounds Qq, Rr, Ss

Directions: Say the sound that the letters Qq, Rr, Ss make.
(Qq = quh, Rr = ruh, Ss = sss.) Draw a line from each picture to
its matching letter.

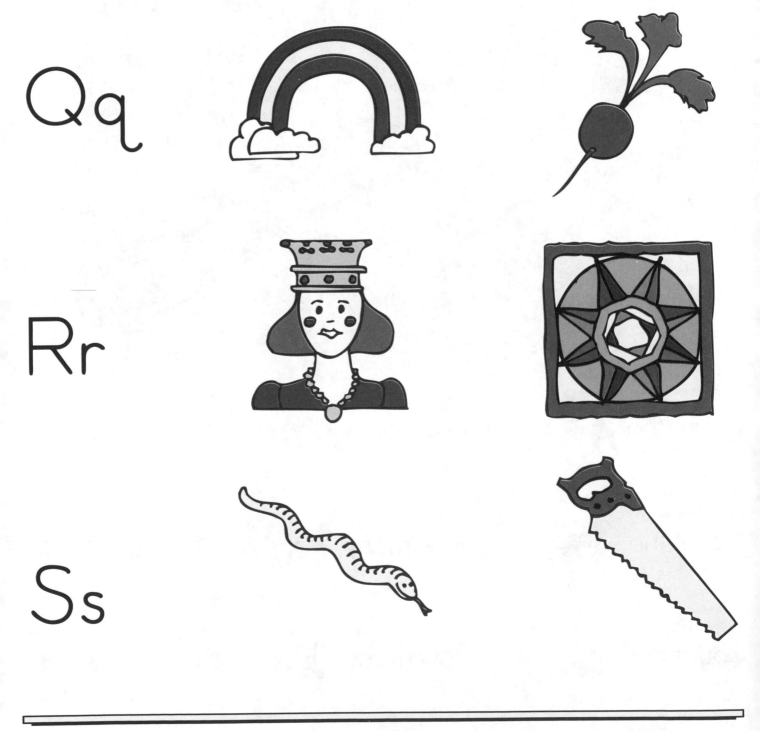

Words That Begin With r

Directions: Color the picture. Circle the six things that start with the sound of the letter **r**.

More Counting

Directions: Study each picture. Read the questions. Draw a circle around the right number.

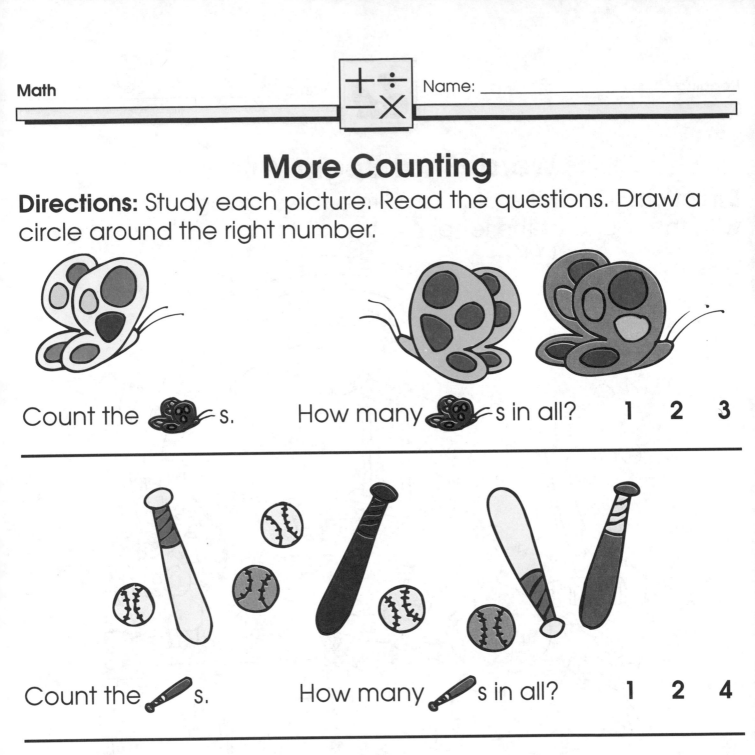

Count the s.   How many s in all?   **1   2   3**

Count the s.   How many s in all?   **1   2   4**

Count the s.   How many s in all?   **1   3   5**

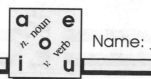
Beginning Consonant Sounds Tt, Vv, Ww

Directions: Say the sound that the letters Tt, Vv, Ww make. (T t= tuh, Vv = vuh, Ww = wuh.) Color each picture if it has the same beginning sound as the letter.

Name: _____

LESSON 7

The Statue of Liberty

The Statue of Liberty was a gift of friendship from the people of France to the people of the United States. Over the years, many people came to the United States on ships from other countries. As they passed the Statue of Liberty in New York Harbor, the people cheered and waved. The Statue of Liberty became a symbol of hope and freedom for these people who dreamed of becoming United States citizens.

What do you think the people on the ships said as they saw the Statue of Liberty in the harbor?

ACTIVITY 7

The Statue of Liberty

Directions: The Statue of Liberty is a symbol of friendship between two countries. Color the Statue of Liberty's torch. Cut out the friendship torch. Give your torch to a friend in another classroom as a symbol of friendship between two classes.

Beginning Sounds

Directions: Look at each picture. Say its name. Circle the
letter the word begins with.

d f	g s	d m
r n	m f	k b
l h	s w	t k
n d	l p	y w

Name: _____

First

Directions: Draw a circle around the first one in each row.

Example:

Name: _____

Beginning Consonant Sounds Xx, Yy, Zz

Directions: Say the sound that the letters Xx, Yy, Zz make. (Xx = zuh, as in xylophone; Yy = yuh; Zz = zuh. Sometimes Xx says its own name, as in xray.) Draw a circle around each picture if its beginning sound matches the letter.

Name: _____

Review

Directions: Circle the pairs that start with the same letter.

Name: _____

Review

Directions: Connect the dots in order from 1-10.
Color the finished drawing.

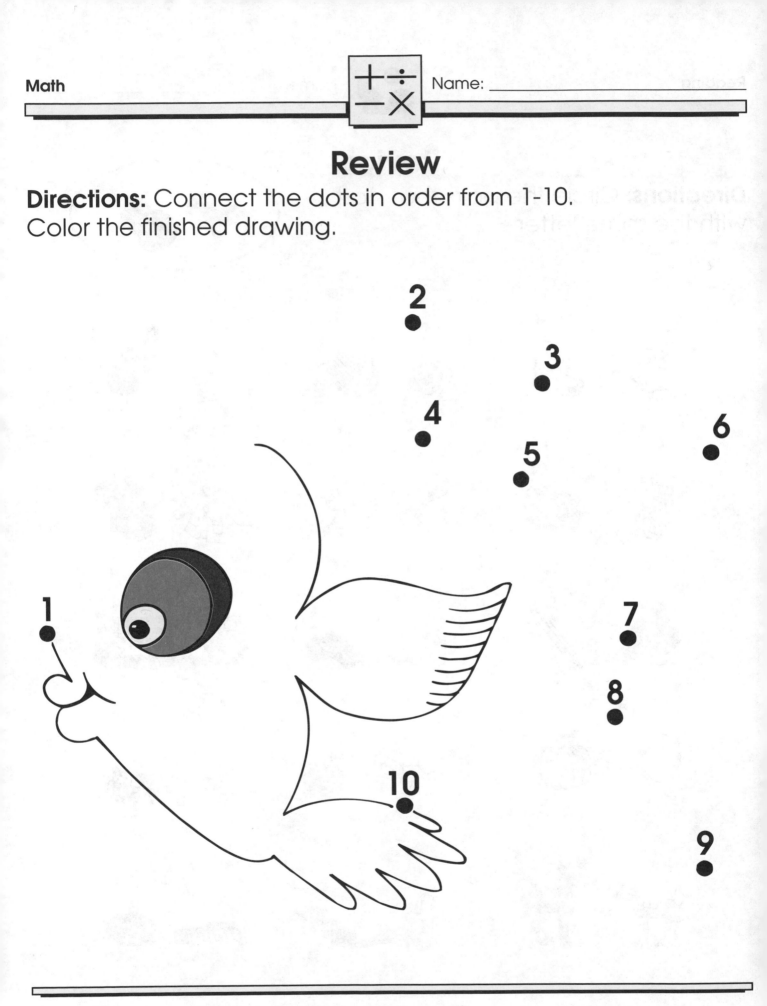

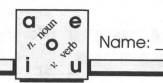

Name: _____

Review

Directions: Look at each picture. Say its name. Write the lower case letter for the beginning sound in each picture.

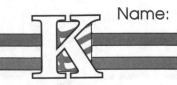

LESSON 8

The Liberty Bell

The Liberty Bell rang out in 1776 to tell everyone that the United States had become a new country.

Some years later, the Liberty Bell cracked. It could no longer be rung. Today Americans cannot hear the bell, but they can see it on display. Americans know the bell still stands for freedom.

The Liberty Bell is a symbol of our country.

Do you think the Liberty Bell will ever ring again? Why or why not?

ACTIVITY 8

The Liberty Bell

Directions: Color the Liberty Bell. Then cut it out. Use your Liberty Bell as a bookmark.

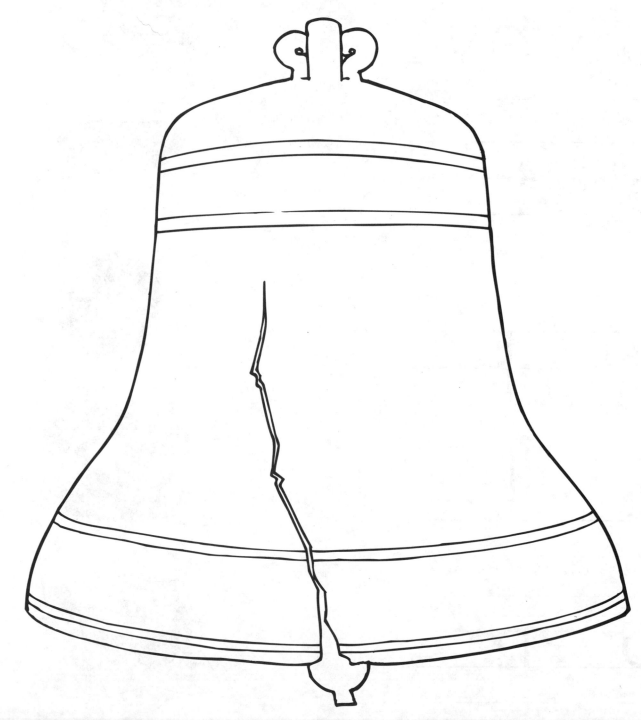

Name: _____

Words With a

Directions: Write the letter **a** to finish each word. Draw a line to match the word and its picture.

b___by

c___t

m___p

b___ll

p___n

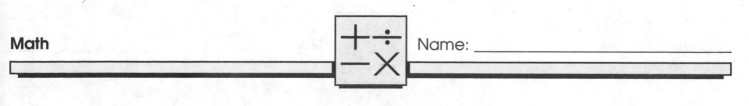
Circles

Directions: We see many circles every day. Circles can be different sizes. Find the circles on the drawings and trace over them. Color the finished drawings.

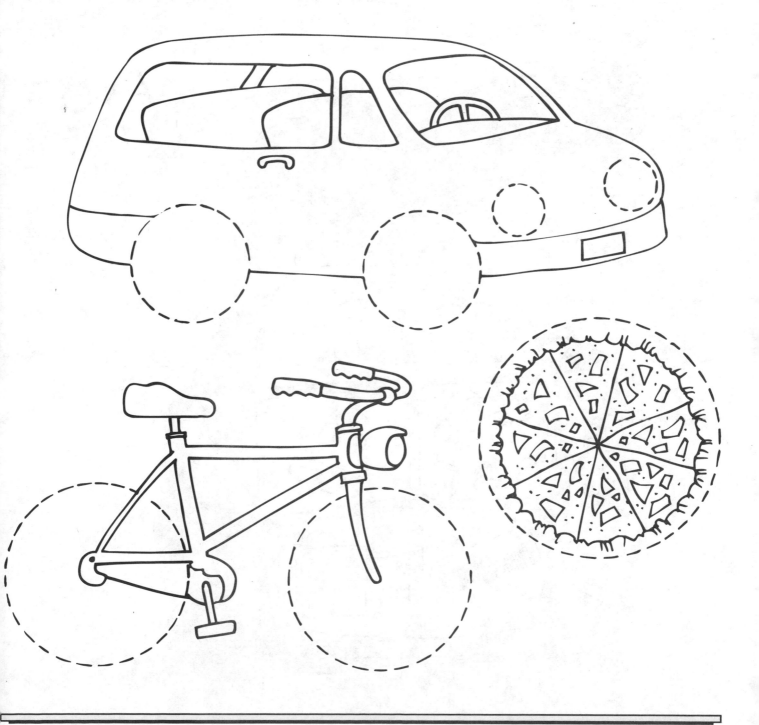

Name: _____

Beginning Short Vowel Sounds: A

Directions: Say the sound for the letter Aa. (The short vowel sound for Aa is heard at the beginning of the word alligator.) Color the pictures that begin with the short vowel sound.

Aa

Name: _____

Words With e

Directions: Color the pictures. Say the name of each picture. Write the letter **e** to finish each word.

n ___ t

b ___ d

b ___ ll

p ___ n

j ___ t

h ___ n

t ___ n

s ___ d

f ___ nce

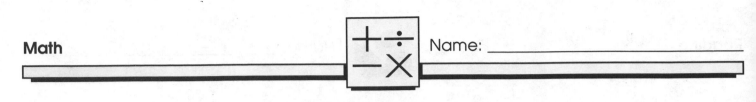

Squares

Directions: All squares have 4 sides. All 4 sides are the same length. Squares can be different sizes. Help Sue get home by coloring in the path that has only □ s.

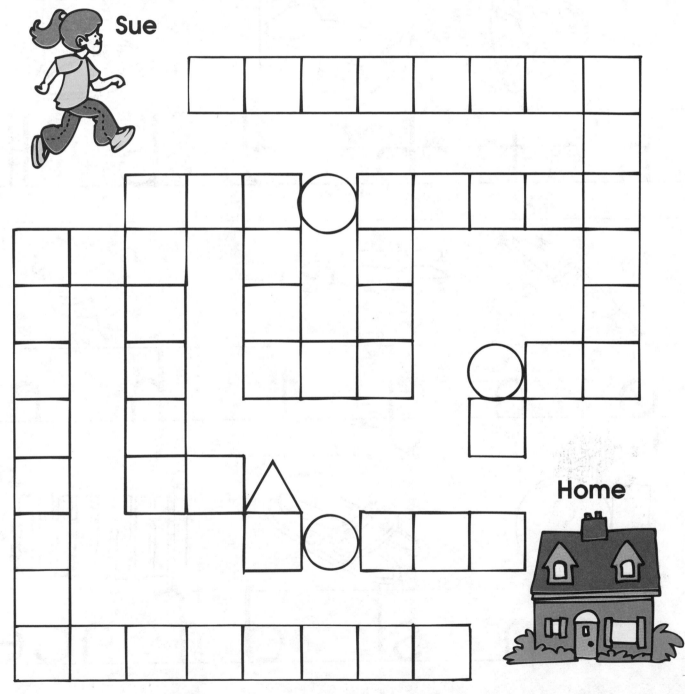

Beginning Short Vowel Sounds: Ee

Directions: Say the short vowel sound for the letter Ee. (It makes the same sound as the "e" in the word egg.) Look at the pictures. Color the pictures if they begin with the sound of the short vowel Ee.

LESSON 9

The Bald Eagle

The bald eagle is a big, strong bird. It stands for freedom and power. The bald eagle is the national bird of the United States. It is a symbol of our country.

Why do you think Americans chose the bald eagle to be a symbol of our country?

Name: _____

ACTIVITY 9

The Bald Eagle

Directions: Look at our national bird. The bald eagle is feeding its babies. The babies are called eaglets. Can you think of good names for the eaglets?

Name: _____

Words With i

Directions: Say the name of each picture. Draw lines from the dish to the pictures with the same middle sound.

Directions: Write the letter **i** to finish each word. Say the words.

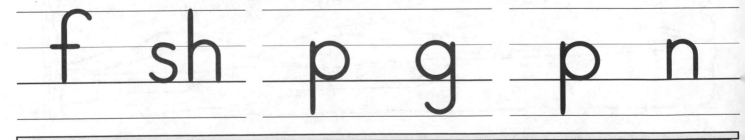

f___sh   p___g   p___n

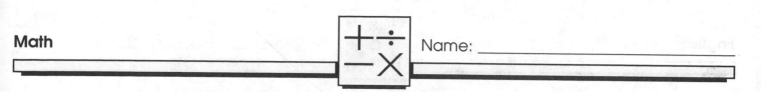
Rectangles

Directions: Like squares, all rectangles have 4 sides but only the opposite sides have to be the same length. Rectangles can be different sizes. Follow the instructions.

1. Study the shapes. Find the rectangles and color them.

2. Draw a circle around each picture that has the shape of a rectangle.

Example:

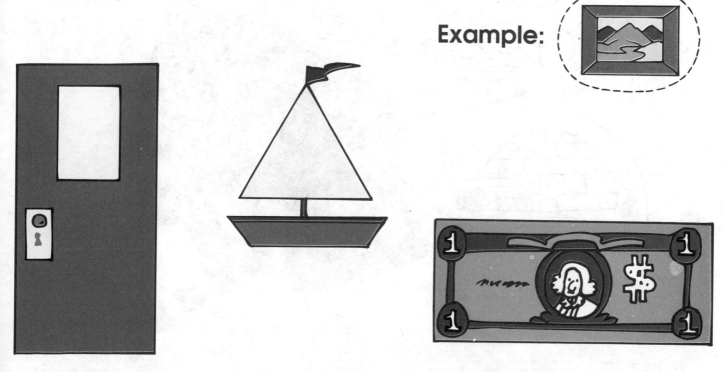

Name: _____

Beginning Short Vowel Sounds: I i

Directions: Say the short vowel sound for the letter **I** i. (The short vowel sound for the letter **I** i sounds like the "**I**" in Indian.) Look at the pictures. Color the pictures that begin with the short vowel sound of **I** i.

Name: _____

Words With o

Directions: Write the letter **o** to finish each word. Say the word.

f ___ x   l ___ g

d ___ g   fr ___ g

Directions: Find the pictures of the words you just wrote and circle them.

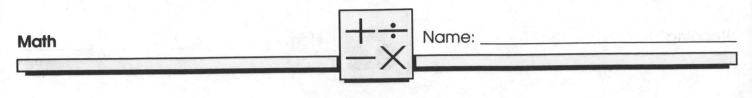
Triangles

Directions: All triangles have 3 sides. Triangles can be different sizes. Color the triangle shapes in the pictures.

Win

Beginning Short Vowel Sounds: Oo

Directions: Say the short vowel sound for Oo. (It makes the same sound as the "O" in Oscar.) Look at the pictures. Color the pictures that begin with the sound of Oo.

LESSON 10

The Fourth of July

Each year on the Fourth of July, Americans celebrate the birthday of the United States. Citizens remember that long ago other Americans worked and fought so that our country would be free. Citizens celebrate the Fourth of July in all kinds of ways.

Happy Birthday, United States!

How does your family celebrate the Fourth of July?

ACTIVITY 10

The Fourth of JULY

Directions: It is the Fourth of July. Fireworks are lighting up the night sky. Take part in the celebration. Add more safe fireworks to our country's birthday show.

Words With u

Directions: Write the letter **u** to finish each word. Say the word.
Draw a line to match each word with its picture.

g___m

b___s

c___p

d___ck

b___g

Name: _____

Shapes

Directions: Color the shapes to finish this picture.

These are the shapes you will need to color.

Color □ s yellow.   Color ○ s blue.
Color △ s red.   Color ▭ s green.

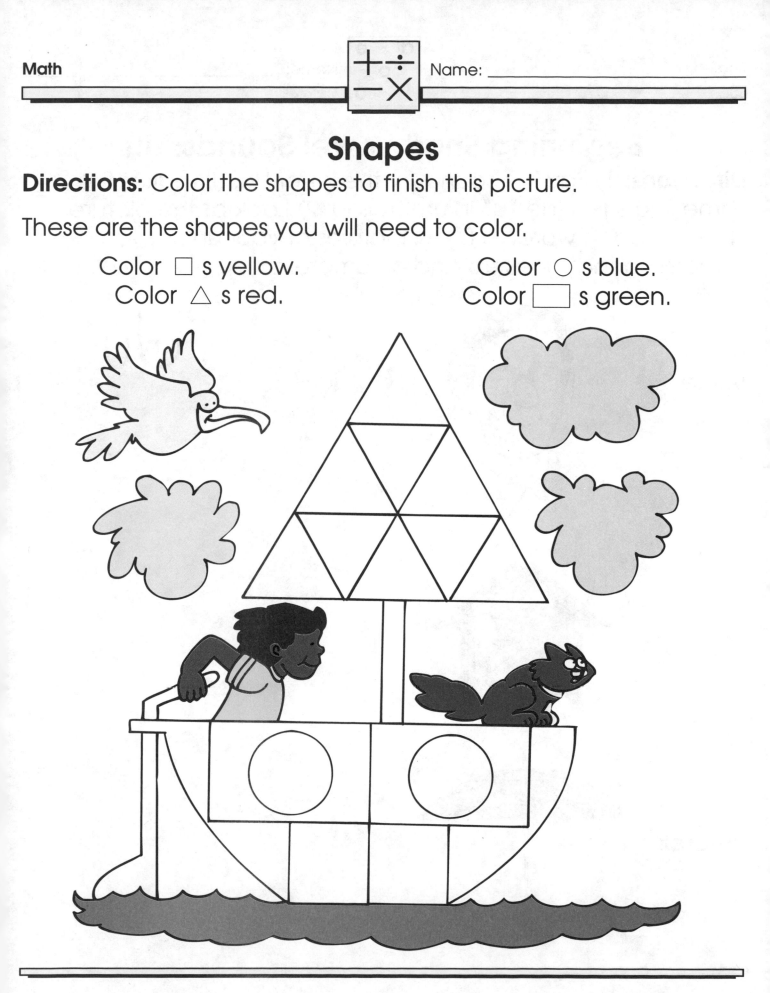

Beginning Short Vowel Sounds: Uu

Directions: 1) Say the sound for the letter Uu. (It makes the same sound as the "u" in umbrella.) 2) Look at the pictures and say each word. 3) Draw pictures of your uncle, something that goes up and an umbrella.

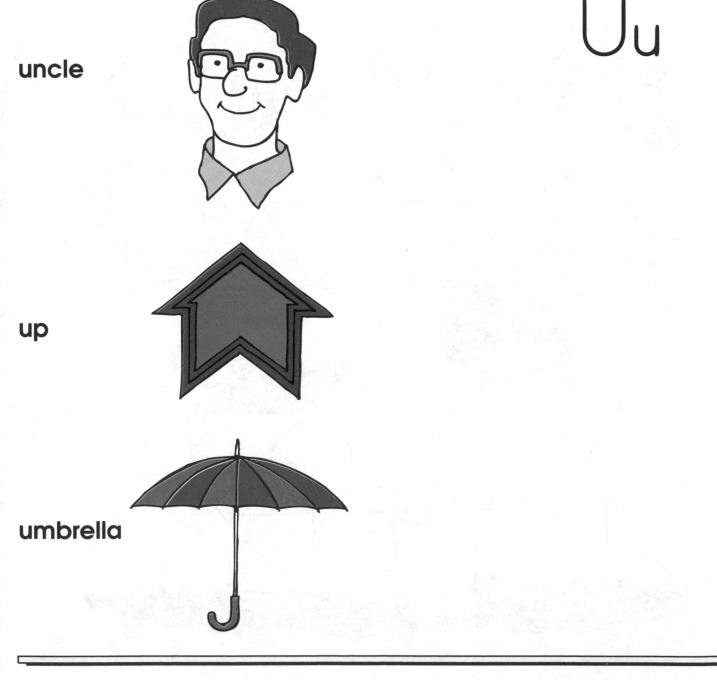

uncle

up

umbrella

Uu

Name: _____

Middle Sounds

Directions: Look at the picture in each box. Say its name. Color the pictures in that row that have the same middle sound.

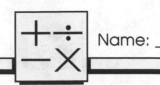 Name: _____

Matching Shapes

Directions: Draw a line from the shapes on the left to their matching shapes on the right.

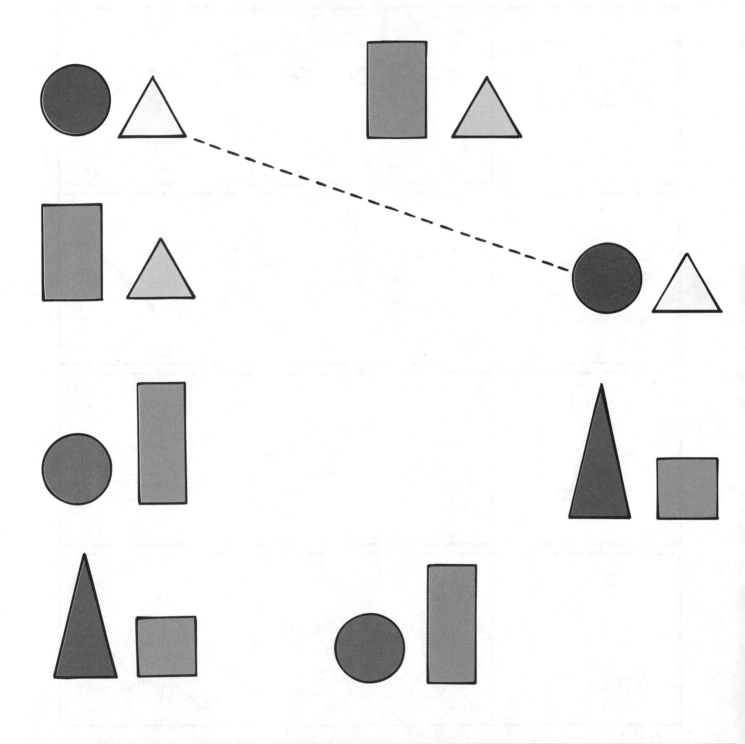

Name: _____

Middle Sounds With Short Vowels

Directions: Say the name of each picture. Listen for the middle sound. Draw a line between the picture and its matching letter.

Name: _____

LESSON 11

The Lincoln Memorial

The Lincoln Memorial stands at the top of a long flight of steps in front of a large pool in Washington, D.C.

The Lincoln Memorial honors Abraham Lincoln, the 16th President of the United States. On the inside of the memorial is a huge statue of Abraham Lincoln.

Abraham Lincoln believed that all people were important. He believed that all Americans should have equal chances to do their best.

How can you show your friends that they are important?

Name: _____

ACTIVITY 11

The Lincoln Memorial

Directions: Look at President Abraham Lincoln and the Lincoln Memorial on the pennies. Count the pennies. Write the numeral on the line.

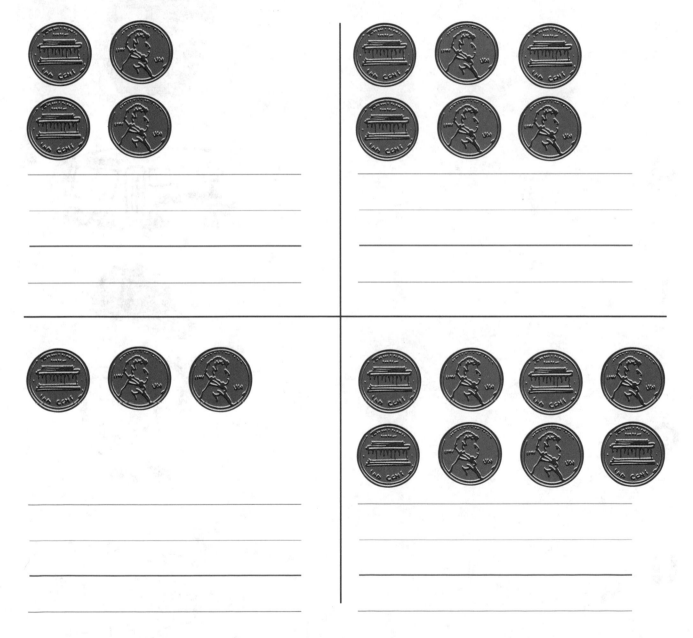

Middle Sounds

Directions: Look at the picture. Say its name. Draw a line to the letter that makes its middle sound.

a

e

i

o

u

Finding Patterns

Directions: See how the shapes are arranged in each row. Circle the one that completes the pattern. The first one is done for you.

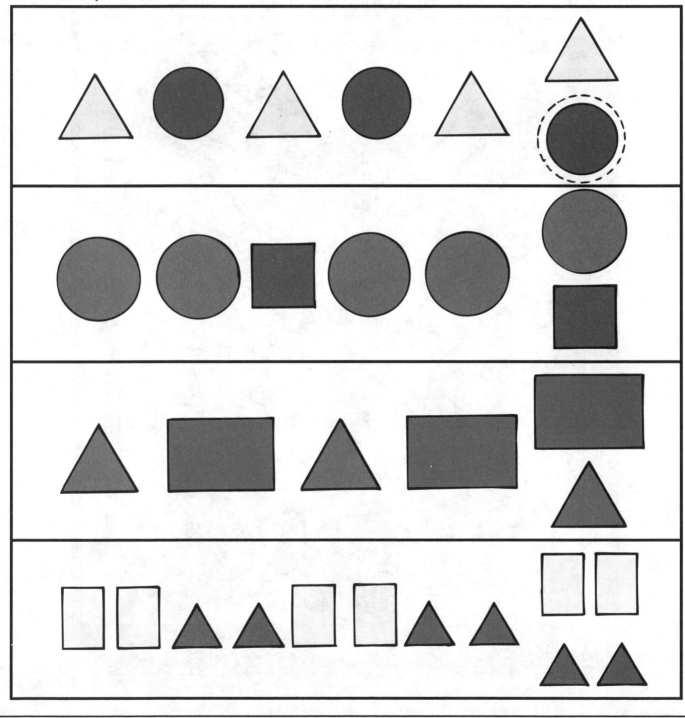

Name: _____

Middle Sounds: Short Vowel Sounds

Directions: Look at the pictures. Write the letter for the sound you hear in the middle of the word.

Name: _____

Review

Directions: Trace the letters.

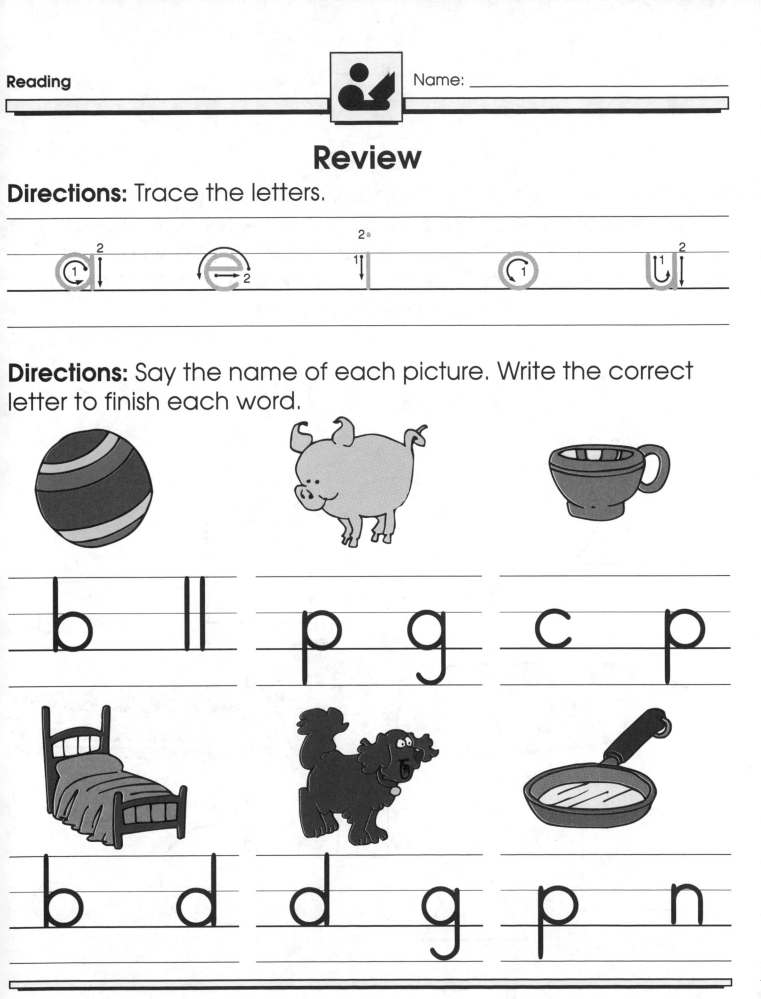

Directions: Say the name of each picture. Write the correct letter to finish each word.

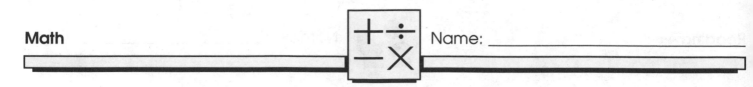

Name: _____

Review

Directions: Look at all the shapes in the picture. 1. Color the ◯ s blue. Color the ☐ s red. Color the △ s green. 2. Draw a line under the small blue ◯ above the rocket. 3. Draw a circle around the large red ☐ below the rocket. 4. Put an **X** on the small green △ below the rocket.

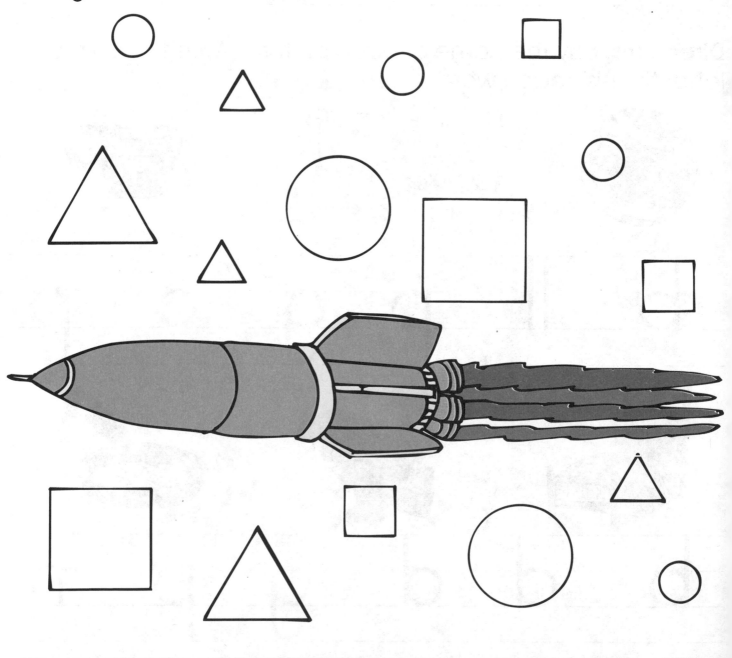

Review

Directions: 1) Look at each picture and say its name. 2) Write the beginning or middle vowel sound that you hear. 3) If you hear the sound at the beginning of the word, color the picture blue. 4) If you hear the sound in the middle of the word, color the picture yellow.

LESSON 12

The Bill of Rights

The Constitution of the United States is the law that tells us how our government works. The Bill of Rights is part of the Constitution that protects all Americans. It says that each person is important. The Bill of Rights says people deserve certain rights.

Americans can worship as they want.

Citizens can write and speak openly.

Americans can meet to talk about ways to make our government better.

What might happen if United States citizens did not have the Bill of Rights?

Name: _____

ACTIVITY 12

The Bill of Rights

Directions: The Bill of Rights says that you are an important citizen. In the center of the blue ribbon, draw a picture of something you do that makes you feel important. Cut out your citizenship award. Wear it proudly!

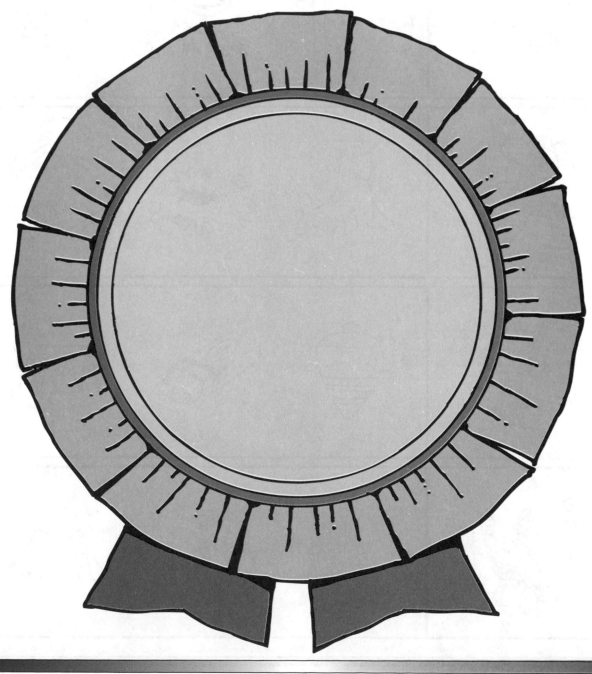

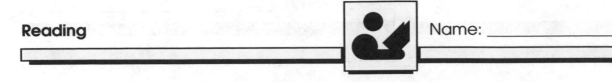

Ending Sounds

Directions: Look at the picture in each box. Say its name.
Color the pictures in each row that end with the same sound.

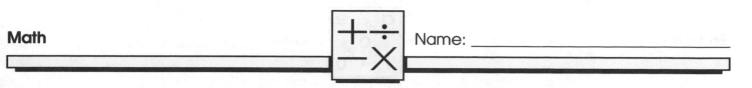

Name: _____

First, Second, Third

Directions: Study the pictures on the right. What happens first? What happens second? What happens third? Draw a line from the correct word to the picture.

first

second

third

Name: _____

Words With Short Vowel Aa

Directions: Read the words. Draw a line from the picture to its matching word.

Name: _____

Ending Sounds

Directions: Look at the picture in each box. Say its name.
Circle the letter that the word ends with.

d t	b p	x s
n m	g f	s b
r t	d r	g v
l p	k m	t n

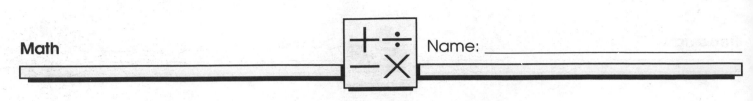
Time

Directions: Trace the numbers on the clock. What time do you wake up in the morning? Draw the clock hands to show when.

Name: _____

Words With Short Vowel Ee

Directions: Read the words. Circle the picture whose sound has short vowel e.

net

fence

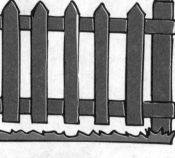

bell

ten

LESSON 13

The United States Flag

The United States flag stands for our country and its people. Americans display, or show, the red, white, and blue flag because they are proud of the United States.

Circle the United States flag in the pictures.

When do you think the United States flag should be displayed? Why?

ACTIVITY 13

The United States Flag

Directions: Color the United States flag red, white, and blue. Proudly display our country's flag in a classroom parade.

Name: _____

Word Families

Directions: Say the name of the picture in the box. Color the pictures in each row that have the same ending sound.

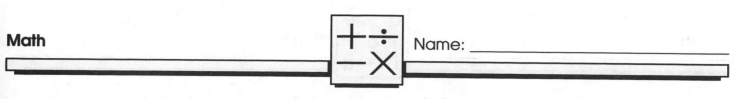

More Time

Directions: Study the pictures. Which picture in each row happens first? Draw a circle around the picture that shows what happens first.

Words With Short Vowel Ii

Directions: Read the words. Draw a line from each word to its matching picture.

Name: _____

Words That End With an

Directions: Say the name of each picture. Draw a line to match each picture with its word.
Write the missing letter.

f n

c n

p n

Directions: Can you write the word that matches this picture?

_____

_____

How Much Time?

Directions: Study the pictures. Circle the picture that takes more time in each row.

Name: _____

Words With Short Vowel Oo

Directions: Look at the pictures and read the words. Draw a line from each picture to the word that describes it.

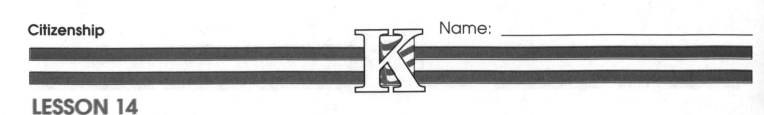

LESSON 14

Children Drummers

Long ago children were allowed to serve in American armies. Some young people helped by beating their drums. Their drums called the troops to battle. The drummers signaled important messages. Drummers sounded beats for marching drills too.

Was a drummer's job dangerous? Tell why you think as you do.

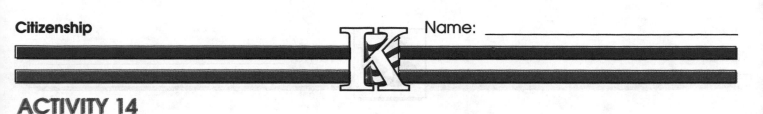

Name: _____

ACTIVITY 14

Children Drummers

Directions: Pretend you are a drummer for your country. Decorate a drum with the pictures below. Beat your drum to let others know you are proud to be a United States citizen.

Name: _____

Words That End With at

Directions: Say the name of the picture. Write the missing letters.

h _____ t

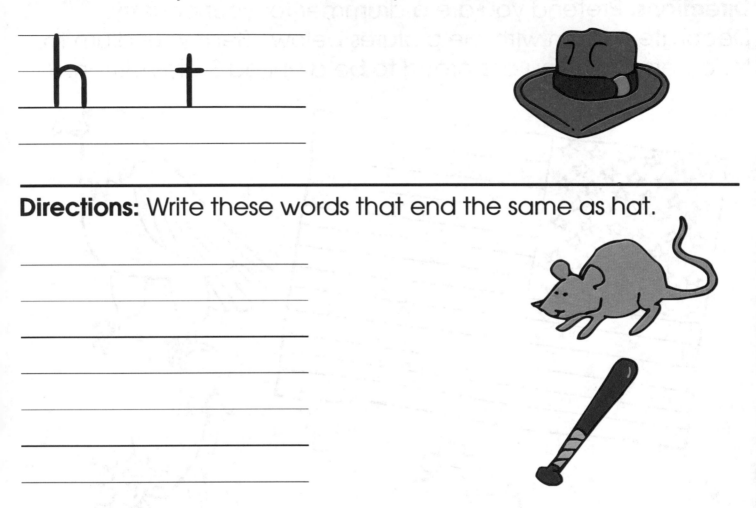

Directions: Write these words that end the same as hat.

Directions: Can you think of another word that sounds like hat? Write the word. Draw the picture.

Name: _____

Penny, Nickel, Dime

Directions: Color each penny brown. Draw a line under each nickel. Draw a circle around each dime.

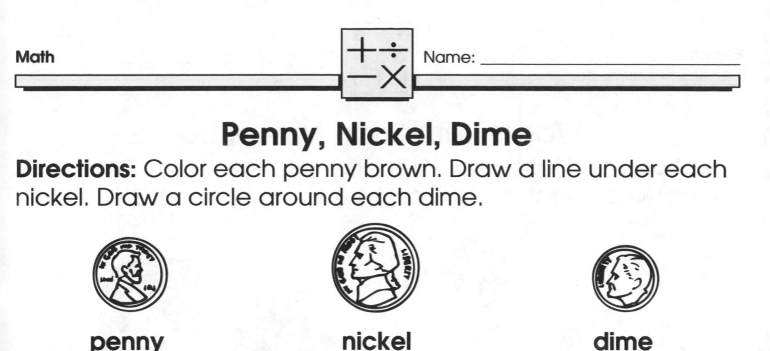

penny   **nickel**   **dime**

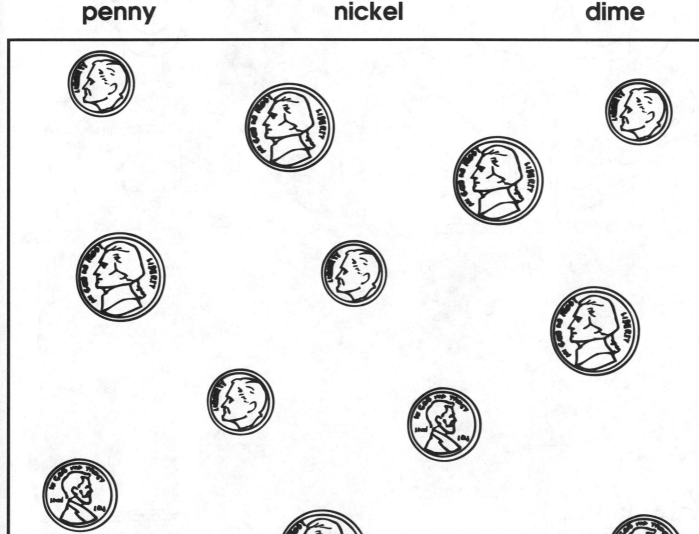

Name: _____

Words With Short Vowel Uu

Directions: Look at the pictures and read the words. Draw a line between each picture and the word that describes it.

bus

cup

gum

bug

LESSON 15

Labor Day

All citizens working together help to keep our country strong. Labor Day is a holiday that honors working people. On Labor Day citizens are reminded that all jobs are important.

Look at the many working people in this school. Name their important jobs.

Think of other school workers and add one to the picture.

Name: _____

ACTIVITY 15

Labor Day

Directions: Color and cut out the citizen worker finger puppets. Make one look like you. Paste the tabs together. Then put on a puppet play that shows how Americans working together, including children who are **Citizens Now**, help to make our country great.

Name: _____

Review

Directions: Trace the words.

fat red big

Directions: Look at each picture. Say the word. Pick a word from the top with the same ending as the word in the picture. Write the words to finish the sentences.

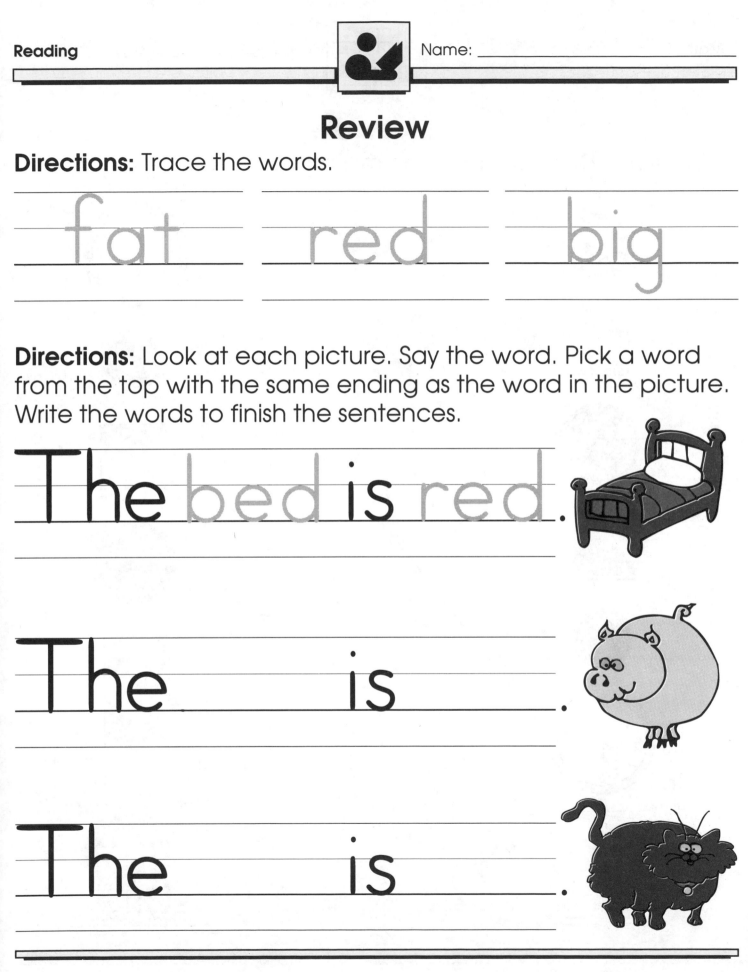

The bed is red.

The _____ is _____.

The _____ is _____.

Name: _____

Review

Directions: Draw a line to the matching pictures.

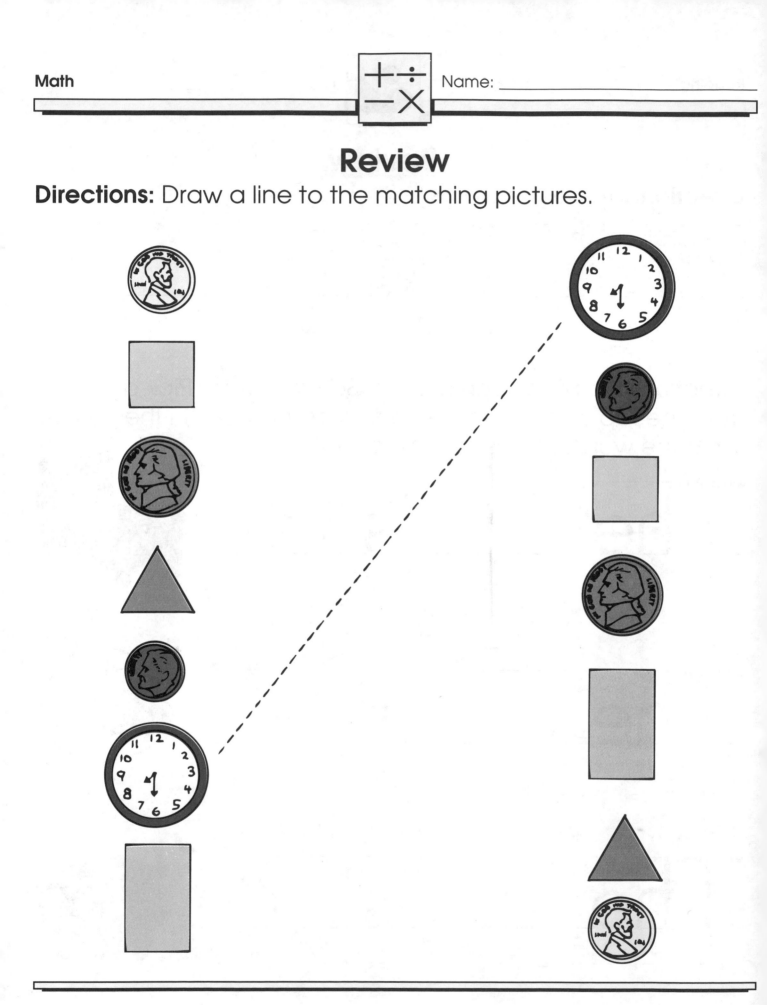

Review

Directions: Look at the pictures and read the words. Draw a line between each picture and the word that describes it.

pig

fox

fish

bus

top

map

bed

duck

net

cat

Glossary

Reading Glossary

Beginning Sounds. The sounds made by the first letters of words.

Classifying. Putting similar things into categories.

Ending Sounds. The sounds made by the last letters of words.

Middle Sounds. The sounds made by the vowels.

Opposites. Things that are different in every way.

Rhymes. Words with the same ending sounds.

Sequencing. Putting things in logical order.

Words Families. Words with the same ending sounds, i.e., words that rhyme.

Math Glossary

Addition. The adding of two or more numbers to find the sum.

Customary System. A measurement system that measures length in inches, feet, yards and miles; capacity is measured using cups, pints, quarts and gallon; temperature is measured in degrees Fahrenheight.

Metric System. A measurement system that measures length in millimeters, centimeters, meters, and kilometers; capacity in milliliters and liters; mass in grams and kilograms; and temperature in degrees Celsius.

Place Value. The value of a digit determined by its position in a number.

Subtraction. The taking away or deducting of one number from another.

English Glossary

ABC Order. Putting objects or words in the same order in which they appear in the alphabet.

Lower Case Letters. The letters which are often called "small" letters.
They are: a b c d e f g h i j k l m n o p q r s t u v w x y z

Upper Case Letters. The letters of the alphabet which are called the "capital" letters.
They are: A B C D E F G H I J K L M N O P Q R S T U V W X Y Z

NOTES

NOTES

NOTES

NOTES

NOTES

NOTES

NOTES

NOTES

NOTES

NOTES

NOTES

NOTES

NOTES

NOTES

NOTES

NOTES

ANSWER KEY

COMPREHENSIVE CURRICULUM
OF BASIC SKILLS
K

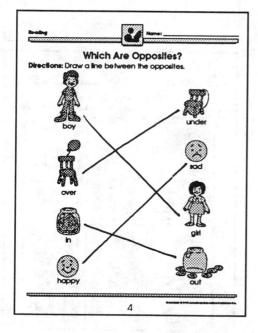

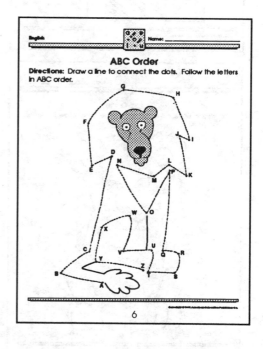

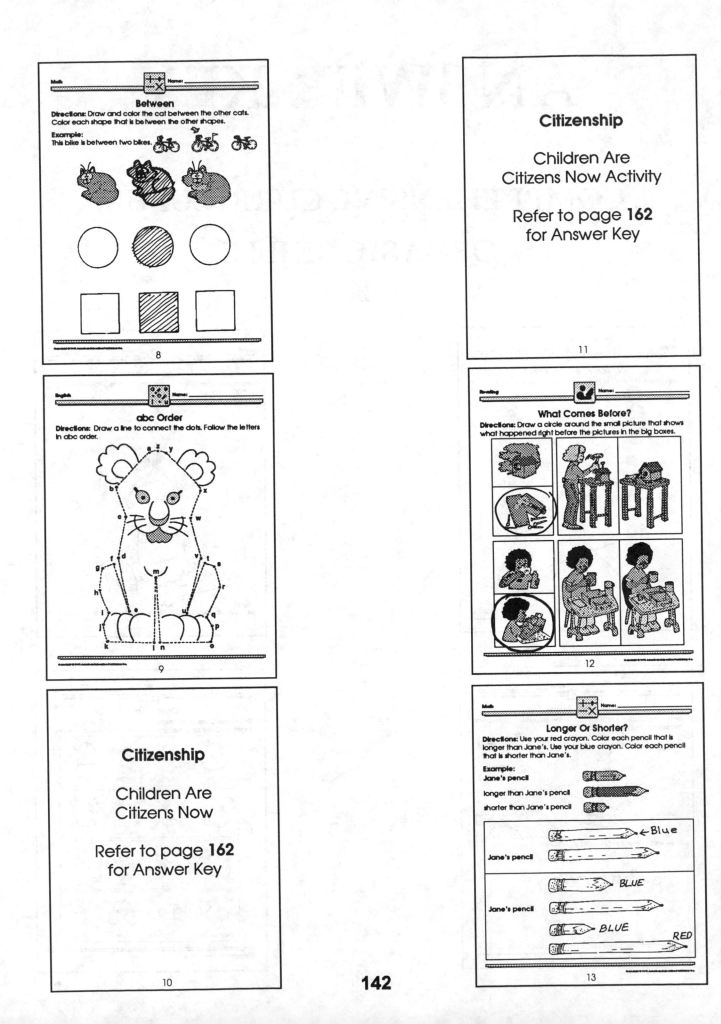

Between

Directions: Draw and color the cat between the other cats. Color each shape that is between the other shapes.

Example:
This bike is between two bikes.

8

abc Order

Directions: Draw a line to connect the dots. Follow the letters in abc order.

9

Citizenship

Children Are
Citizens Now

Refer to page **162**
for Answer Key

10

Citizenship

Children Are
Citizens Now Activity

Refer to page **162**
for Answer Key

11

What Comes Before?

Directions: Draw a circle around the small picture that shows what happened right before the pictures in the big boxes.

12

Longer Or Shorter?

Directions: Use your red crayon. Color each pencil that is longer than Jane's. Use your blue crayon. Color each pencil that is shorter than Jane's.

Example:
Jane's pencil

longer than Jane's pencil

shorter than Jane's pencil

Jane's pencil ← Blue

Jane's pencil BLUE

BLUE

RED

13

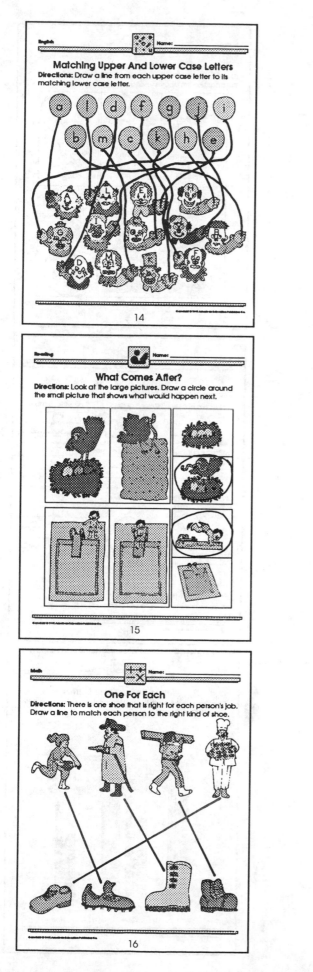

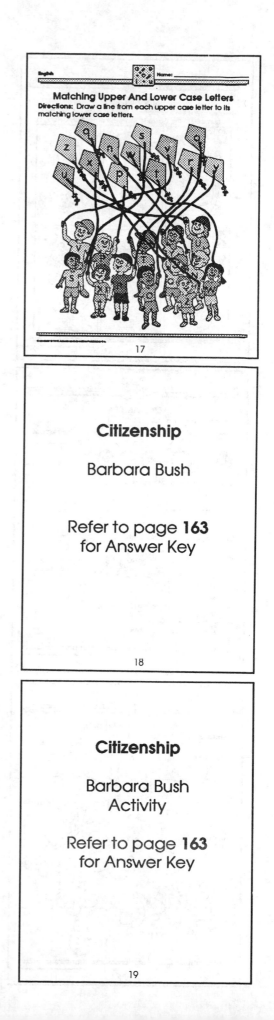

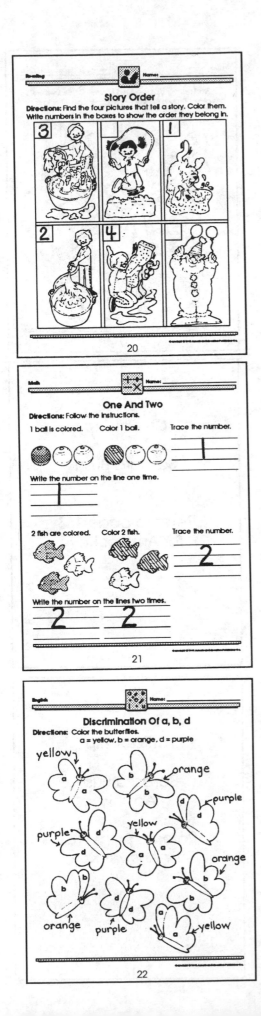

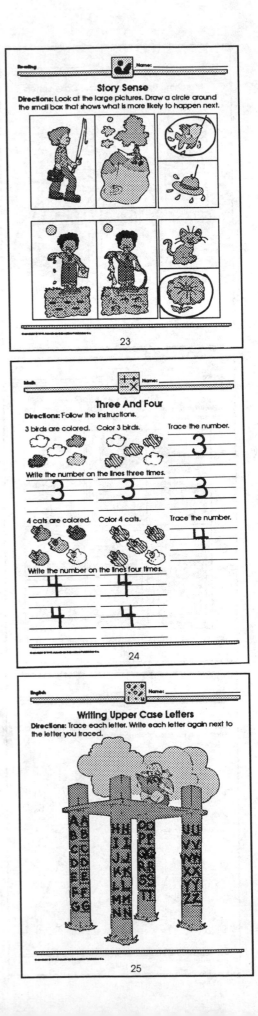

Story Order

Directions: Find the four pictures that tell a story. Color them. Write numbers in the boxes to show the order they belong in.

20

One And Two

Directions: Follow the instructions.

1 ball is colored.   Color 1 ball.   Trace the number.

Write the number on the line one time.

2 fish are colored.   Color 2 fish.   Trace the number.

Write the number on the lines two times.

21

Discrimination Of a, b, d

Directions: Color the butterflies.
a = yellow, b = orange, d = purple

yellow

orange

purple

purple

yellow

orange

orange   purple   yellow

22

Story Sense

Directions: Look at the large pictures. Draw a circle around the small box that shows what is more likely to happen next.

23

Three And Four

Directions: Follow the instructions.

3 birds are colored.   Color 3 birds.   Trace the number.

Write the number on the lines three times.

4 cats are colored.   Color 4 cats.   Trace the number.

Write the number on the lines four times.

24

Writing Upper Case Letters

Directions: Trace each letter. Write each letter again next to the letter you traced.

25

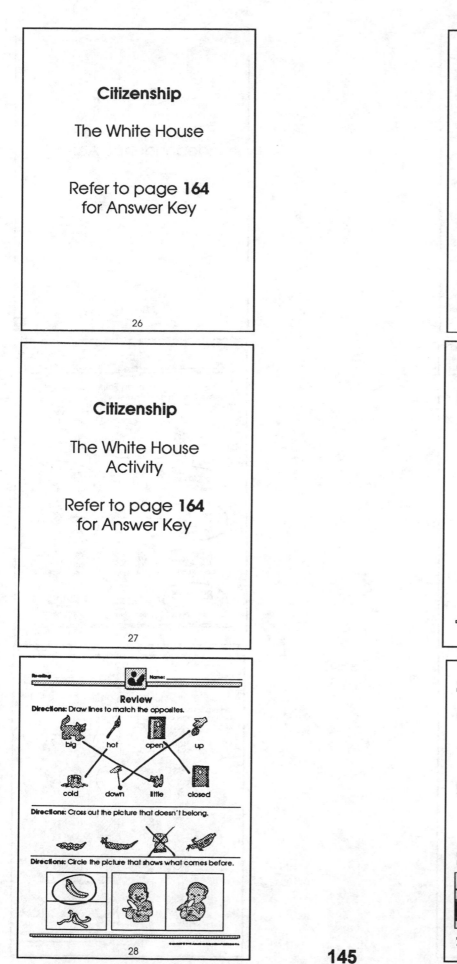

Citizenship

The White House

Refer to page **164**
for Answer Key

26

Citizenship

The White House
Activity

Refer to page **164**
for Answer Key

27

Review
Directions: Draw lines to match the opposites.

big   hot   open   up

cold   down   little   closed

Directions: Cross out the picture that doesn't belong.

Directions: Circle the picture that shows what comes before.

28

Five
Directions: Follow the instructions.

5 dogs are colored.

Color 5 dogs.

Trace the number. Write it on the lines five times.

29

Writing Lower Case Letters
Directions: Trace each letter. Write each letter again next to the letter you traced.

30

Review
Directions: Circle the picture that shows what comes after.

Directions: Write numbers in the boxes to show what order they belong in.

Directions: Circle the picture that shows what is likely to happen next.

31

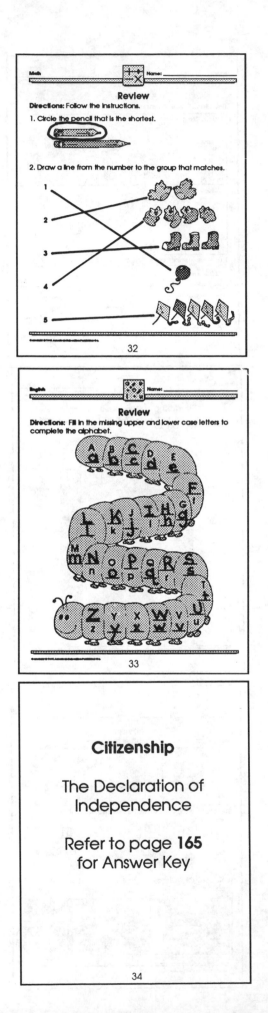

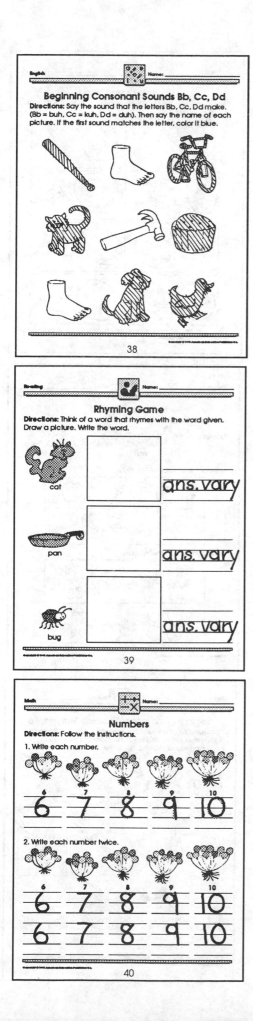

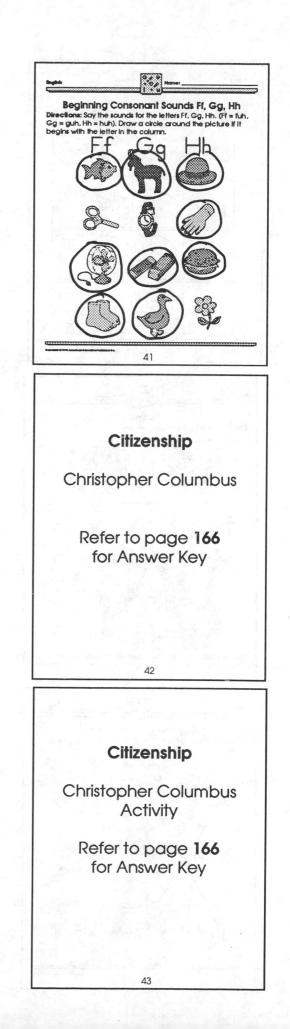

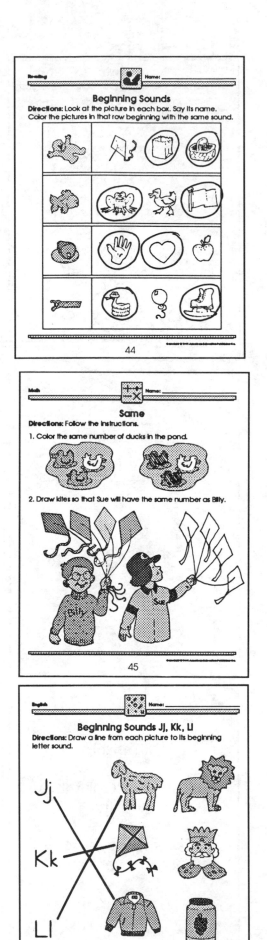

Beginning Sounds

Directions: Look at the picture in each box. Say its name. Color the pictures in that row beginning with the same sound.

44

Same

Directions: Follow the instructions.

1. Color the same number of ducks in the pond.

2. Draw kites so that Sue will have the same number as Billy.

45

Beginning Sounds Jj, Kk, Ll

Directions: Draw a line from each picture to its beginning letter sound.

Jj

Kk

Ll

46

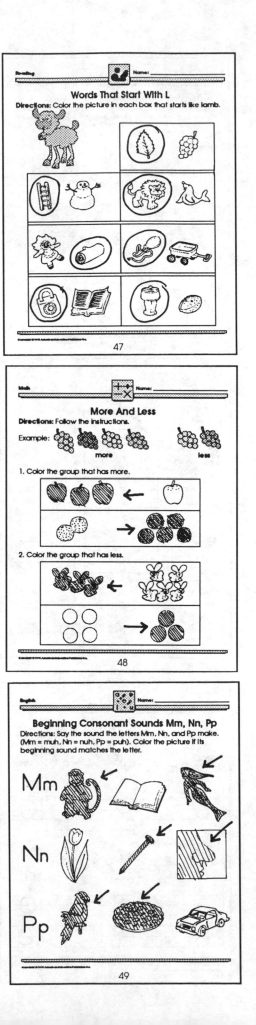

Words That Start With L

Directions: Color the picture in each box that starts like lamb.

47

More And Less

Directions: Follow the instructions.

Example: more   less

1. Color the group that has more.

2. Color the group that has less.

48

Beginning Consonant Sounds Mm, Nn, Pp

Directions: Say the sound the letters Mm, Nn, and Pp make. (Mm = muh, Nn = nuh, Pp = puh). Color the picture if its beginning sound matches the letter.

Mm

Nn

Pp

49

Citizenship

Thanksgiving Day

Refer to page **167**
for Answer Key

50

Citizenship

Thanksgiving Day
Activity

Refer to page **167**
for Answer Key

51

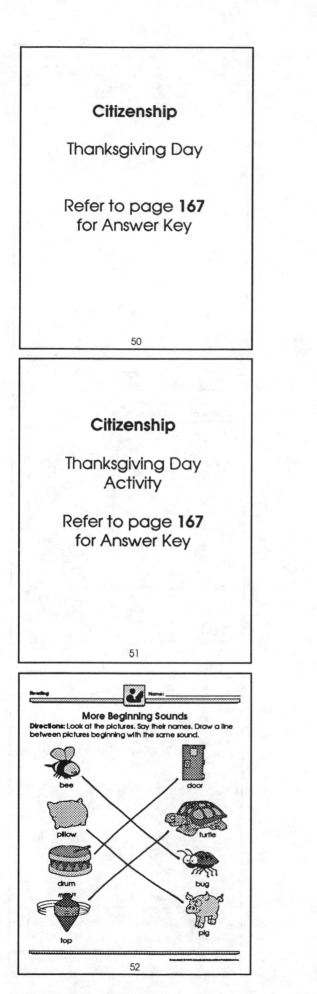

More Beginning Sounds

Directions: Look at the pictures. Say their names. Draw a line between pictures beginning with the same sound.

bee — door
pillow — turtle
drum — bug
top — pig

52

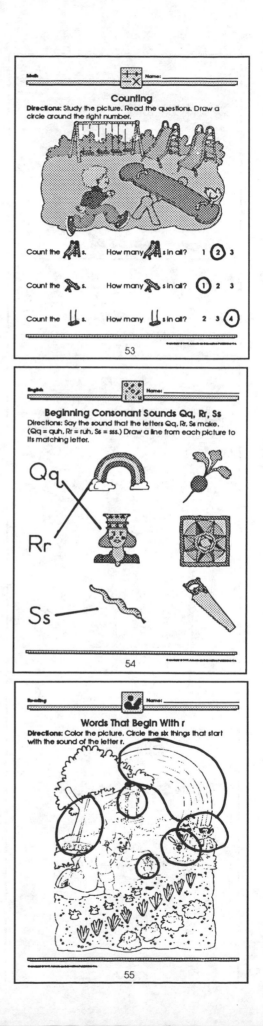

Counting

Directions: Study the picture. Read the questions. Draw a circle around the right number.

Count the 🪜s. How many 🪜s in all? 1 ② 3

Count the 🔭s. How many 🔭s in all? ① 2 3

Count the 👢s. How many 👢s in all? 2 3 ④

53

Beginning Consonant Sounds Qq, Rr, Ss

Directions: Say the sound that the letters Qq, Rr, Ss make. (Qq = quh, Rr = ruh, Ss = sss.) Draw a line from each picture to its matching letter.

Qq

Rr

Ss

54

Words That Begin With r

Directions: Color the picture. Circle the six things that start with the sound of the letter r.

55

149

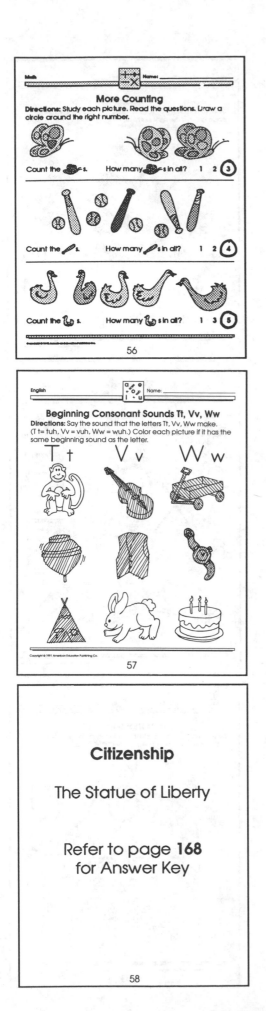

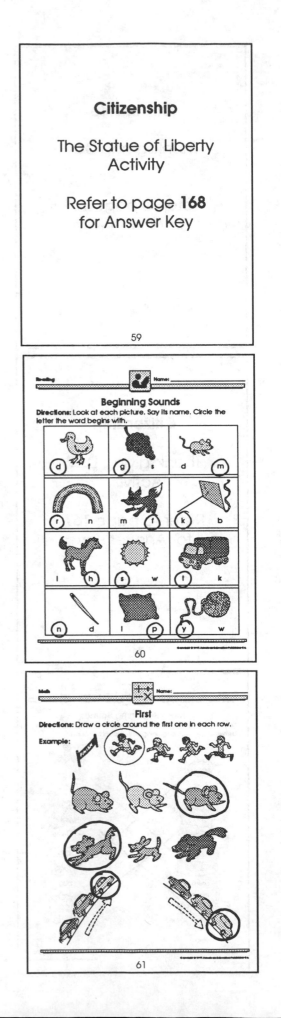

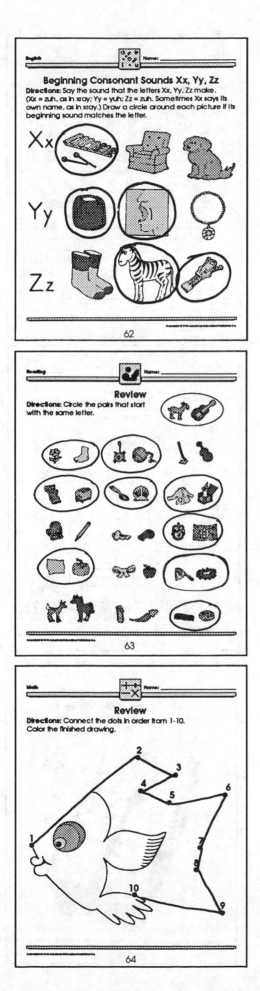

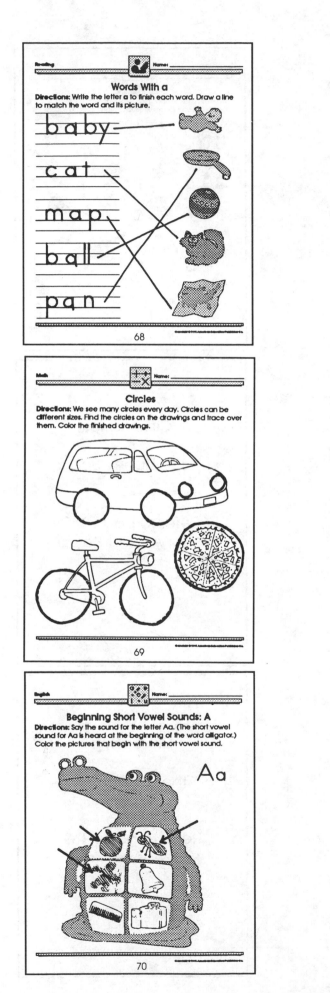

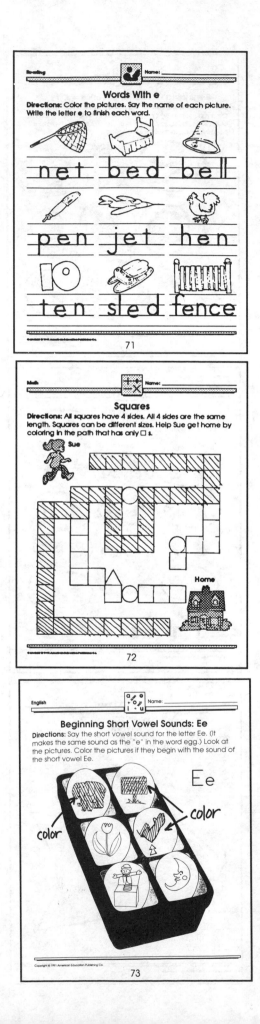

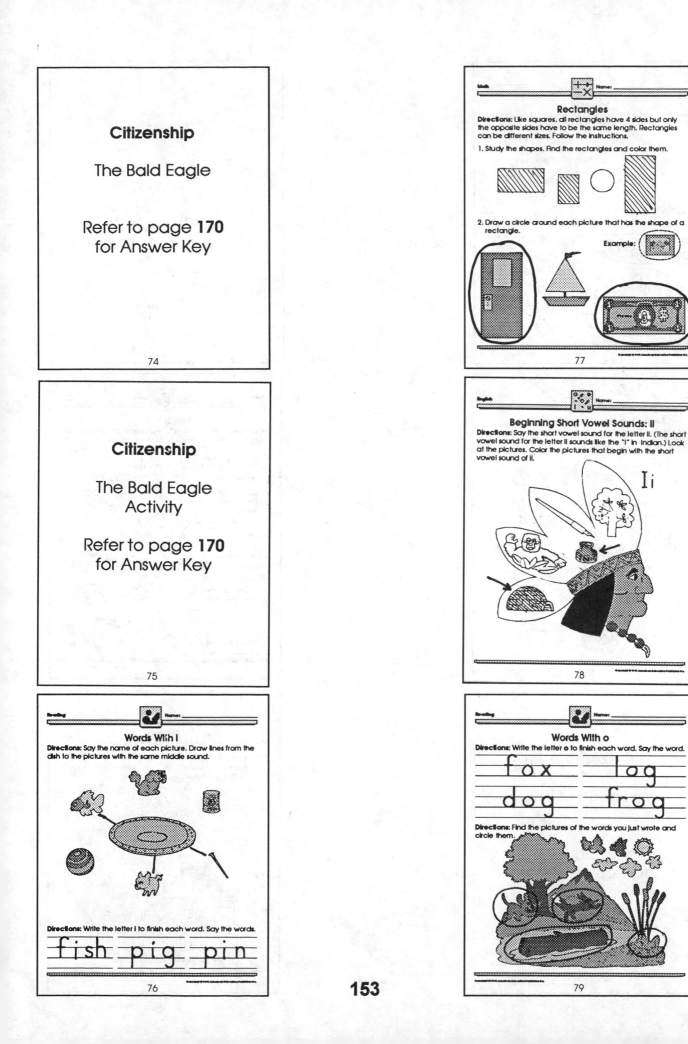

Citizenship

The Bald Eagle

Refer to page **170**
for Answer Key

74

Citizenship

The Bald Eagle
Activity

Refer to page **170**
for Answer Key

75

Rectangles

Directions: Like squares, all rectangles have 4 sides but only the opposite sides have to be the same length. Rectangles can be different sizes. Follow the instructions.

1. Study the shapes. Find the rectangles and color them.

2. Draw a circle around each picture that has the shape of a rectangle.

Example:

77

Beginning Short Vowel Sounds: Ii

Directions: Say the short vowel sound for the letter Ii. (The short vowel sound for the letter Ii sounds like the "I" in Indian.) Look at the pictures. Color the pictures that begin with the short vowel sound of Ii.

Ii

78

Words With i

Directions: Say the name of each picture. Draw lines from the dish to the pictures with the same middle sound.

Directions: Write the letter i to finish each word. Say the words.

fish pig pin

76

Words With o

Directions: Write the letter o to finish each word. Say the word.

fox log

dog frog

Directions: Find the pictures of the words you just wrote and circle them.

79

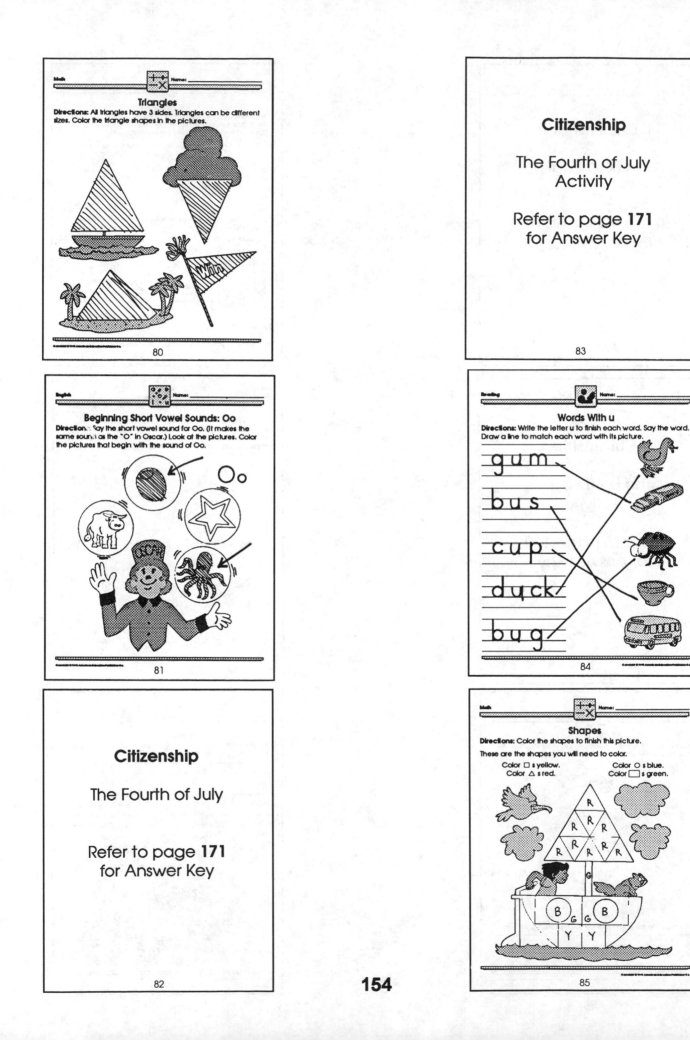

Triangles

Directions: All triangles have 3 sides. Triangles can be different sizes. Color the triangle shapes in the pictures.

80

Beginning Short Vowel Sounds: Oo

Directions: Say the short vowel sound for Oo. (It makes the same sound as the "O" in Oscar.) Look at the pictures. Color the pictures that begin with the sound of Oo.

Oo

81

Citizenship

The Fourth of July

Refer to page **171**
for Answer Key

82

Citizenship

The Fourth of July
Activity

Refer to page **171**
for Answer Key

83

Words With u

Directions: Write the letter u to finish each word. Say the word. Draw a line to match each word with its picture.

gum

bus

cup

duck

bug

84

Shapes

Directions: Color the shapes to finish this picture.

These are the shapes you will need to color.

Color □ s yellow.   Color ○ s blue.
Color △ s red.   Color ▭ s green.

85

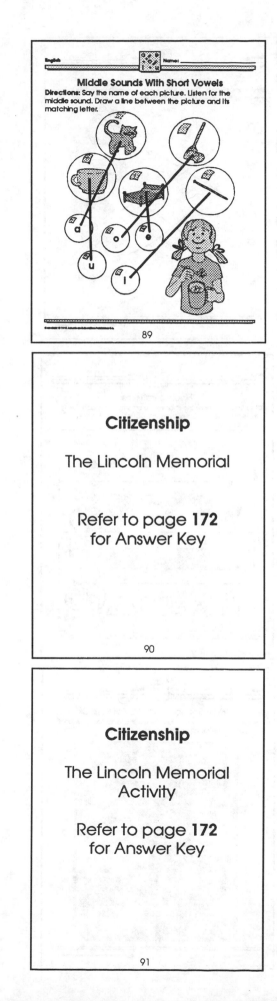

Middle Sounds

Directions: Look at the picture. Say its name. Draw a line to the letter that makes its middle sound.

a

e

i

o

u

92

Review

Directions: Trace the letters.

Directions: Say the name of each picture. Write the correct letter to finish each word.

ball   pig   cup

bed   dog   pan

95

Finding Patterns

Directions: See how the shapes are arranged in each row. Circle the one that completes the pattern. The first one is done for you.

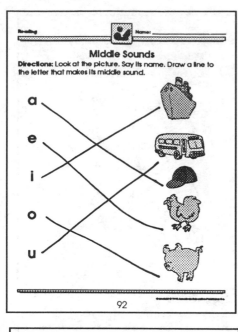

93

Review

Directions: Look at all the shapes in the picture. 1. Color the ○ s blue. Color the □ s red. Color the △ s green. 2. Draw a line under the small blue ○ above the rocket. 3. Draw a circle around the large red □ below the rocket. 4. Put an X on the small green △ below the rocket.

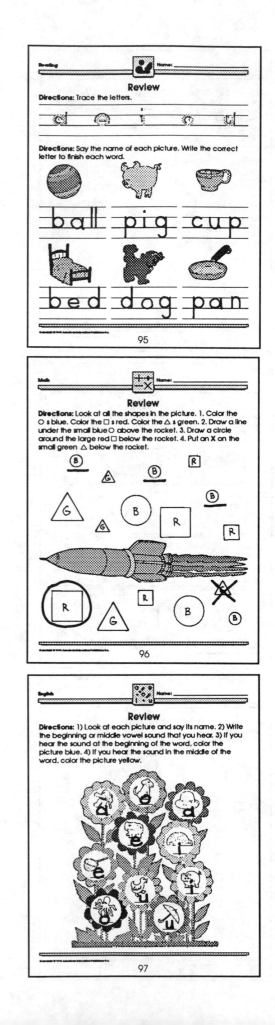

96

Middle Sounds: Short Vowel Sounds

Directions: Look at the pictures. Write the letter for the sound you hear in the middle of the word.

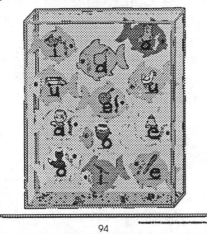

94

Review

Directions: 1) Look at each picture and say its name. 2) Write the beginning or middle vowel sound that you hear. 3) If you hear the sound at the beginning of the word, color the picture blue. 4) If you hear the sound in the middle of the word, color the picture yellow.

97

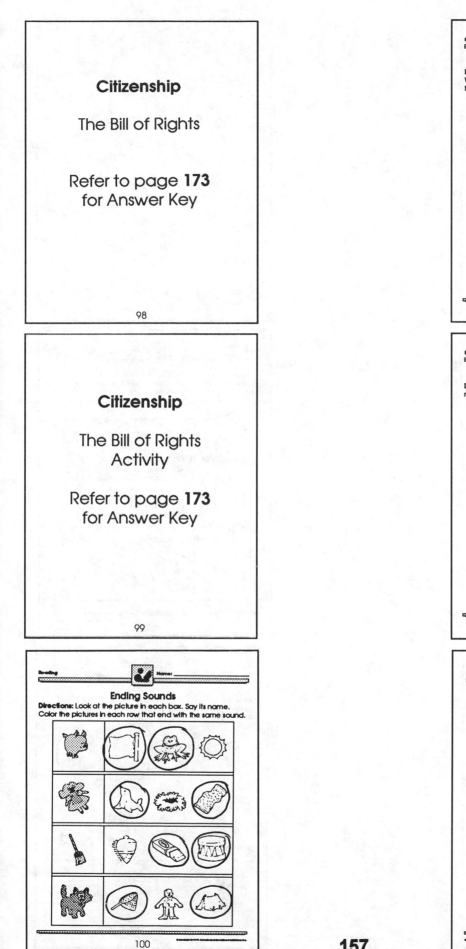

Ending Sounds

Directions: Look at the picture in each box. Say its name. Color the pictures in each row that end with the same sound.

100

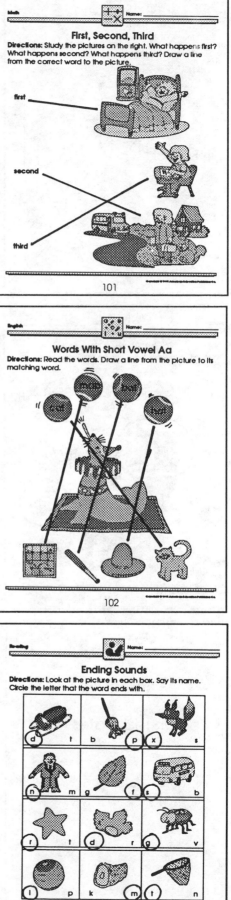

First, Second, Third

Directions: Study the pictures on the right. What happens first? What happens second? What happens third? Draw a line from the correct word to the picture.

first

second

third

101

Words With Short Vowel Aa

Directions: Read the words. Draw a line from the picture to its matching word.

102

Ending Sounds

Directions: Look at the picture in each box. Say its name. Circle the letter that the word ends with.

103

Directions: Trace the numbers on the clock. What time do you wake up in the morning? Draw the clock hands to show when.

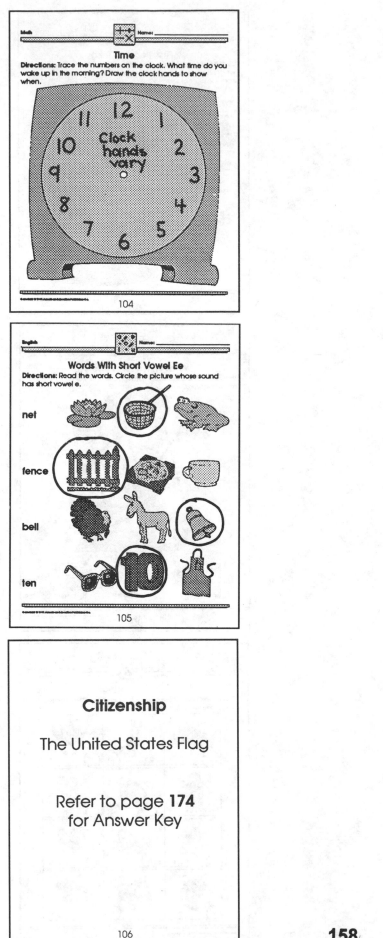

Clock hands vary

104

English ◫ Name: _____

Words With Short Vowel Ee

Directions: Read the words. Circle the picture whose sound has short vowel e.

net

fence

bell

ten

105

Citizenship

The United States Flag

Refer to page **174** for Answer Key

106

Citizenship

The United States Flag Activity

Refer to page **174** for Answer Key

107

Reading ◫ Name: _____

Word Families

Directions: Say the name of the picture in the box. Color the pictures in each row that have the same ending sound.

108

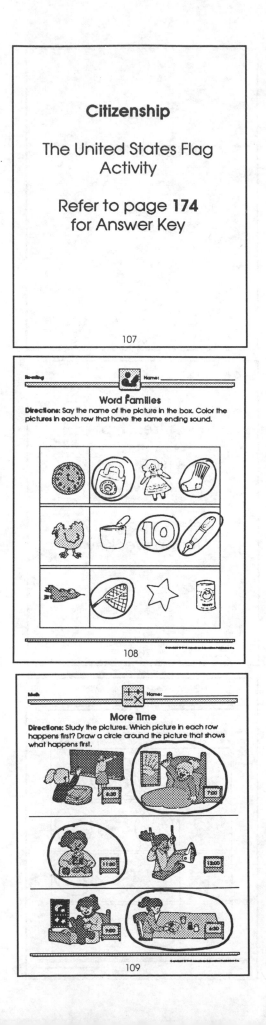

Math ⊠ Name: _____

More Time

Directions: Study the pictures. Which picture in each row happens first? Draw a circle around the picture that shows what happens first.

109

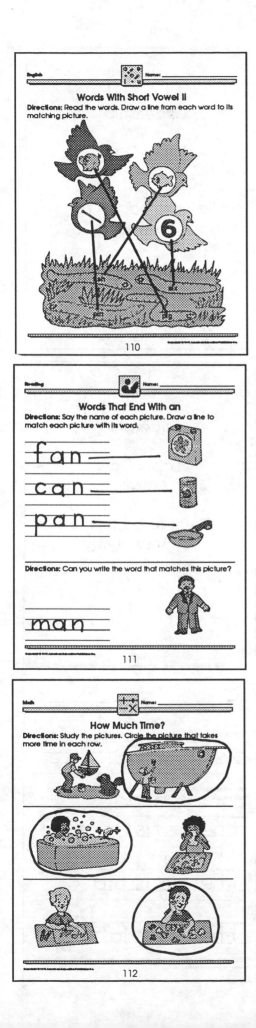

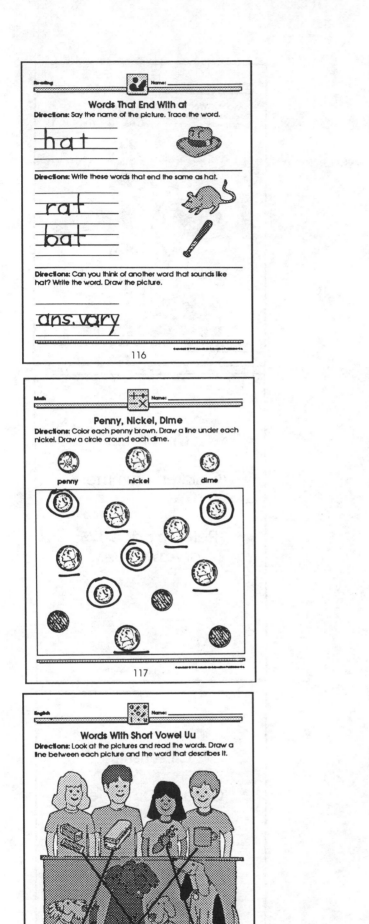

Words That End With at

Directions: Say the name of the picture. Trace the word.

hat

Directions: Write these words that end the same as hat.

rat

bat

Directions: Can you think of another word that sounds like hat? Write the word. Draw the picture.

ans. vary

116

Penny, Nickel, Dime

Directions: Color each penny brown. Draw a line under each nickel. Draw a circle around each dime.

penny   nickel   dime

117

Words With Short Vowel Uu

Directions: Look at the pictures and read the words. Draw a line between each picture and the word that describes it.

bus   cup   gum

118

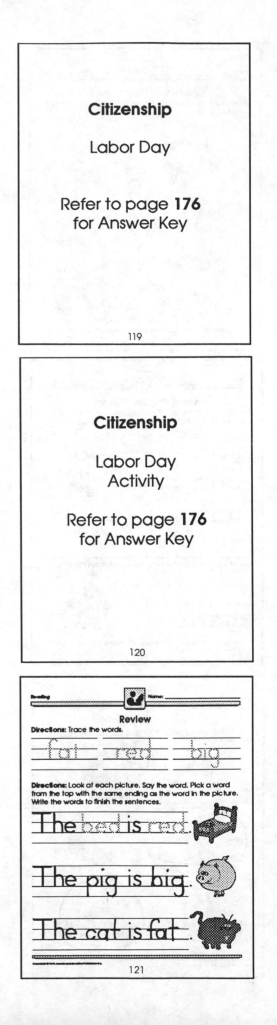

Citizenship

Labor Day

Refer to page **176** for Answer Key

119

Citizenship

Labor Day
Activity

Refer to page **176** for Answer Key

120

Review

Directions: Trace the words.

fat   red   big

Directions: Look at each picture. Say the word. Pick a word from the top with the same ending as the word in the picture. Write the words to finish the sentences.

The bed is red.

The pig is big.

The cat is fat.

121

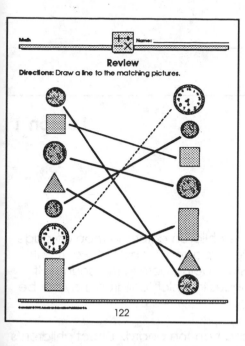

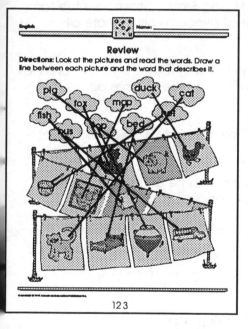

TEACHING SUGGESTIONS

Citizens Now

Lesson 1

Purposes: To recognize that children are citizens
To identify the United States on a map

Materials: classroom map, crayons, paste

Prework: Locate the United States on the classroom map. Then have children color the map on page 1 using a key, such as blue = water, red = United States. Read page 10 together. Point out that most people become citizens of the United States just by being born in this country. If the situation warrants, you may want to discuss circumstances in which children may not be United States citizens.

Instructions: Display the citizen chain. Make a comparison/contrast chart on the board. Direct children's attention to the citizen chain and invite them to tell how United States citizens are the same and how they are different. Lead children to conclude that although citizens are all different, they all live and work together in the same country.

Extensions:
- Reading: Place *Anno's U.S.A.* by Mitsumasa Anno on the reading table. Invite children to look at the book to see citizens doing things in other times and other places across the United States.

- Speaking: Organize the class into small groups. Ask: If the citizens dolls could talk, what might they say to each other?

- Music: Play a recording of "This Land is Your Land." Point out some of the places mentioned in the song. Encourage children to join in the refrain.

- Family: Invite children to find out the names of the first members of their families to become United States citizens.

NOTE: The Activity page requires cutting out objects on the page.
Lesson on following page should be completed before cutting.

162

Barbara Bush   Lesson 2

Purpose: To recognize that reading is important

Materials: several familiar picture books, crayons

Prework: Invite children to share their experiences with reading by asking: Who reads to you? What are some of your favorite stories? Do you like to listen to some stories over and over again? Why?

Instructions: Display several familiar picture books. Discuss the titles and the cover designs. Then read and discuss the directions on page 19. When the page is completed, display the covers on a bulletin board titled: Good Citizens Read! Read! Read!

Extensions:
- Reading: Read and discuss a children's classic such as Caldecott Medal winners *Make Way for Ducklings* by Robert McCloskey or *The Little House* by Virginia Lee Burton. Ask the children why some stories never grow old.

- Writing: Help children complete a semantic map that asks: How do people learn to read? Record their suggestions such as listening to others read and looking at books.

- Language Arts: Read the poem "Good Books, Good Times!" by Lee Bennett Hopkins from *Good Books, Good Times!* selected by Lee Bennett Hopkins. Invite children to add more "goods" to the poem.

- Family: Encourage children to share a favorite book with a family member. You may want to send home copies of a major goal of the Barbara Bush Foundation for Family Literacy: "Help every family in the nation understand that the home is the child's first school, that the parent is the child's first teacher, and that reading is the child's first subject."

TEACHING SUGGESTIONS

White House

Purpose: To recognize that the White House is where the President of the United States lives and works

Materials: crayons

Prework: Draw attention to the illustration on page 26. Ask children to tell about times when they have visited or seen pictures of the White House.

Instructions: Before beginning the activity, point out that the President's family lives in the White House too. Ask children to describe other rooms that might be in the White House. After the children follow the maze, invite them to draw pictures of what the President might do that day in the Oval Office. Display the pictures.

Extensions:
- Reading: Read *Arthur Meets the President* by Marc Brown and challenge children to identify the White House and other famous buildings and monuments in Washington, D.C. Discuss Arthur"s winning essay on "How I Can Help Make America Great." Ask children how they can be good **Citizens** by helping others.

- Writing: Design a poster that tells some things children will need to do to become President of the United States and live in the White House. Point out that females may also hold the job. Write: Study hard in school. Plan to go to college. Ask small groups to think of another idea to add to the poster before displaying it under the caption: The Way to the White House.

- Language Arts: Have small groups of children role play situations that could happen in the White House: the President giving a medal to a hero, the First Family eating dinner, the President holding a meeting in the Oval Office, the First Family watching TV.

- Family: Encourage children to ask family members if they would like to live in the White House and why. Allow the children to share families' comments with the class.

Declaration of Independence   Lesson 4

Purpose: To recognize that the Declaration of Independence said that a new country called the United States of America had been formed

Materials: crayons

Prework: Discuss ways children celebrate the Fourth of July. Tell them that people celebrate the Fourth of July because of what happened on July 4, 1776. Read and discuss page 34.

Instructions: Point out the colonies on the map. Explain that this was the size of the United States at the time the Americans approved the Declaration of Independence. Invite children to color the colonies. Ask them to work with a partner to think of a name for the country. Circulate and give spelling and writing assistance.

Extensions:
- Reading: Read *The Many Lives of Benjamin Franklin* by Aliki. Discuss Franklin's ideas and how many of them affect us today.

- Speaking: Ask: What do you think Americans said when they heard they were living in a new, free country? Encourage children to role play the new citizens as they heard the news.

- Art: Invite children to draw pictures of themselves doing things that make them feel free.

- Family: Tell children that just as the Declaration of Independence tells about the birth of a new country their birth certificates are important papers that tell about their births. Encourage children to ask their parents to show them copies of their birth certificates. You may want to send a note home explaining the tie-in to the Declaration of Independence.

TEACHING SUGGESTIONS

Christopher Columbus

Purpose: To realize that Columbus's voyage changed the world

Materials: crayons

Prework: Draw attention to the illustration on page 42. Tell children that the man is Christopher Columbus. Read and discuss page 42. Point out that the natives, pineapples, parrots, and corn were people and things that Columbus and his men had never seen before. Ask how Columbus and the sailors may have felt when they landed.

Instructions: Invite children to talk about times when they did something for the first time (ate a new food, went to school, swam without water wings). Help children visualize what it would be like to leave on a ship. After they share the pictures, you may want to have them cut out the ships and display them on a blue background.

Extensions:
- Reading: Read and discuss *In 1492* by Jean Marzollo. Encourage children to look at the illustrations and repeat the rhyming couplets about Columbus's voyage to the New World.

- Writing: Invite children to think about a plant that no one has ever seen. Ask them to draw the plant. Then help each child write a name for the plant. Ask them to share their drawings.

- Social Studies: Use the classroom map to point out important places connected with Columbus's voyage: the Bahamas, Cuba, Spain, Europe, North, South, and Central America.

- Family: Invite children to make a checklist with the words *pineapple*, *sweet potato*, and *corn* on it. Ask them to make a check next to the word each time their families eat the item. Encourage them to tell their families the story of how Christopher Columbus and his sailors may have been the first Eurpoeans to see these plants.

Thanksgiving Day   Lesson 6

Purpose: To recognize that the Pilgrims and Native Americans celebrated the first New England Thanksgiving

Materials: crayons, scissors, paper plates, paste

Prework: Ask children to discuss ways their families celebrate Thanksgiving.

Instructions: After children finish pasting the "food" on the paper plates, organize the class into small groups. Ask each group to pretend they are the Pilgrims and the Native Americans at the first Thanksgiving table talking about what they are thankful for.

Extensions:
- Reading: Read the poems from *It's Thanksgiving* by Jack Prelutsky. Do an echo reading with some of the shorter poems, in which you read one section of a poem and the children repeat it after you.

- Speaking: Ask small groups to talk about ways to help those who do not have enough food to eat on Thanksgiving and other days.

- Science: Seasons—Discuss things that children do in the winter in places where the weather is cold. Point out that the Pilgrims did not have a good winter when they first came to America because they did not have enough food. Invite children to make drawings of some good and bad things about cold winters. Display the drawings on a bulletin board titled: Welcome Winter/Worst Winter. You may want to tie in the letter *w* with this lesson.

- Family: Assist children in writing thank-you notes to present to family members.

NOTE: The Activity page requires cutting out objects on the page.
Lesson on following page should be completed before cutting.

TEACHING SUGGESTIONS

Statue of Liberty   Lesson 7

Purpose: To recognize that the Statue of Liberty was a gift of friendship from France

Materials: crayons, scissors, chart paper

Prework: Draw attention to the illustration on page 58. Tell children they will be learning why the statue is important to American Citizens.

Instructions: After children complete their torches, ask them to discuss why it is important to be friendly to children in other classrooms. Record their responses on chart paper. Share the responses with the students to whom the torches are presented.

Extensions: • Reading: Read and discuss *Watch the Stars Come Out* by Riki Levinson. In this story a grandmother tells of her mother's voyage to America. Encourage children to share experiences they have had with their grandparents or other older people.

• Speaking: Present several simple French words to the class, and invite children to use them throughout the day. Examples: *bonjour* = hello, *oui* = yes, *merci* = thank you, *non* = no

• Math: Tell children that the mouth of the Statue of Liberty is 3 feet wide. Ask children to work cooperatively with yard sticks and mural paper to draw mouths the size of the Statue of Liberty's mouth. As they measure and draw, invite children to talk about what Lady Liberty might say as she saw a shipload of people coming to the United States.

• Family: Invite children to ask their parents to tell stories of family members who came to the United States from other countries. Encourage them to share the stories with the class.

NOTE: **The Activity page requires cutting out objects on the page.**
Lesson on following page should be completed before cutting.

The Liberty Bell

Lesson 8

Purposes: To identify the Liberty Bell
To recognize that the Liberty Bell is a symbol of our country

Materials: small bell, crayons, scissors, laminating material or tag board

Prework: Ring a small bell. Ask children to tell about times when they have heard bells being rung, such as in school, at a concert, in church, on the ice cream truck. Ask them why people ring bells. Tell them they will be learning about a special bell that is a symbol of our country.

Instructions: As children color and cut out the Liberty Bell on page 67 circulate and give help when needed. If possible, laminate the shape before cutting along the crack. As an alternative, mount the bells on tag board and recut them. Show children how to place the crack over a book page to mark a place. Encourage children to use the bookmarks while looking at their favorite books.

Extensions:
• Reading: Read the poem "Bells" from *Children of Long Ago* by Lessie Jones Little. As you read, ask children to close their eyes and listen for the sounds the bells are making. You may also wish to read the poems "Paper Dolls" and "Reading Glasses," which correlate with Lessons 1 and 2 in **Citizenship.**

• Listening: Display several different kinds of bells. Encourage children to explore the different sounds the bells make. Invite them to ring the "liberty bells" to announce a new country. You may want to have children move outdoors for this activity.

• Science: Challenge children to explore vibrations by touching their throats as they are talking, putting their hands over a stereo or radio speaker, and feeling the bells. Lead them to conclude that when the vibrations stop, the sound stops too.

• Family: Invite children to bring bells from home. Encourage them to tell the class how the bells are used in their homes.

NOTE: **The Activity page requires cutting out objects on the page.**
Lesson on following page should be completed before cutting.

TEACHING SUGGESTIONS

The Bald Eagle

Lesson 9

Purpose: To identify the bald eagle as a symbol of our country

Materials: crayons

Prework: Ask children to look at the picture of the bird on page 74. Tell them that like the United States flag and the Liberty Bell, the bald eagle stands for our country.

Instructions: Remind students that the bald eagle is a symbol of the United States. Read the directions on page 18. Then have children brainstorm for names. Encourage them to think of names that have a patriotic theme. Examples: Star and Stripe, U and S, Yankee and Doodle. Write the responses on the board. You may want capable children to copy two names under the nest on page 18. Finally, invite children to color the picture.

Extensions:
- Reading: Read and discuss the chapter "Eaglets" from *Bald Eagles* by Emilie U. Lepthien. Encourage partners to look at the book and talk about our national bird.

- Writing: Write this story starter on a chart: I looked up and saw a huge nest. Just then two eaglets peeked over the edge. Invite children to finish the story orally as you record their suggestions on the chart.

- Art: Ask children to use thin paper, dark crayons, and quarters to design eagle place mats. Have children place a quarter, eagle side up, under the paper and rub over the top with a crayon until the eagle appears on the paper. Use the place mats at lunch or snack time.

- Family: Invite children to play the traditional game of "Button, Button, Who Has the Button?" with family members. Ask them to substitute a quarter for the button and have them repeat the refrain "Eagle, eagle, who has the eagle?" as they pass the quarter "secretly" and take turns trying to guess who has it.

The Fourth of July
Lesson 10

Purpose: To recognize that the Fourth of July is the birthday of the United States

Materials: crayons (neon optional), glue, sparkles (optional)

Prework: Discuss ways children celebrate their birthdays. Explain that the United States has a birthday too. Ask children to look at the pictures on page 82 to find out how citizens celebrate our country's birthday.

Instructions: If possible, provide neon crayons or glue and sparkles for the drawings. When the drawings are complete, display them near the classroom ceiling.

Extensions:
- Reading: Read and discuss the poems in *My First Fourth of July Book* by Harriet W. Hodgson. Ask children to join in the refrains.

- Listening: Invite the children to listen and sing along with contemporary patriotic music, such as "Born in the USA," "Proud to Be An American," and "Voices That Care."

- Art: Allow the children to create patriotic decorations with red or blue finger paints. Encourage them to combine symbols they have learned with their own ideas. Display their work in the classroom for parents to see.

- Family: Encourage the children to ask their families about special Fourth of July celebrations they remember from childhood. Allow the children to share the stories with the class.

TEACHING SUGGESTIONS

The Lincoln Memorial

Purposes: To identify the Lincoln Memorial
To realize that Abraham Lincoln believed that all people are important

Materials: pennies (optional)

Prework: Draw attention to the illustrations on page 90. Invite children to tell what they know about Abraham Lincoln. Encourage them to think about what they would like to know about Lincoln.

Instructions: After completing several exercises with the class on counting from 1-10, invite children to work with partners to finish page 91. You may want to have pennies available for pairs to manipulate. Go over the answers.

Extensions:
- Reading: Read and discuss *A Picture Book of Abraham Lincoln* by David Adler. After children listen to the book, ask: How do we know that Abraham Lincoln believed that all people are important?

- Speaking: Ask partners to talk about what they think Abraham Lincoln would say if he saw the Lincoln Memorial.

- Art: Invite groups of children to use building blocks or recycled boxes to design a memorial for a past President of the United States.

- Family: Glue a penny to a 3 X 5 note card for each child. Invite children to decorate around the pennies. Ask them to give the card to a family member. Encourage them to tell the person about Abraham Lincoln and his memorial.

The Bill of Rights   Lesson 12

Purpose: To recognize that the Bill of Rights is based on the idea that every person is important

Materials: crayons, scissors, paper punch, yarn

Prework: Discuss classroom and playground rules. Lead children to conclude that the rules protect all students.

Instructions: Discuss children's drawings. After they have cut out the ribbons, punch a hole in each award. Then put yarn through the holes. Encourage children to wear the blue ribbons.

Extensions:
- Reading: Read Steven Kellogg's version of *Chicken Little*. Encourage the children to discuss whether Chicken Little used the right of freedom of speech wisely.

- Speaking: Remind children that the Bill of Rights promises that Americans can meet to make changes. Hold a classroom meeting. Invite children to talk about changes they would like to make in the classroom or playground rules.

- Art: Ask children to draw scenes of what might happen if citizens do not use freedom of speech wisely. Use examples like yelling "fire" in a crowded building or "help" in the swimming pool when it isn't necessary.

- Family: Encourage children to ask family members to name things they do that make them feel important. Invite children to share their comments with the class.

NOTE: The Activity page requires cutting out objects on the page.
Lesson on following page should be completed before cutting.

TEACHING SUGGESTIONS

The United States Flag

Purpose: To identify the flag of the United States

Materials: United States flag, world map, red and blue crayons, scissors, tape, used paper, patriotic recordings

Prework: Display the United States flag. Ask children to tell what they think of when they see the flag. Locate the United States on a world map. Explain that the United States flag stands for our country and its people.

Instructions: When children are coloring the flags, circulate and give help when necessary. Then ask them to cut out the flags. Tape each flag to a piece of rolled recycled paper. Play patriotic music as the children march around the classroom with their flags.

Extensions:
- Reading: Read and discuss *The Star-Spangled Banner* by Peter Spier. Help the children learn the meaning of the words from the national anthem and challenge them to identify the many places illustrated.

- Listening: After the children are through parading, ask them to listen to the patriotic music. Prompt them to tell how the music makes them feel.

- Math: Tell children that red, white, and blue are our country's colors. Ask children who are wearing red to stand. Have children count those who are standing. Record the total number on the board with red chalk. Repeat this procedure for children wearing white and blue. Discuss the results.

- Family: Invite children to take their flags home and display them. Encourage children to discuss with family members what they think the flag stands for. Allow them to share answers with the class.

Children Drummers   Lesson 14

Purpose: To recognize that children participated as drummers in early American armies

Materials: crayons, scissors, recycled cylindrical containers, paste, pencils or spoons, (felt, sparkles, yarn, foil - optional)

Prework: Tell children that in early American armies children participated as drummers. Ask them to look at the picture on page 114 to find out what the drummers looked like.

Instructions: Invite children to tell what the symbols stand for before they color and cut them out. Then have them glue the symbols to recycled cylindrical containers. Encourage children to use other available items, such as sparkles, felt, yarn, or foil to decorate their drums. Have them use pencils or spoons to beat the drums during a classroom march.

Extensions:
- Reading: Do a dramatic reading of the colorfully illustrated Caldecott Medal winner *Drummer Hoff* adapted by Barbara Emberley. Direct the children to respond, "Drummer Hoff fired it off" in unison each time. Allow them to use their drums for a drum roll just before General Border cries, "Ready! Aim! Fire!" and they all shout "KAHBAHBLOOOM!"

- Speaking: Ask groups of children to pretend they are trying to convince their parents to allow them to be a drummer in the army.

- Music: Display and discuss drums or pictures of drums, such as snare, bass, timpani and bongo.

- Family: Invite children to ask their parents about family members who served in the armed forces. Encourage them to share their stories and memorabilia.

NOTE: The Activity page requires cutting out objects on the page.
Lesson on following page should be completed before cutting.

TEACHING SUGGESTIONS

Labor Day

Purpose: To recognize that Labor Day is an American holiday that honors working people

Materials: crayons, scissors, paste

Prework: Ask children: What is your job now? What job do you want to have when you grow up?

Instructions: Discuss the jobs of each of the community workers. Point out that each job could be done by both males and females. After children make the finger puppets, organize the class into small groups. Invite each group to present a short play that shows why each worker's job is important. You may want to model first with a construction worker repairing a window or a policeman helping a lost child.

Extensions:
- Reading: Read and discuss *How a House Is Built* by Gail Gibbons and show the illustrations of the many kinds of workers involved in building a house.

- Listening: Invite a school worker to talk to the class about his or her job. Encourage children to ask questions after the talk.

- Health/Safety: Explain that some jobs are so important that all people who do them cannot stay home from work on Labor Day. Ask children to brainstorm for examples (doctors, ambulance drivers, telephone operators, police workers, fire fighters).

- Family: Distribute note cards to the class. Invite children to ask family members to write a few sentences describing his or her job on the cards. Encourage children to share the cards with the class.

NOTE: The Activity page requires cutting out objects on the page.
Lesson on following page should be completed before cutting.

Table of Contents

continued on next page

continued on next page

continued on next page

Glossary

Reading Glossary

Alphabetical Order.   Putting words in a-b-c order.

Auditory Discrimination. The skill of identifying sounds in words.

Beginning Sounds.   The sounds made by the first letters of words.

Blends. Two consonant sounds put together.

Classifying. Putting similar things into categories.

Compound Words. When two words are put together to make one.

Consonants. Letters that are not vowels (a, e, i, o, and u).

Digraphs. Two consonants that make one special sound at the beginning of a word.

Ending Sounds. The sounds made by the last letters of words.

Following Directions. Doing what the directions say to do.

Opposites. Things that are different in every way.

Phonics. Using the sounds letters make to decode unknown words.

Plural. More than one.

Rhymes. Words with the same ending sounds.

Riddles. A puzzling question.

Sequencing. Putting things in logical order.

Visual Clues. Looking at the pictures to figure out meaning.

Vowels. The letters a, e, i, o, and u.

Comprehension Glossary

Classifying. Putting things that are alike into categories.

Comprehension. Understanding what is seen, heard or read.

Following Directions. Doing what the directions say to do.

Same/Different. Being able to tell how things are the same and different.

Sequencing. Putting things in order.

Math Glossary

Addition. "Putting together" or adding two or more numbers to find the sum.
For example, $3 + 5 = 8$

Glossary continued on next page

Math Glossary continued

Circle. A figure that is round. It looks like this: ◯

Diamond. A figure with four sides of the same length. Its corners form points at the top, sides, and bottom. It looks like this: ◇

Digit. The symbols used to write numbers: 1, 2, 3, 4, 5, 6, 7, 8, and 9.

Dime. Ten cents. It is written **10¢** or **$.10**.

Fraction. A number that names part of a whole, such as **1/2** or **1/3**.

Half-hour. Thirty minutes. When the long hand of the clock is pointing to the six, the time is on the half-hour. It is written **:30**, such as **5:30**.

Hour. Sixty minutes. The short hand of a clock tells the hour.

Nickel. Five cents. It is written **5¢** or **$.05**.

Ordinal number. Numbers that indicate order in a series, such as first, second, or third.

Oval. A figure that is egg shaped. I looks like this: ⬭

Penny. One cent. It is written **1¢** or **$.01**.

Place Value. The value of a digit, or numeral, shown by where it is in the number. For example, in the number **123**, **1** has the place value of **hundreds**, **2** is **tens**, and **3** is **ones**.

Rectangle. A figure with four corners and four sides. Sides opposite each other are the same length. It looks like this: ▭

Sequencing. Putting numbers in the correct order, such as 7, 8, 9.

Square. A figure with four corners and four sides of the same length. It looks like this: ☐

Subtraction. "Taking away" or subtracting one number from another. For example, 10 - 3 = 7.

Triangle. A figure with three corners and three sides. It looks like this: △

English Glossary

ABC Order. Putting objects or words in the same order in which they appear in the alphabet.

Antonyms. Words that are opposites.

Asking Sentences. An asking sentence begins with a capital letter, ends with a question mark and asks a question.

Beginning Consonants. Sounds that come at the beginning of words that are not vowel sounds. (Vowels are the letters a, e, i, o, u and sometimes y.)

Glossary continued on next page

English Glossary continued

Capital Letters. Letters that are used at the beginning of names of people and places. They are also used at the beginning of sentences. These letters (**A B C D E F G H I J K L M N O P Q R S T U V W X Y Z**) are sometimes called the "big" letters.

Compound Words. When two words are put together to make one word. Example: house + boat = houseboat

Describing Words. Words that tell us more about a person, place or thing.

Ending Consonants. Sounds, which are not vowel sounds, that come at the end of words.

Homonyms. Words that sound the same but are spelled differently and mean different things. Example: blue and blew.

Nouns. Words that tell the name of persons, places or things.

Sound Discrimination. Being able to identify the differences between sounds.

Super E. When you add an e to some words and the vowel changes from a short vowel sound to a long vowel sound. Example: rip + e = ripe.

Synonyms. Words that mean the same thing. Example: small and little.

Telling Sentences. These sentences begin with a capital letter, end with a period and tell us something.

Verbs. Words that tell what a person or thing can do.

Words Order. The logical order of words in sentences.

Thinking Skills Glossary

Classifying. Putting things that are alike into categories.

Duplicating. Copying.

Opposites. Things that are different in every way.

Finding Patterns. Recognizing similar shapes.

Finding Similarities. Finding items that are almost the same.

Following Directions. Doing what the directions say to do.

Inference. Using logic to figure out what is unspoken but evident.

Predicting Outcome. Telling what is likely to happen based on available facts.

Same/Different. Being able to tell how things are the same and different.

Sequencing. Putting things in order.

Tracking. Following a path.

Glossary continued on next page

Environmental Science Glossary

Conservationist. A person who takes care of the environment.

Conserve. To keep from being wasted or used up.

Earth. The planet we live on.

Environment. Everything around you.

Polluted. Air, land or water that is very dirty.

Pollution. Things that make the environment unclean.

Recycle. Saving things and using them over and over.

Refuge. A safe place for wild animals.

School Custodians. Men and women who keep the school clean.

NOTES

Name: _____

Color Code

Directions: Color the B words orange. Color the M words yellow. Color the L words blue. Color the S words black.

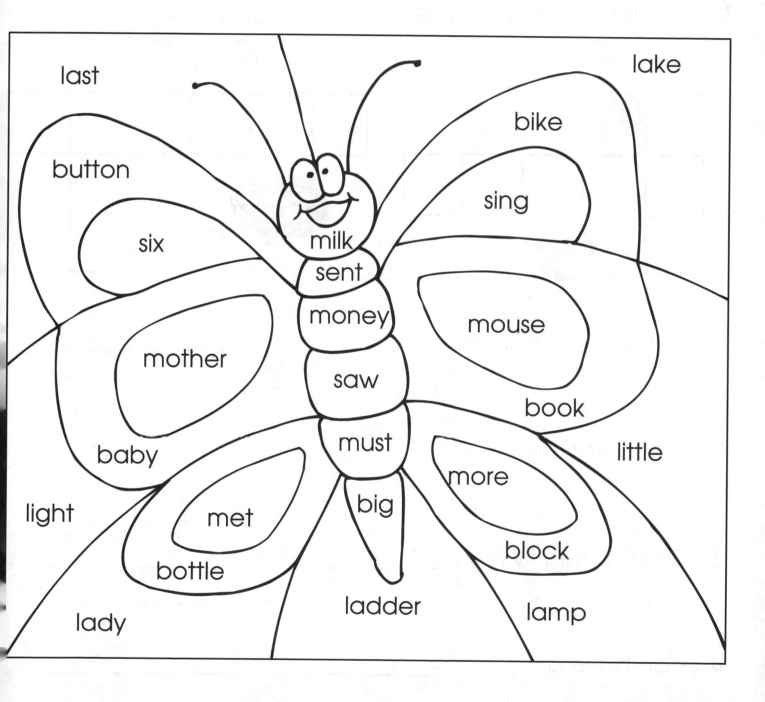

Name: _____

Things I Know About

Directions: 1. Say each of the 4 words aloud. 2. Write each word where it belongs in the blanks. 3. Now write each word beside its picture in the puzzle.

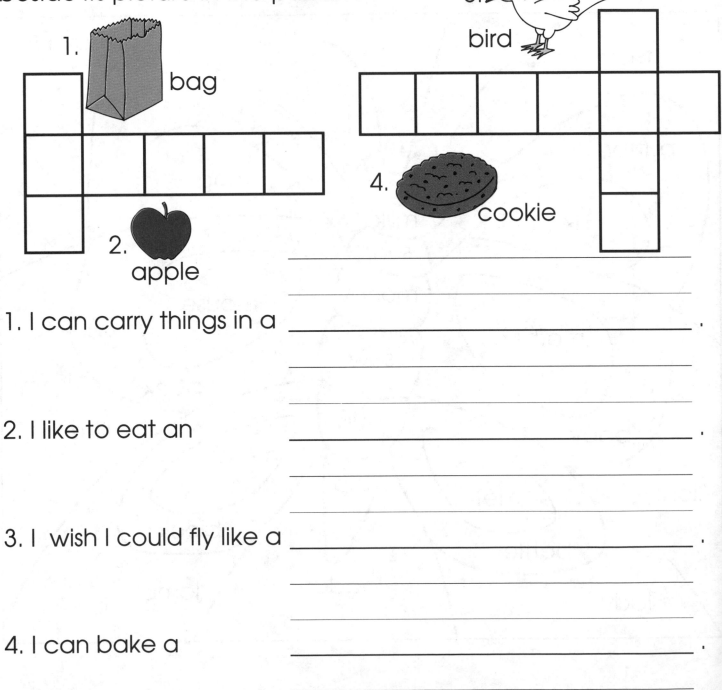

1. bag

2. apple

3. bird

4. cookie

1. I can carry things in a _____.

2. I like to eat an _____.

3. I wish I could fly like a _____.

4. I can bake a _____.

Name: _____

Number Recognition

Directions: Write the numbers 1-10. Color the bear.

Name: _____

ABC Order

Directions: Draw a line to connect the dots. Follow the letters in **ABC** order.

I Can Write The Names Of Pets!

Directions: 1. Follow the lines to write the name of each pet.
2. Write each name again by yourself. 3. Color the pictures.
4. Read the words to someone.

Like this:

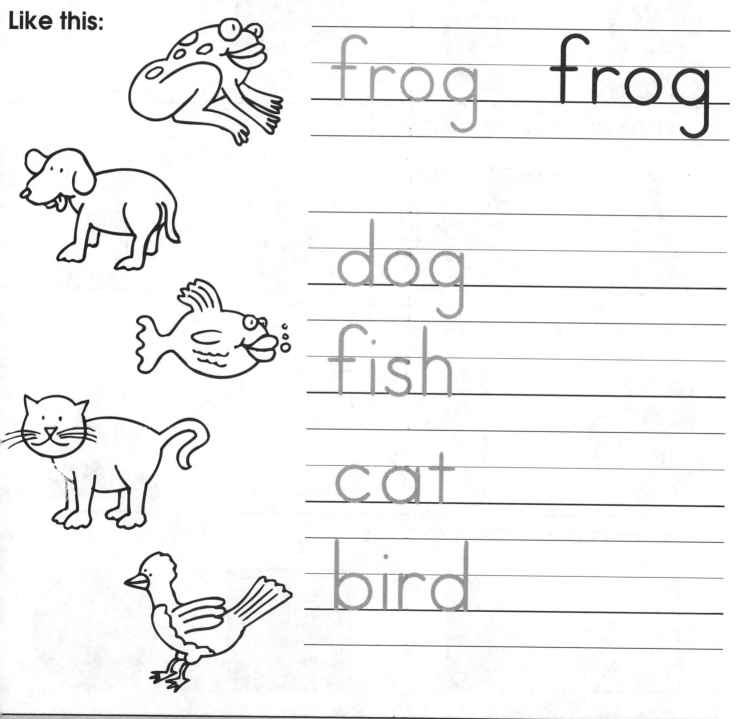

frog   frog

dog

fish

cat

bird

Name: _____

Following Directions

Directions: Put a box around the circle ○.

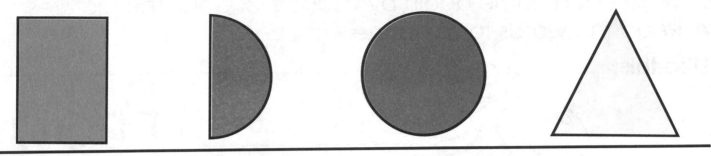

Put a box around the square □.

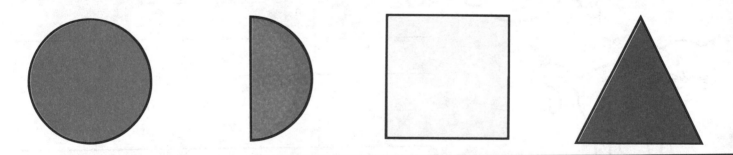

Put a box around the triangle △.

  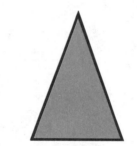 

Put a box around the half-circle ⅅ.

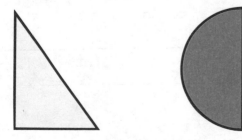  

Name: _____

Building A Snowman

Directions: Read the sentences. Do what they tell you to do.

Bob is making a snowman. He needs your help. Draw a black hat on the snowman. Draw red buttons. Now, draw a green scarf. Draw a happy face on the snowman.

1. BLACK
2. RED
3. GREEN

Snow Is Cold!

Directions: Read about snow. Then answer the questions.

When you play in snow, dress warmly. Wear a coat. Wear a hat. Wear gloves. Do you wear these when you play in snow?

1. Snow is

         warm.
         cold.

2. When you play in snow, dress

         warmly.
         quickly.

3. List 3 things to wear when you play in snow.

_____

_____

_____

_____

Name: _____

Number Recognition 1, 2, 3, 4, 5

Directions: Use the color code to color the parrot.

Color:
1's red
2's blue
3's yellow
4's green
5's orange

Name: _____

abc Order

Directions: Draw a line to connect the dots. Follow the letters in **abc** order.

I Can Finish A Sentence!

A sentence tells about something.

Directions: These sentences tell about pets. Write the word that finishes each sentence.

Like this:

My _____frog_____ jumps high.

1. I take my _____ for a walk.

2. My_____ lives in water.

3. My_____ can sing.

4. My_____ has a long tail.

Name: _____

Following Directions

Directions: Color the squares ☐ purple.

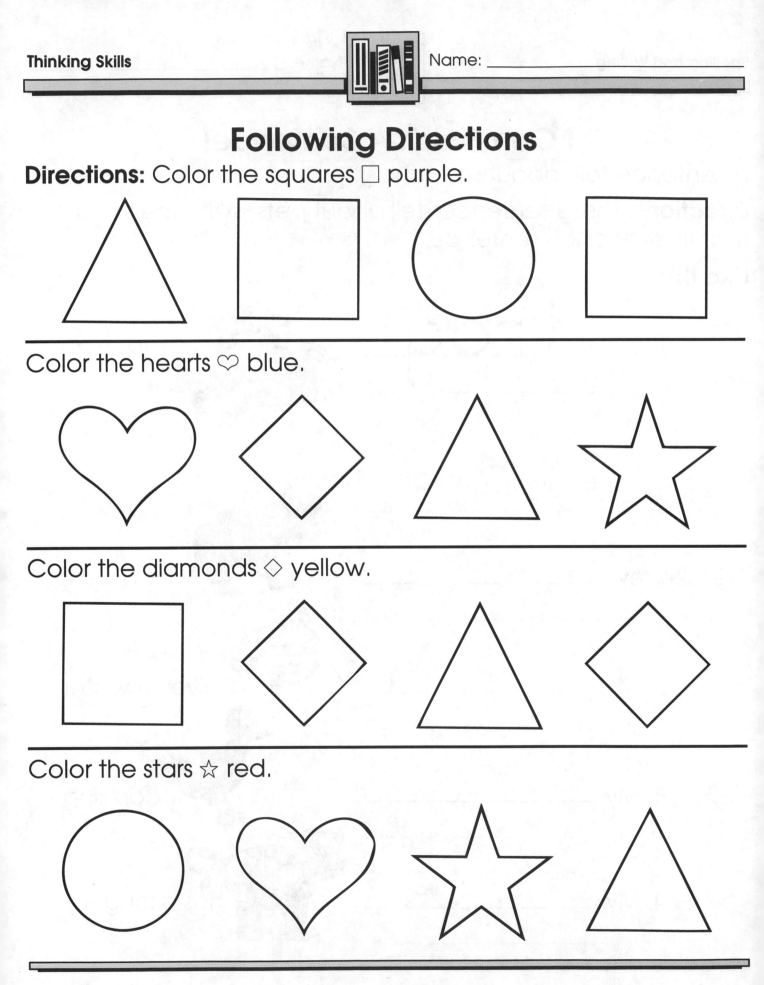

Color the hearts ♡ blue.

Color the diamonds ◇ yellow.

Color the stars ☆ red.

Name: _____

LESSON 1

Citizens Now

Your country is called the United States of America. The United States of America is different from most other countries because it is made up of people from all over the world.

People who are members of our country are called citizens. Did you know that you don't have to wait until you are a grown-up to become an American citizen? You already are a citizen of the United States of America. You are a **citizen now**!

Do you think it is good that the United States has all kinds of citizens? Tell why you think as you do.

Name: _____

ACTIVITY 1

Citizens Now

Directions: Look at the citizen's face. Make the face look like yours. Next, cut it out and paste it on a large outline map of the United States with other citizens' faces to show that you are all **Citizens Now**!

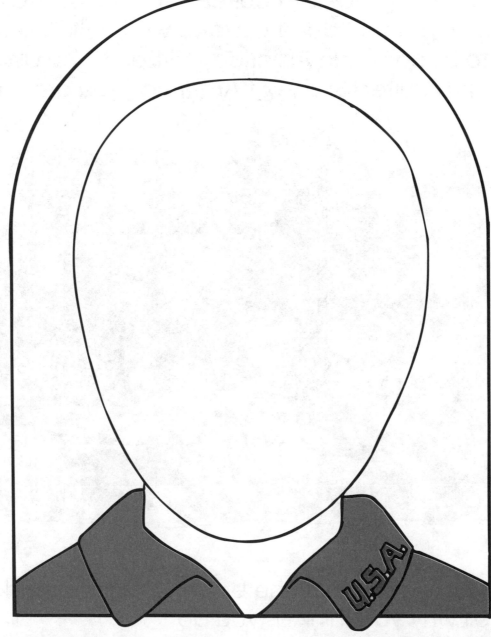

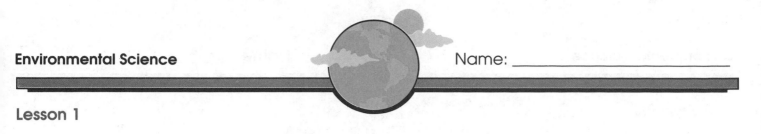

Name: _____

Your Environment

The Earth is where we live. The Earth is made of many things. People made some of the things. Other things were made by nature. Some of these things are living. Others are not alive.

Your environment is everything around you. People, plants and animals are all parts of your environment. Air, water and soil are parts of your environment, too.

Name some things in your school environment.

Name: _____

Activity 1

All Around Me

Directions: Mark an **X** next to the picture of each thing you see in your environment. Then draw two pictures of other things you see in the boxes at the bottom of the chart.

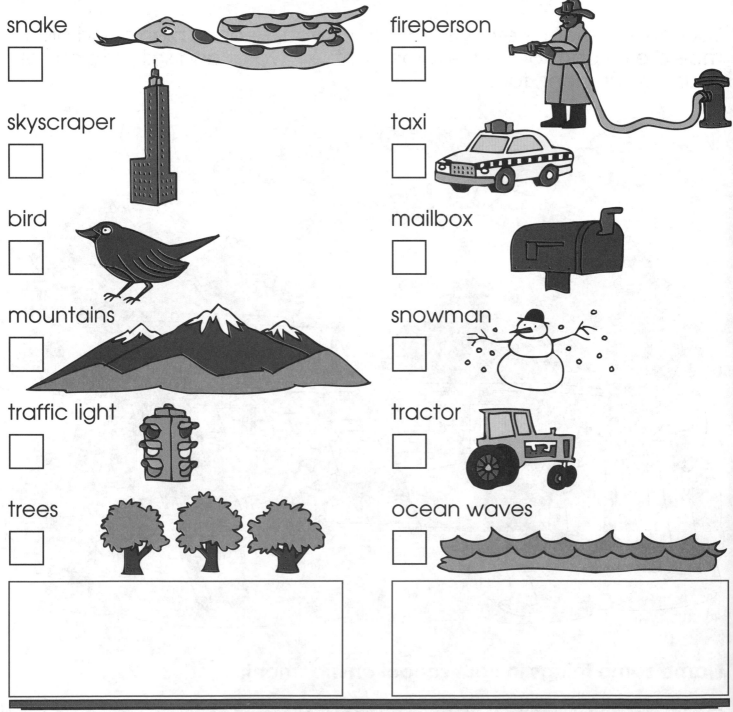

snake ☐

skyscraper ☐

bird ☐

mountains ☐

traffic light ☐

trees ☐

fireperson ☐

taxi ☐

mailbox ☐

snowman ☐

tractor ☐

ocean waves ☐

Name: _____

Color The Eggs

Directions: Read the words. Color the picture.

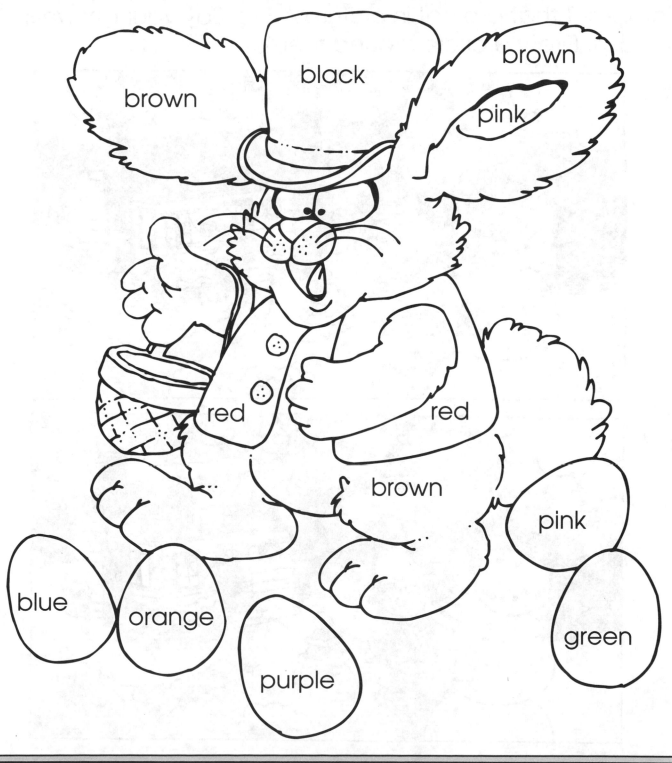

brown

black

brown

pink

red

red

brown

pink

blue

orange

green

purple

Look And See

Directions: 1. Look at both pictures. 2. Find five things in picture # 1 that are not in picture # 2. 3. Say your answers aloud. 4. Draw a circle around them.

1

2

Number Recognition 6, 7, 8, 9, 10

Directions: Use the code to color the carousel horse.

Color:
6's purple
7's yellow
8's black
9's pink
10's brown

Beginning Consonants Bb, Cc, Dd, Ff

Beginning consonants make the sounds that come at the beginning of words. Consonants are the letters b, c, d, f, g, h, j, k, l, m, n, p, q, r, s, t, v, w, x, y, z.

Directions: Say the name of each letter. Say the sound each letter makes. Draw a circle around the letters that make the beginning sound for each picture. Say the name of someone you know whose name begins with each letter.

Bb   Cc   Dd   Ff

Bb Dd   Ff Cc   Cc Dd   Ff Bb

Bb Dd   Ff Cc   Cc Dd   Ff Bb

I Know Which Words Begin The Same!

Directions: 1. Say the name of the pet and write the first letter under the name. 2. Find the two pictures in each row that begin the same as the pet. 3. Write the same first letter under them.

Like this:

frog

f____ f____ ____ f____ ____

cat

____ ____ ____ ____ ____

fish

____ ____ ____ ____ ____

dog

____ ____ ____ ____ ____

bird

____ ____ ____ ____

Name: _____

Following Directions

Directions: Color the picture.
red crayon for □.
blue crayon for ○.
purple crayon for △.

green crayon for D.
yellow crayon for ☆.
black crayon for ♡.
pink crayon for ◇.

Color The Pictures

Directions: Color each picture the correct colors. Draw and color another picture like the first one.

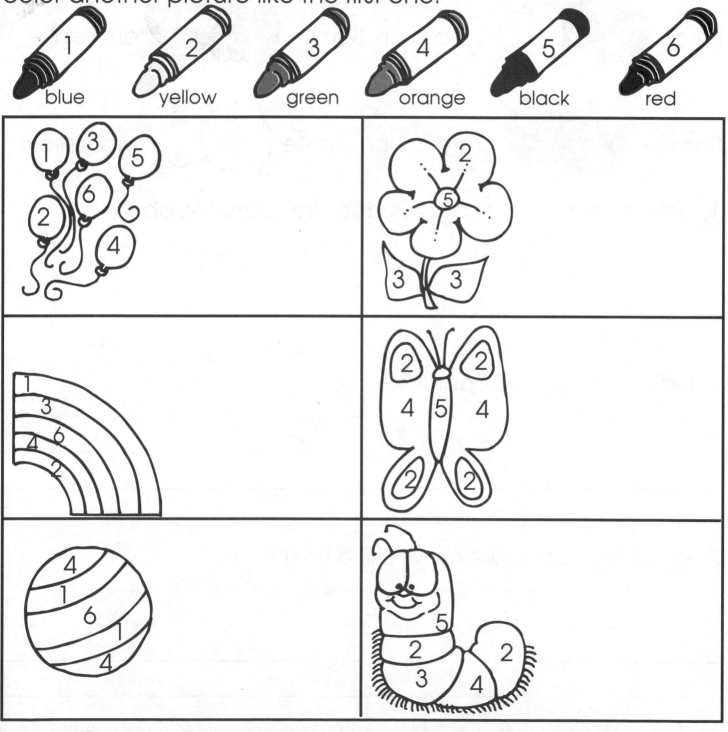

blue   yellow   green   orange   black   red

I Like Apples

Directions: Read about apples. Then answer the questions.

I like _____ . Do you? Some _____ are red. Some _____ are green. Some _____ are yellow.

1. How many kinds of apples does the story tell about?

_____

_____

_____

_____

2. Name the kinds of apples.

_____ _____ _____

_____ _____ _____

_____ _____ _____

3. What kind of apple do you like best?

_____

_____

_____

_____

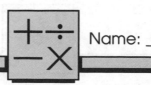

Name: _____

Number Recognition

Directions: Count the number of objects in each group. Draw a line to the correct number.

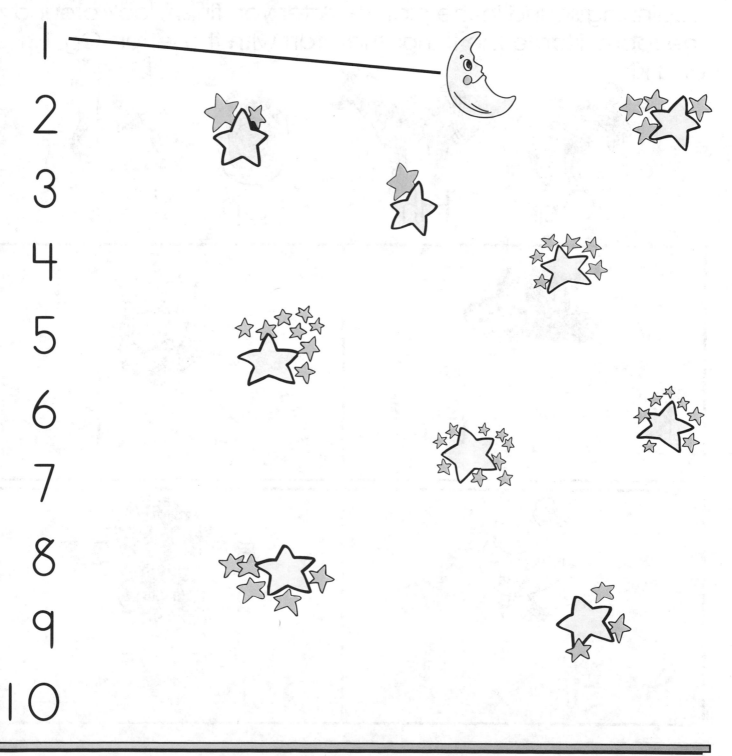

1
2
3
4
5
6
7
8
9
10

Beginning Consonants Gg, Hh, Jj, Kk

Directions: Say the name of each letter. Say the sound that each letter makes. Then, trace the letter that makes the beginning sound in the picture. After you finish, look around the room. Name the things that start with the letters Gg, Hh, Jj, and Kk.

Gg   Hh   Jj   Kk

K k   H h   G g   K k

G g   H h   J j   G g

Name: _____

I Can Write A Whole Sentence!

A telling sentence ends with a period.

Directions: 1. Write the name of the pet on the line with the same number. 2. Find a picture that shows the pet doing something. 3. Write that word on the line to make a whole sentence. 4. Put a period at the end of each sentence.

Like this:

The frog   jumps

The frog jumps.

1. The fish   sleeps

2. The bird   runs

3. The cat   flies

4. The dog   eats

1. _____

2. _____

3. _____

4. _____

Following Directions

Directions: Trace a circle ○, a square □ , a triangle △, and a half-circle Ɔ. Color each one. Draw other shapes. Color them.

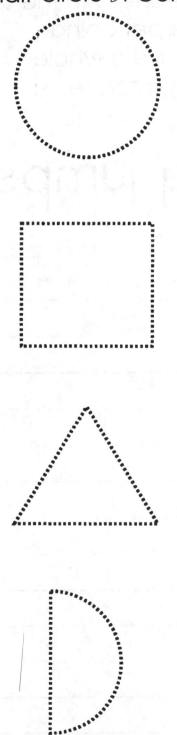

Name: _____

Following Directions

Directions: Look at the pictures. Follow the directions in each box.

Draw a circle around the caterpillar.
Draw a line under the stick.

Put an **X** on the mother bird.
Draw a triangle around the baby birds.

Put a box around the rabbit.

Color the flowers. Count the bees.

These Keep Me Warm

Directions: Look at the pictures. Color only the things that keep you warm.

Name: _____

Sequencing Numbers

Sequencing is putting numbers in the correct order.

Directions: Write the missing numbers.

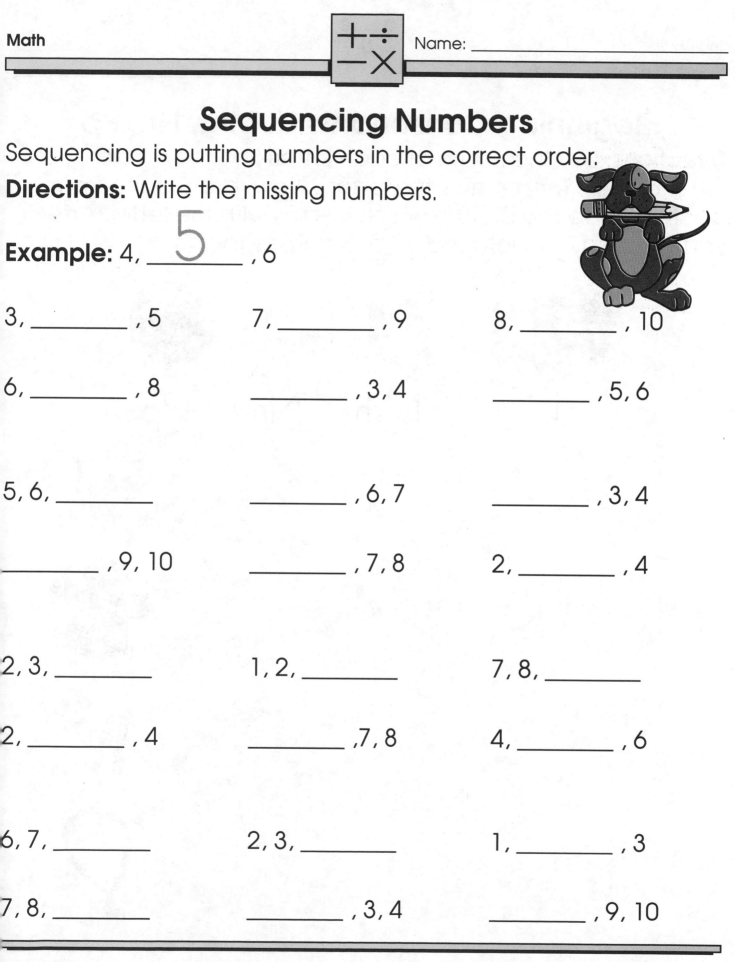

Example: 4, ___5___ , 6

3, _____ , 5   7, _____ , 9   8, _____ , 10

6, _____ , 8   _____ , 3, 4   _____ , 5, 6

5, 6, _____   _____ , 6, 7   _____ , 3, 4

_____ , 9, 10   _____ , 7, 8   2, _____ , 4

2, 3, _____   1, 2, _____   7, 8, _____

2, _____ , 4   _____ , 7, 8   4, _____ , 6

6, 7, _____   2, 3, _____   1, _____ , 3

7, 8, _____   _____ , 3, 4   _____ , 9, 10

Beginning Consonants Ll, Mm, Nn, Pp

Directions: Say the name of each letter. Say the sound each letter makes. Then, trace the letters. Now, draw a line from each letter to the picture which begins with the letter. After you finish, say the letters Ll, Mm, Nn, Pp again.

Ll   Mm   Nn   Pp

Ll

Mm

Nn

Pp

Name: _____

I Know Which Letters Are Missing!

Directions: Fill in the missing letters for each word. Then write the word by yourself.

Like this:

frog frog frog

fi___ f___ ___h

d___ ___g o___g

bi___ d___ b___d

___at c___ ___t

43

Name: _____

Same/Different

Directions: Color the shape next to it that looks the same as the first shape in each row.

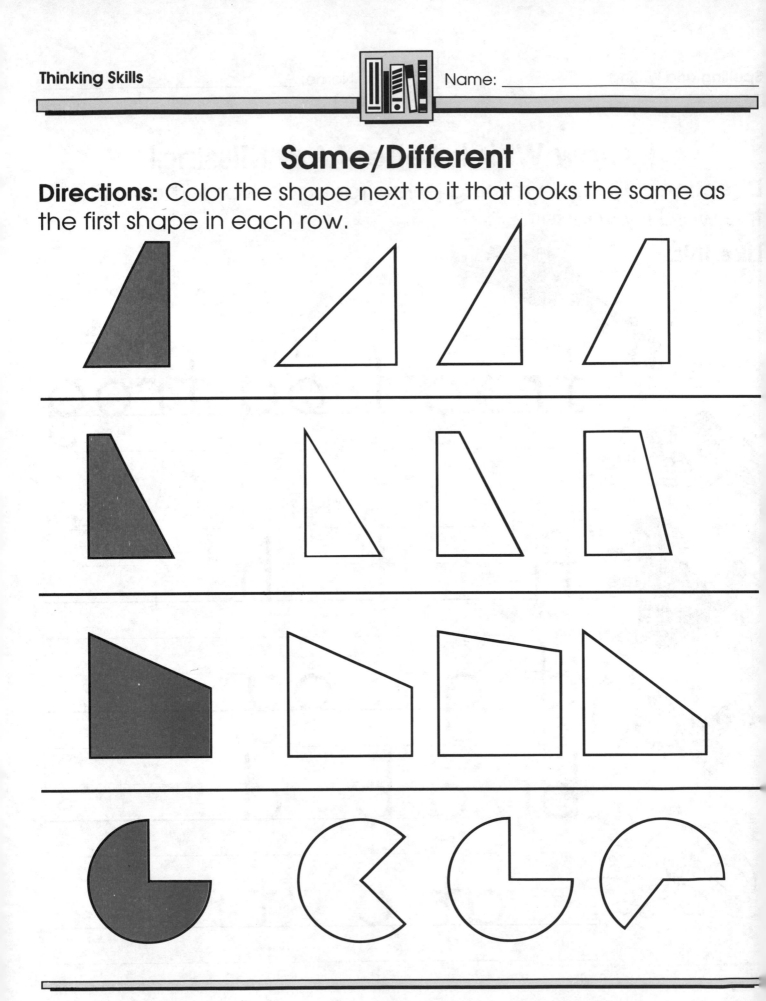

Finish The Pictures

Directions: Read the words. Finish the pictures.

a red ball

a black hat

a yellow sun

a pink kite

an orange balloon

a blue umbrella

I Like To Rake Leaves

Directions: Read about raking leaves. Then answer the questions.

I like to rake leaves. Do you? Leaves die each year. They get brown and dry. They fall from the trees. Then we rake them up.

1. What color are leaves when they die?

_____

_____

_____

2. What happens when they die?

_____

_____

_____

3. What do we do when they fall?

_____

_____

_____

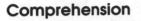

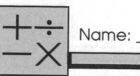

Name: _____

Counting

Directions: How many are there of each shape? Write the answers in the boxes. The first one is done for you.

Name: _____

Beginning Consonants Qq, Rr, Ss, Tt

Directions: Say the name of each letter. Say the sound that each letter makes. Then, trace each letter in the boxes. Color the picture which begins with the sound of the letter.

Qq   Rr   Ss   Tt

T t   Q q

R r   S s

I Know Which Words Make A Sentence!

Directions: 1. Finish writing the names of the pets. 2. Draw a line from the pet's name to the end of the sentence. 3. Put a period at the end of each sentence. 4. Read your sentences to someone.

Like this:

A green ___frog___ jumps in the water ☐

1. Ken's ___c_____ climbs trees ☐

2. My friend's ___d_____ barks a lot ☐

3. Pat's ___f_____ swims in the water ☐

4. My little ___b_____ sits on his finger ☐

Name: _____

Same/Different

Directions: Put an **X** on the shapes in each row that do not match the first shape.

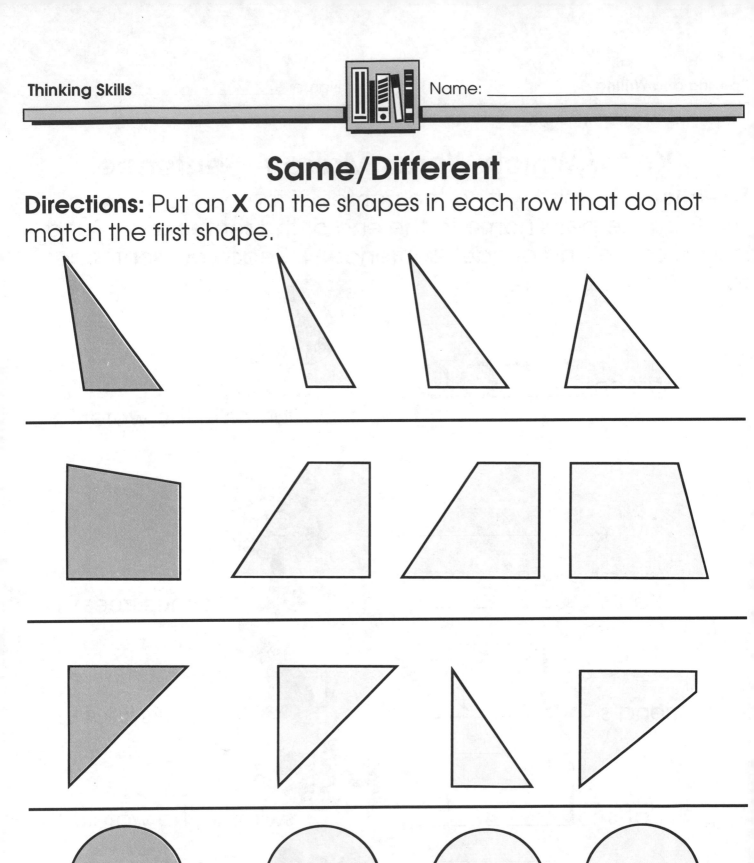

LESSON 2

AMERICA 2000

In 1989, George Bush became President of the United States. President Bush thought that education was important, so he helped make a plan for the future called AMERICA 2000.

Since people need to learn to read to be good citizens, part of the plan says that every grown-up will know how to read by the year 2000.

Look at the citizens waiting to vote. Name the different items in the picture that can be read.

Why do you think it is important for citizens to know how to read?

ACTIVITY 2

AMERICA 2000

Directions: Pretend it is the year 2000. You are much older now and want to share a book with someone you know who is in first grade. Draw a picture of the cover of the book you would read with the first grader.

Lesson 2

Water

People need water to stay alive.
People use water for drinking, cooking and cleaning.
People use water for fun, too.

Animals need water to live.
Plants need water to grow.
Some animals and plants live in water.
All living things need clean water.

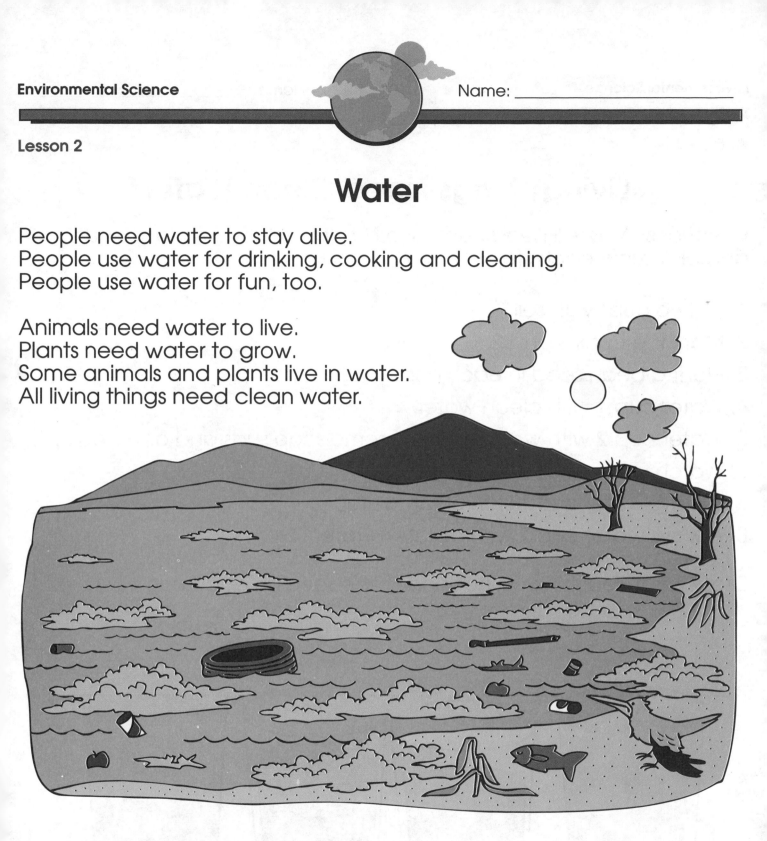

But not all water is clean.
Some water is very dirty, or polluted.
Polluted water makes people sick.
Animals and plants that live in polluted water can die.

How does water become polluted?

Activity 2

Living Things Need Clean Water

Directions: You will need cups, two bean seeds, water, soap suds, and oil. Follow each step in order.

1. Fill two cups with soil.

2. Mark the cups 1 and 2.

3. Plant a bean seed in each cup.

4. Water cup 1 with clean water.

5. Water cup 2 with water that has some soap suds and oil mixed in it.

6. Watch your seeds each day.

7. Always water cup 1 with clean water.

8. Always water cup 2 with polluted water.

Draw what you think will happen to the seeds in each cup?

CUP 1   **CUP 2**

Name: _____

Fill In The Blank

Directions: Look at the pictures. Pick the correct word from the word box and write it on the line.

bike	truck	wagon	bird	bear

1. a blue _____

2. a green _____

3. a red _____

4. a yellow _____

5. a brown _____

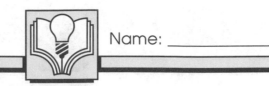

I Can Rake Leaves

Directions: Look at the pictures. Then number them in 1-2-3-4 order.

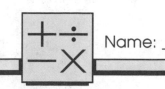

Name: _____

Counting

Directions: How many are there of each shape? Write the answers in the boxes. The first one is done for you.

Beginning Consonants Vv, Ww, Xx, Yy, Zz

Directions: Say the name of each letter. Say the sound the letter makes. Then, trace the letters. Now, draw a line from the letters that match the beginning sound in each picture.

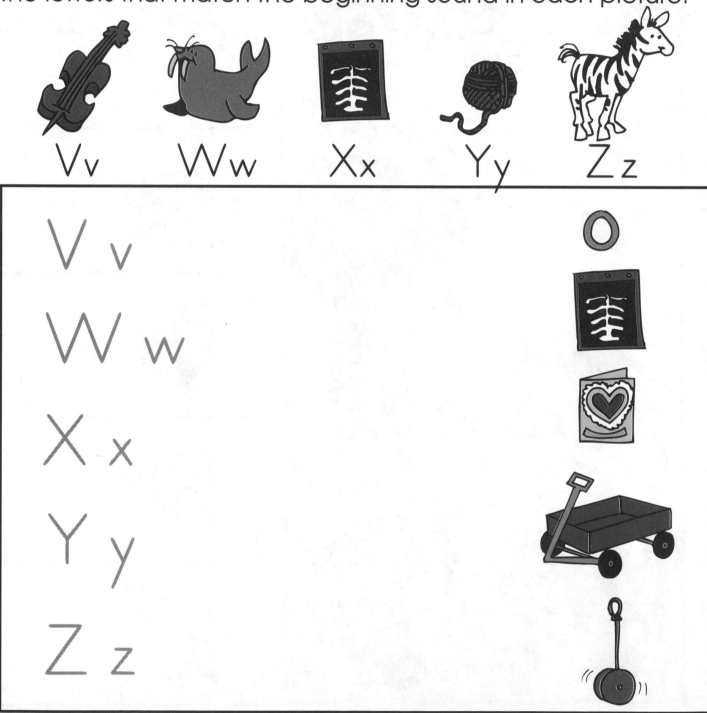

Vv   Ww   Xx   Yy   Zz

I Know How The Letters Go!

Directions: The letters in the name of each pet are mixed up. Write them the way they should be.

Like this:

g f o r

frog

t a c

o d g

i f s h

d i b r

Name: _____

Same/Different

Directions: Color the shape that does not belong in each group.

Example:

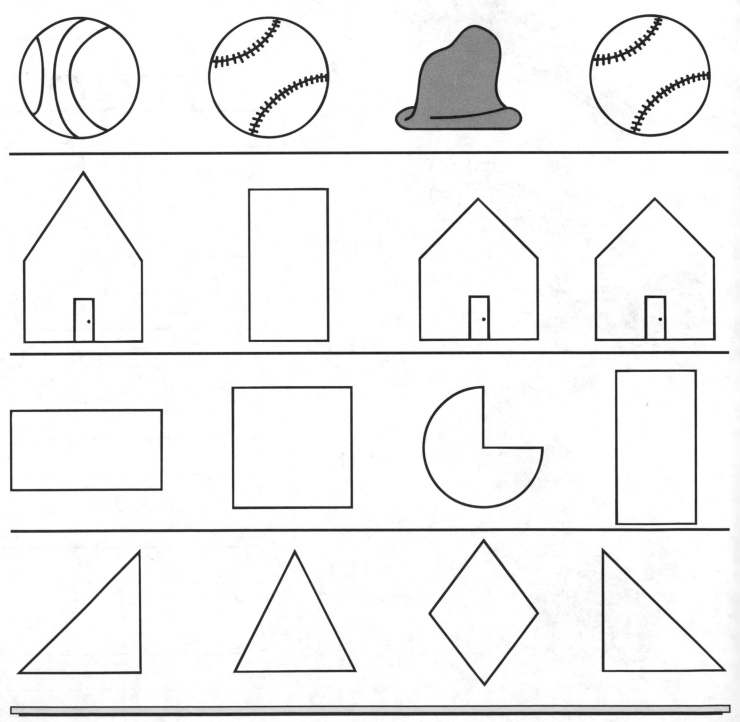

Name: _____

Skills Review: Following Directions, Color Word Vocabulary

Directions: Read the sentences. Follow the directions.

1. Color one house red.
2. Color two cars green.
3. Color two jets blue.
4. Color a big truck orange.
5. Color a bus yellow.

Name: _____

Review

Directions: Read the story. Then follow the instructions.

Some things used in baking are dry. Some things used in baking are wet. To bake a cake, first mix the salt, sugar and flour. Then add the egg. Now add the milk. Stir. Put the cake in the oven.

1. Circle the things that are wet.

2. Tell the order to mix things when you bake.

_____   _____   _____

1) _____   2) _____   3)_____

_____   _____   _____

4) _____   5)_____

3. The first things to mix are

      dry.   wet.

                _____

_____

4. Where are cakes baked? _____

_____

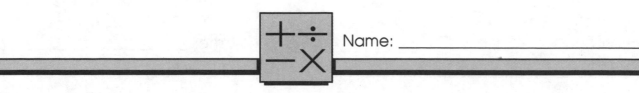

Name: _____

Review

Directions: Count the shapes and write the answers.

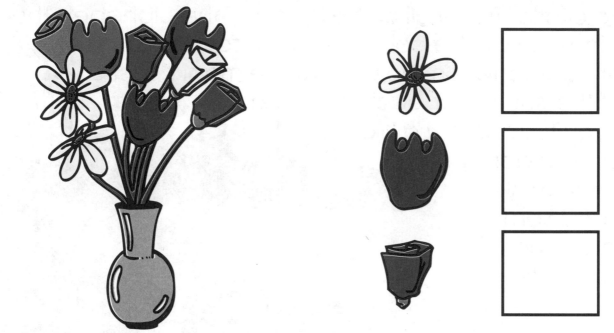

Directions: Fill in the missing numbers. Connect the dots to finish the picture.

Name: _____

Review

Directions: Help Meg and Kent and their dog, Sam, get to the magic castle. Trace all of the letters of the alphabet. Then, write the lower case consonant next to the matching upper case letter on the road to the magic castle. Make the sound for each consonant. After you finish, draw a picture on another paper of what you think Meg and Sam will find in the magic castle.

V__ W__ X__ Y__ Z__

T__

S__

R__ P__ M__ K__

Q__ N__ L__ J__

H__

G__

C__ F__

B__ D__

Review

Directions: Use the words in the pictures to write a sentence about each pet. Can you spell the name of the pet by yourself? Put a period at the end of each sentence.

Like this:

The 🐸 eats bugs   The frog eats bugs.

The 🐱 drinks milk _____

_____

_____

The 🐦 eats an apple _____

_____

_____

The 🐭 jumps out _____

_____

_____

The 🐟🐟 sees a friend _____

_____

_____

Review

Directions: Color the circles ○ red.

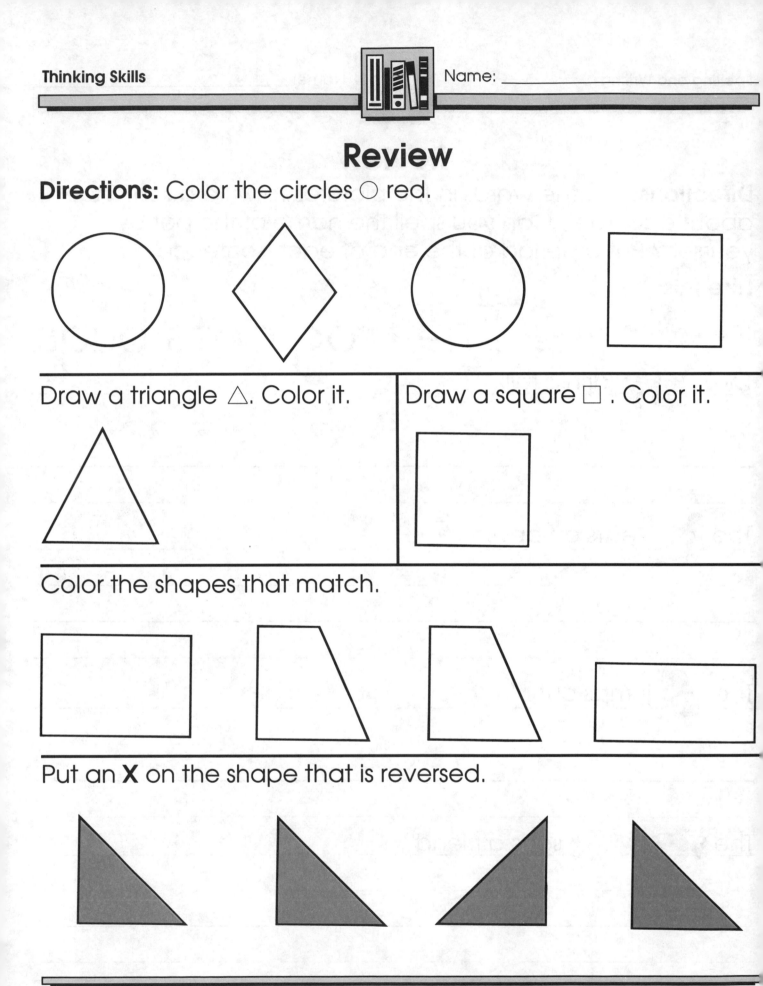

Draw a triangle △. Color it.

Draw a square □ . Color it.

Color the shapes that match.

Put an **X** on the shape that is reversed.

 Name: _____

Which Are Opposites?

Directions: Draw a line between the opposites.

day

happy

big

open

front

little

closed

night

back

sad

I Like Cats

Directions: Read the story. Then answer the questions.

Do you like cats? I do. To pet a cat, move slowly. Hold out your hand. The cat will come to you. Then pet its head. Do not grab a cat! It will run away.

1. To pet a cat, move   fast.

                                   slow.

2. Give directions on how to pet a cat. _____

_____

1) Hold out your _____ .

_____

_____

2) The cat will _____ .

_____

_____

3) Pet the cat's _____ .

_____

_____

3. Do not do this _____
    to a cat! _____

Number Words

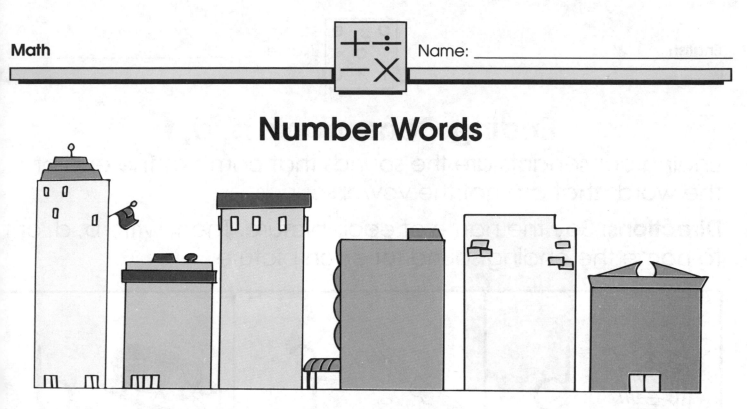

Directions: Number the buildings from one to six.

Directions: Draw a line from the word to the number.

two	1
five	3
six	5
four	6
one	2
three	4

Name: _____

Ending Consonants b, d, f

Ending consonants are the sounds that come at the end of the words that are not the vowel sounds.

Directions: Say the name of each picture. Then, write b, d, or f to name the ending sound for each picture.

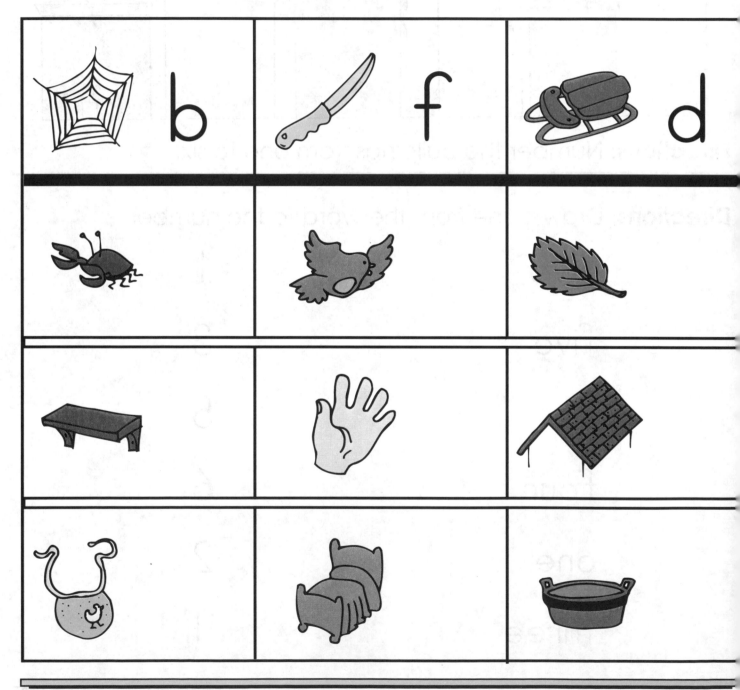

Name: _____

I Can Write The Names Of Colors!

Directions: Follow the lines to print the name of each color.
Then print the name again by yourself.

Like this:

orange   orange

blue

green

yellow

red

brown

Name: _____

Classifying

Directions: Bob is looking for stars. Help him find them. Color all the stars blue.

How many stars did Bob find? _____

Name: _____

Game Of Opposites

Directions: Write each word from the word box under its opposite.

| no | bad | hot | up | in | went | go | off |

good	came

yes	stop

down	on

out	cold

Name: _____

Where Flowers Grow

Directions: Read about flowers. Then answer the questions.

Some flowers grow in pots. Many flowers grow in flower beds. Others grow beside the road. Some flowers begin from seeds. They grow into small buds. Then they open wide and bloom. Flowers are pretty!

1. Name 2 places flowers grow.

_____

_____

_____

2. Some flowers begin from _____.

3. Then flowers grow into small _____.

4. Flowers then open wide and _____.

Name: _____

Number Words

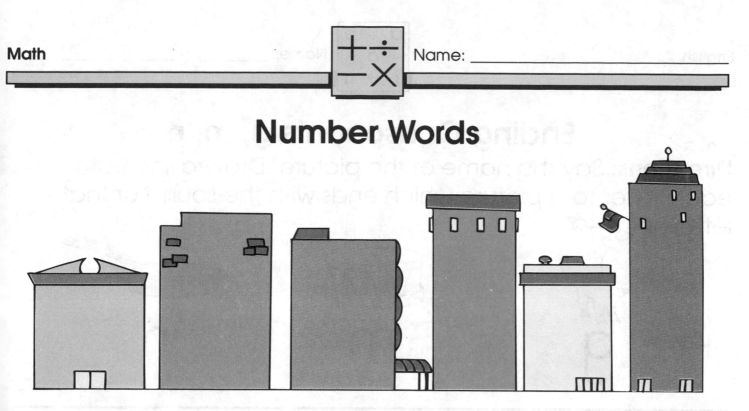

Directions: Number the buildings from five to ten.

Directions: Draw a line from the word to the number.

nine   8

seven   10

five   7

eight   5

six   9

ten   6

Name: _____

Ending Consonants g, m, n

Directions: Say the name of the picture. Draw a line from each letter to a picture which ends with the sound of that letter.

I Can Finish A Sentence!

Directions: Use the color words to finish these sentences. Then put a period at the end.

Like this: My new  are ___orange___ .

| green tree | blue bike | yellow chick | red ball |

1. The baby is _____ ☐

2. This is _____ ☐

3. My is big and _____ ☐

4. My sister's is _____ ☐

77

Name: _____

Classifying

Directions: Color the stars ☆.   How many stars?_____

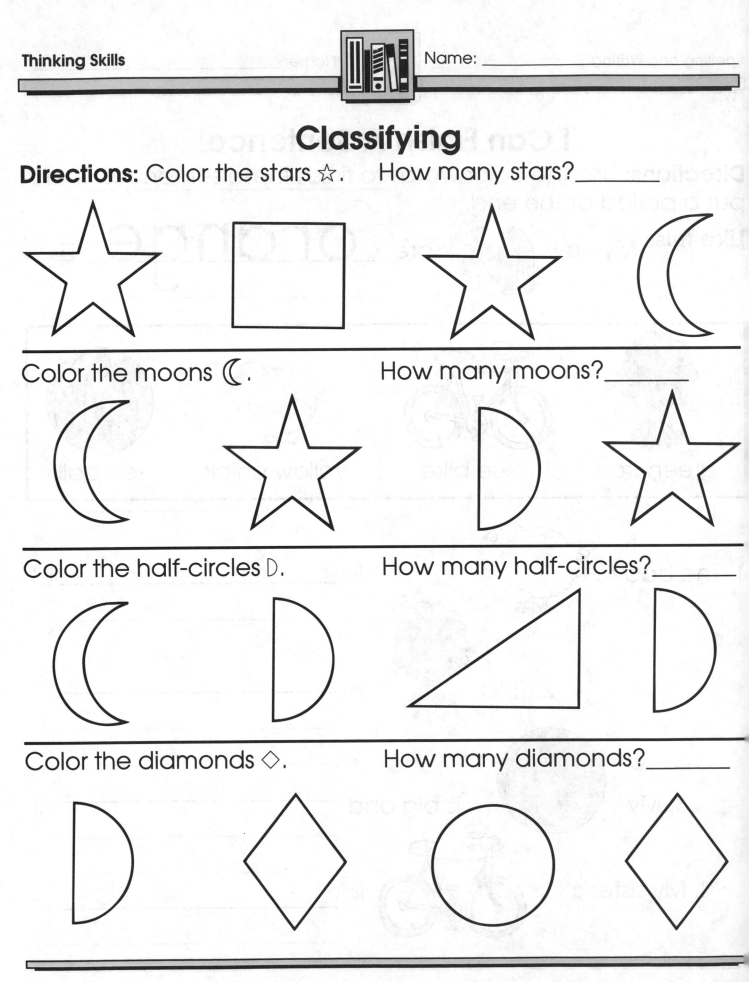

Color the moons ☾.   How many moons?_____

Color the half-circles ᗡ.   How many half-circles?_____

Color the diamonds ◇.   How many diamonds?_____

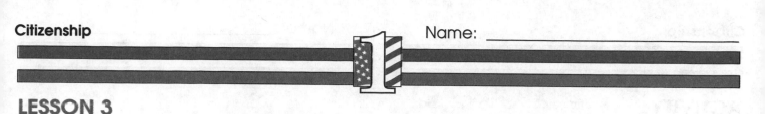

LESSON 3

The United States Flag

The United States flag stands for our country. It is a symbol of the United States and its people.

The flag can be seen in many places. Draw pictures of places where you have seen the American flag.

Why do you think Americans like to display the United States flag?

ACTIVITY 3

The United States Flag

Look at the astronaut on page 79. She is Sally Ride, the first American woman to orbit the earth. Sally Ride went to school for many years. She studied and worked hard to be an American astronaut and wear her country's flag during space travel.

Directions: Make a flag patch like the one on Sally Ride's suit. Wear your flag patch proudly!

Air

Living things need air to live.
People and animals need clean air to breathe.
Plants need clean air to grow.
Some air is not clean.
It is very dirty.

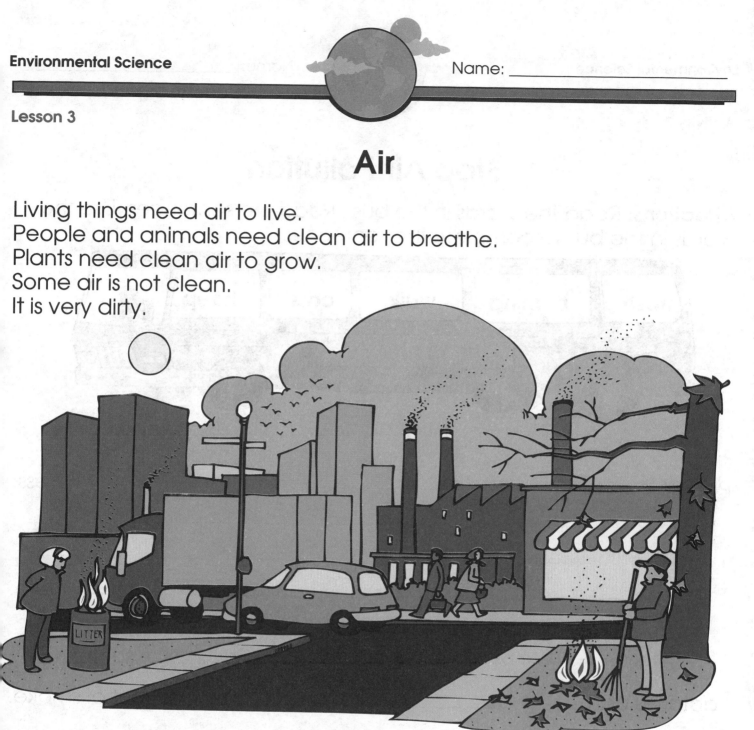

This air is polluted.
It may have dust, dirt and smoke in it.

Polluted air can be harmful to living things. It can make people sick.
Polluted air can harm plants and animals, too.

How can people help to keep our air clean?

Name: _____

Stop Air Pollution

Directions: Read the words in the bus. Read the sentences. Use the words in the bus to complete the sentences.

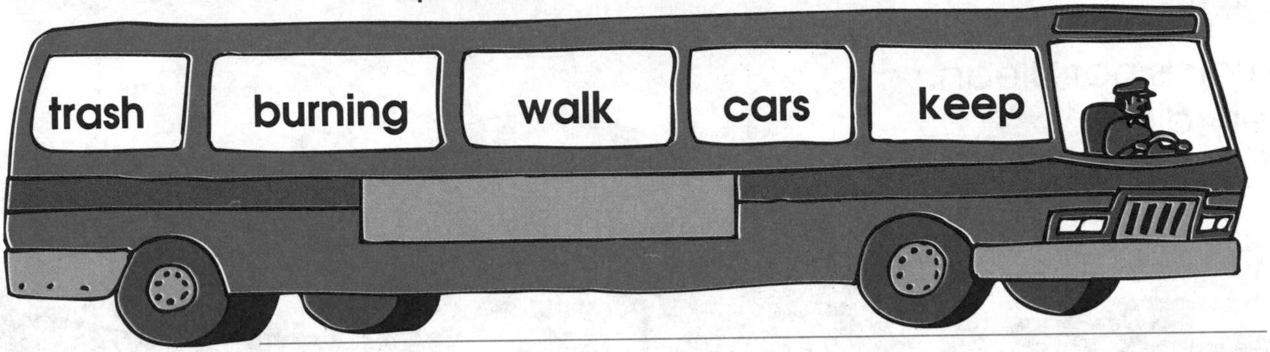

| trash | burning | walk | cars | keep |

People can use _____ less.

They can _____ more.

Factories can _____ dirt out of smoke.

People can stop burning _____

People can stop _____ leaves.

Classifying

Directions: Draw a circle around the correct pictures.

What Can Swim?

What Can Fly?

Flower Puzzle

Directions: Re-read the story about flowers on page 74, Then fill in the puzzle with the right answers about flowers.

Across
1. Flowers do this when they open wide.
2. Some flowers grow from these.

Down
1. Before they bloom, flowers grow ___.
3. A flower can grow in a flower bed or a __.

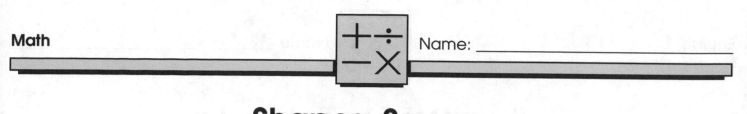
Shapes: Square

A square is a figure with four corners and four sides of the same length. This is a square □.

Directions: Find the squares and circle them.

Directions: Trace the word.   Write the word.

square

Name: _____

Ending Consonants k, l, p

Directions: Say the name of the pictures. Color the pictures in each row that end with the sound of the letter at the beginning of the row. Trace the letters.

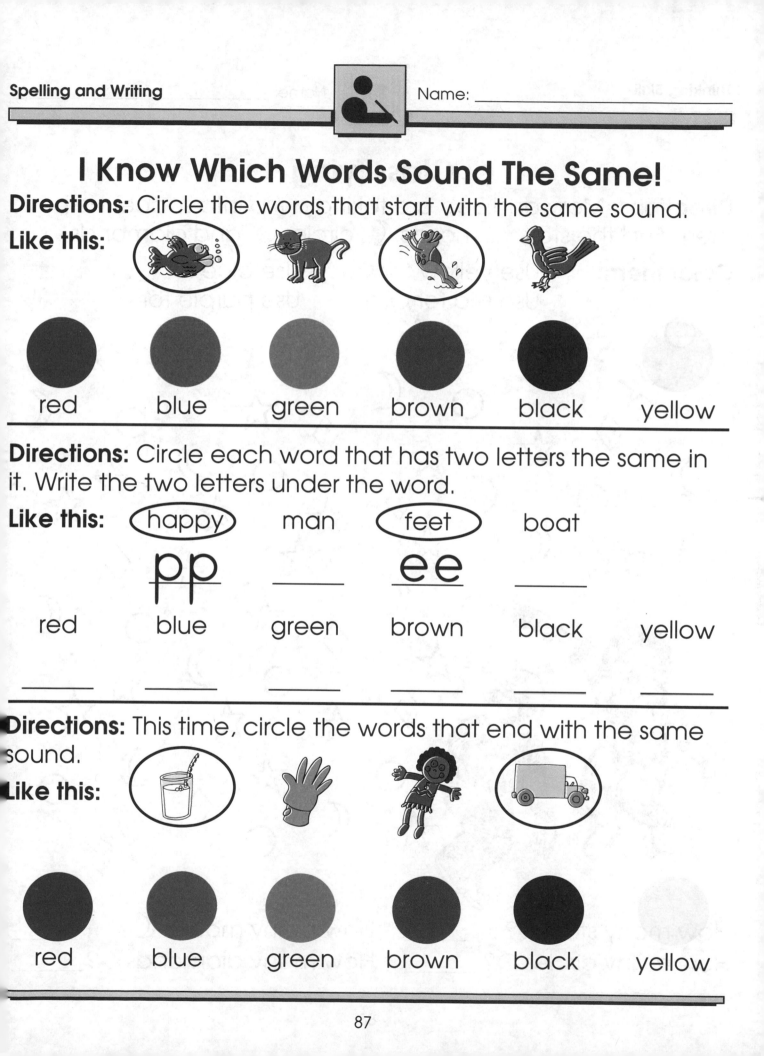

Name: _____

I Know Which Words Sound The Same!

Directions: Circle the words that start with the same sound.

Like this:

red　　blue　　green　　brown　　black　　yellow

Directions: Circle each word that has two letters the same in it. Write the two letters under the word.

Like this:　(happy)　　man　　(feet)　　boat

pp　　___　　___　　ee　　___

red　　blue　　green　　brown　　black　　yellow

___　　___　　___　　___　　___　　___

Directions: This time, circle the words that end with the same sound.

Like this:

red　　blue　　green　　brown　　black　　yellow

Name: _____

Classifying

Directions: Mary and Bob are taking a trip into space. Help them find the stars ☆, moons ☾, circles ○, and diamonds ◇.

Color them: Use yellow for ☆.   Use blue for ☾.
Use red for ○.   Use purple for ◇.

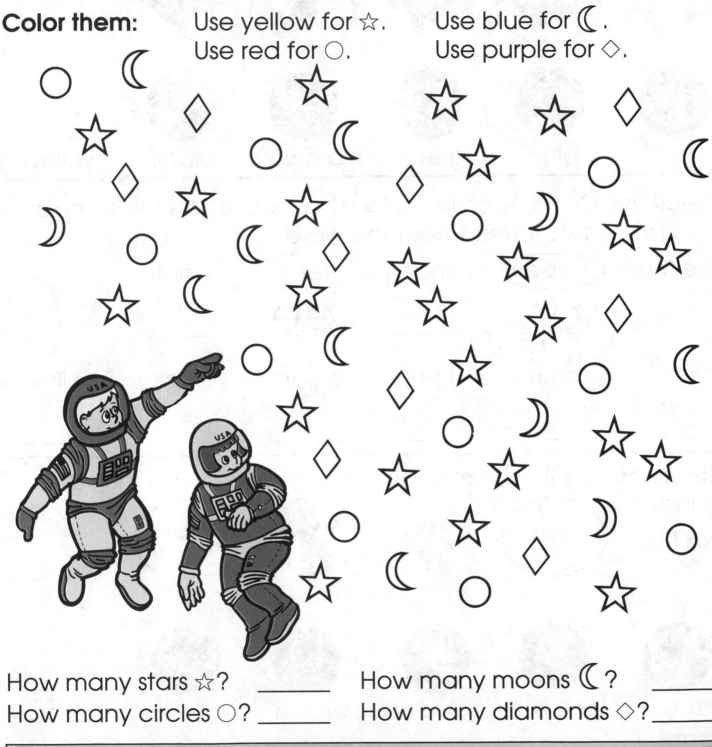

How many stars ☆? _____   How many moons ☾? _____
How many circles ○? _____   How many diamonds ◇? _____

What Are They?

Directions: Read the words in the boxes. Put each word in its correct place.

Joe	cat	blue	Tim
two	dog	red	ten
Sue	green	pig	six

Name
Words

_____

_____

_____

Number
Words

_____

_____

Animal
Words

_____

_____

Color
Words

_____

_____

Name: _____

Balloons

Directions: Read about balloons. Then answer the questions.

Some balloons float. They are filled with gas. Some balloons do not float. They are filled with air. Some clowns carry balloons. The balloons come in many colors. What color do you want?

1. What makes balloons float? _____

_____

2. What is in balloons that do not float? _____

_____

3. What kind of balloons is the clown holding? _____

_____

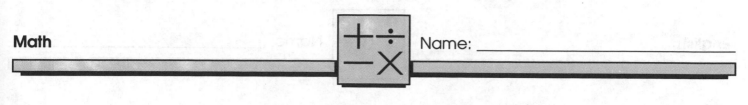
Shapes: Circle

A circle is a figure that is round. This is a circle ○.

Directions: Find the circles and put a square around them.

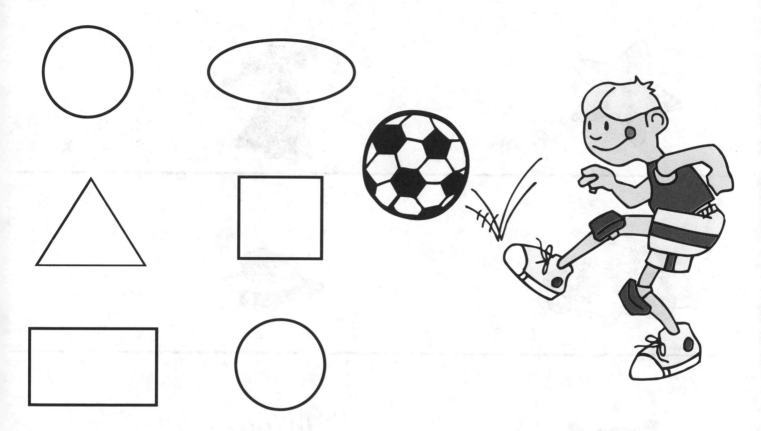

Directions: Trace the word. Write the word.

circle

Ending Consonants r, s, t, x

Directions: Say the name of the picture. Then circle the ending sound for each picture.

r s t x

r s t x

r s t x

r s t x

r s t x

r s t x

r s t x

r s t x

I Know Which Ones Are Sentences!

Directions: Some of these sentences tell the whole idea. Others have something missing. If you think something is missing, draw a line to a word that would finish that sentence. Remember to put a period after the last word in the sentence.

1. He is holding up his

2. Ken has a new puppy.

book

3. I can read a

4. We like to play games.

hand.

5. Pat wants to eat some

tree

6. I will color the

cake

7. This is my birthday.

Name: _____

Classifying

Directions: Help Mary and Bob sort their shapes. Draw a line from each shape to the basket it should go in.

Alphabetical Order

Directions: Look at the words in each box. Circle the word that comes first in a-b-c order.

A-B-C Order

duck four rock	chair apple yellow	peach this walk
game boy pink	light come one	mouse ten orange
angel table hair	zebra watch five	foot boat mine
look blue rope	who dog black	book tan six

Clowning Around

Directions: Look at the pictures of the clowns. Find 4 things that are different in picture 2. Color the things that are different.

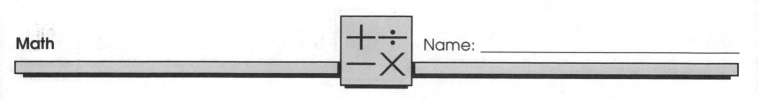

Shapes: Triangle

A triangle is a figure with three corners and three sides. This is a triangle △.

Directions: Find the triangles and put a circle around them.

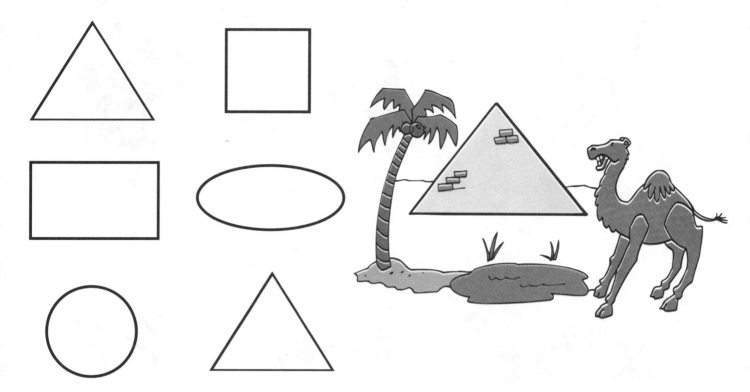

Directions: Trace the word.   Write the word.

triangle

Name: _____

Beginning and Ending Sounds Discrimination

Directions: Say the name of the picture. Draw a blue circle around the picture if it begins with the sound of the letter. Draw a green triangle around the picture if it ends with the sound of the letter.

w   l   m

k   n   u

t   s   z

Name: _____

I Know Which Words Begin The Same!

Directions: Say the name of the color and the picture beside it. If they begin with the same sound, write an **X** in the box.

Like this:

red **X** □ **blue**

yellow □ □ **black**

green □ □ **brown**

Name: _____

Classifying

Directions: Look at the shapes. Answer the questions.

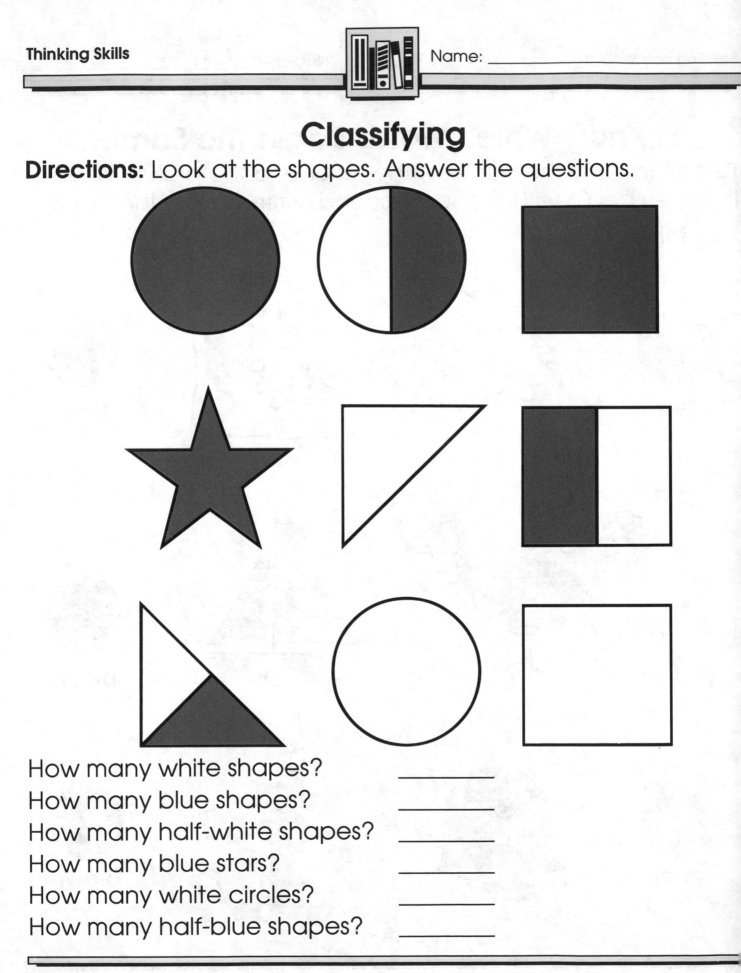

How many white shapes? _____

How many blue shapes? _____

How many half-white shapes? _____

How many blue stars? _____

How many white circles? _____

How many half-blue shapes? _____

Name: _____

Story Order

Directions: The pictures tell a story, but they are in the wrong order. Write a number under each box to show the order they belong in.

_____   _____   _____

_____   _____   _____

Name: _____

Tigers

Directions: Read about tigers. Then answer the questions.

Tigers sleep during the day. They hunt at night. Tigers eat meat. They hunt deer. They like to eat wild pigs. If they cannot find meat, tigers will eat fish.

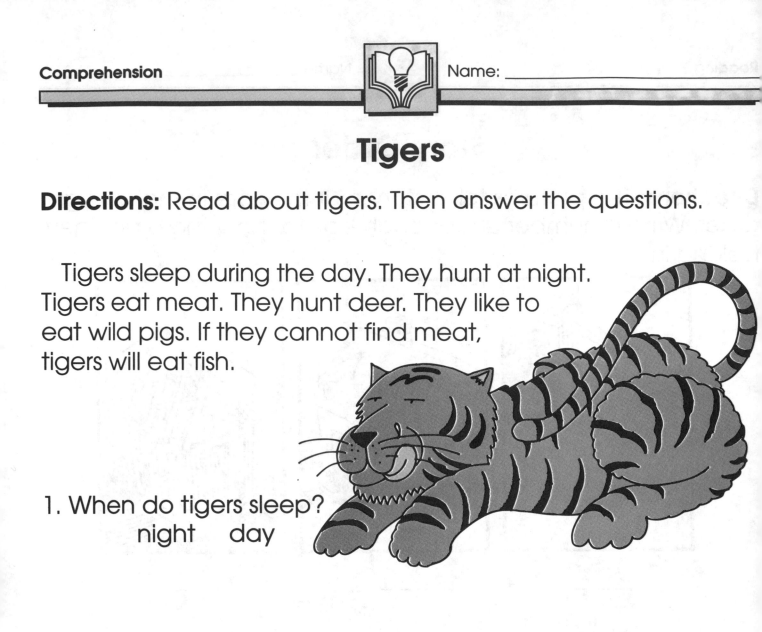

1. When do tigers sleep?
   night   day

2. Name 2 things tigers eat.

_____   _____

_____   _____

_____   _____

3. When do tigers hunt?
   day   night

Shapes: Rectangle

A rectangle is a figure with four corners and four sides. Sides opposite each other are the same length. This is a rectangle ☐ .

Directions: Find the rectangles and put a circle around them.

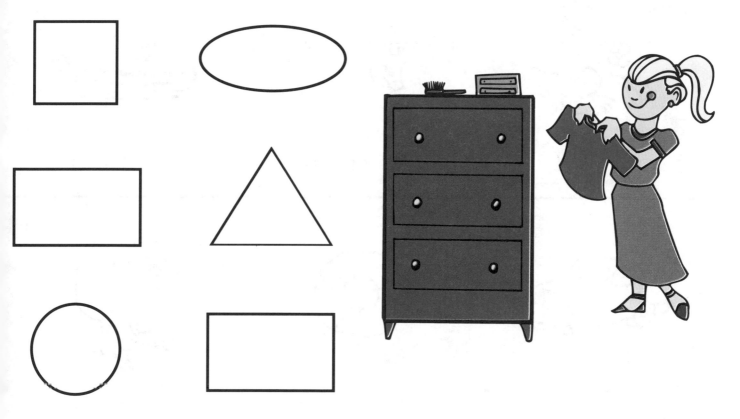

Directions: Trace the word.   Write the word.

Name: _____

Beginning and Ending Sounds Discrimination

Directions: Say the name of each picture. Draw a triangle around the letter that makes the beginning sound. Draw a square around the letter that makes the ending sound. Color the pictures.

o   r   t   f   d   w   v   t   b

x   c   r   t   g   d   d   a   k

l   m   h   x   g   r   p   t   v

I Know How To Start A Sentence!

A sentence starts with a capital letter.

Directions: 1. Read the words by each picture. 2. Write them to make a sentence that tells about the picture. 3. Start each sentence with a capital letter—and end with a period.

Like this: the girl coat a red has

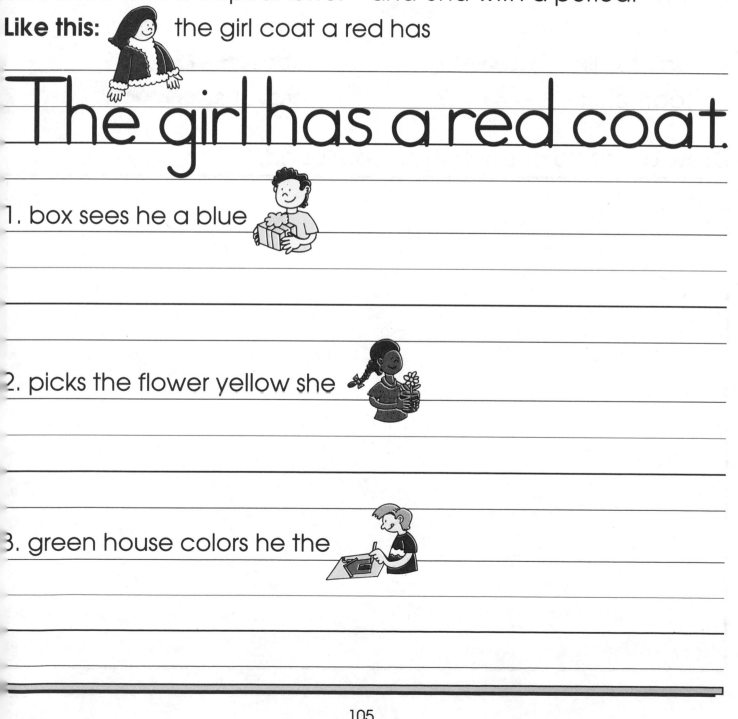

The girl has a red coat.

1. box sees he a blue

2. picks the flower yellow she

3. green house colors he the

Name: _____

Classifying

Directions: Look around your home or school. Find some pencils, pens, straws, toothpicks, paintbrushes, and crayons. Count them.

How many:

pencils   ?_____   straws   ?_____

paintbrushes   ?_____   pens   ?_____

toothpicks   ?____   crayons   ?____

Draw a picture of each thing you found.

LESSON 4

The Declaration of Independence

In 1776, American leaders asked Thomas Jefferson to write the Declaration of Independence. The Declaration of Independence was an important paper. It said a new country called the United States of America had been formed. In the Declaration, Thomas Jefferson wrote that people have the right to be free. American citizens will always remember Jefferson's famous words.

Why do you think American leaders chose Thomas Jefferson to write the Declaration of Independence?

Name: _____

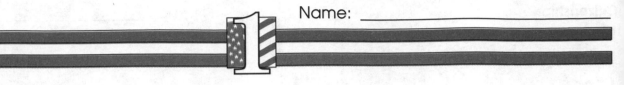

ACTIVITY 4

The Declaration of Independence

Directions: The Declaration of Independence reminds us that we are free. Write a "Declaration" that tells what *being free* means to you.

Keep Our Land Clean

Things people throw away can cause pollution.
Pollution makes the environment unclean.
Junk, garbage and trash pollute the land.
People can help keep the land clean.
They can throw trash in the right place.
They can clean up their environment.

This is a picture of a school playground that shows pollution.

What do you think people can do to make the playground clean?

Activity 4

People Who Help

School custodians are men and women who keep schools clean. They help to get rid of the school's trash. They work to keep the environment clean.

Directions: Invite your custodian to visit your classroom. Ask your custodian to talk about ways that you can help to keep your school clean. Write two questions you will ask on the lines.

1. _____

_____

_____

2. _____

_____

Name: _____

Story Order

Directions: 1) Look at the picture story. 2) Read the sentences. 3) Write 1, 2, 3 or 4 by each sentence to show the order of the story.

Ben rides the bus. _____
Ben is at the bus stop. _____
Ben leaves his house. _____
Ben gets on the bus. _____

Name: _____

Tiger Puzzle

Directions: Re-read the story about tigers on page 102, Then fill in the puzzle with the right answers about tigers.

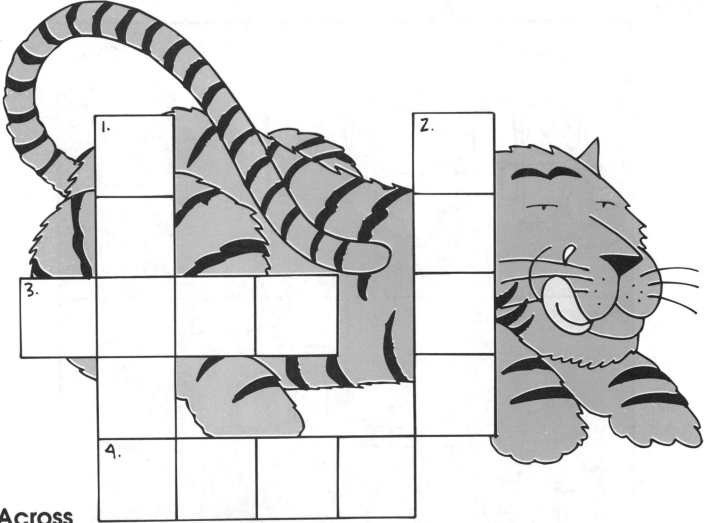

Across
3. The food tigers like best.
4. Tigers like to eat this meat: wild ____.

Down
1. Tigers do this during the day.
2. When tigers cannot get meat, they eat this.

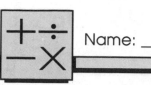

Shapes: Oval And Diamond

An oval is an egg-shaped figure. A diamond is a figure with four sides of the same length. Its corners form points at the top, sides, and bottom. This is an oval ⬭. This is a diamond ◇.

Directions: Color the ovals red. Color the diamonds blue.

Directions: Trace the words. Write the words.

oval

diamond

Name: _____

Beginning and Ending Sounds Discrimination

Directions: Look at the example. Say the beginning and ending sounds for the word **pipe**. Write the letter that makes the beginning and ending sound for each picture.

Name: _____

I Can Play A Word Game!

Directions: Finish the name of each color. Some words go down and some go across. Can you spell them by yourself?

Name: _____

Classifying

Directions: Look at the shapes with Mary. Then answer the questions.

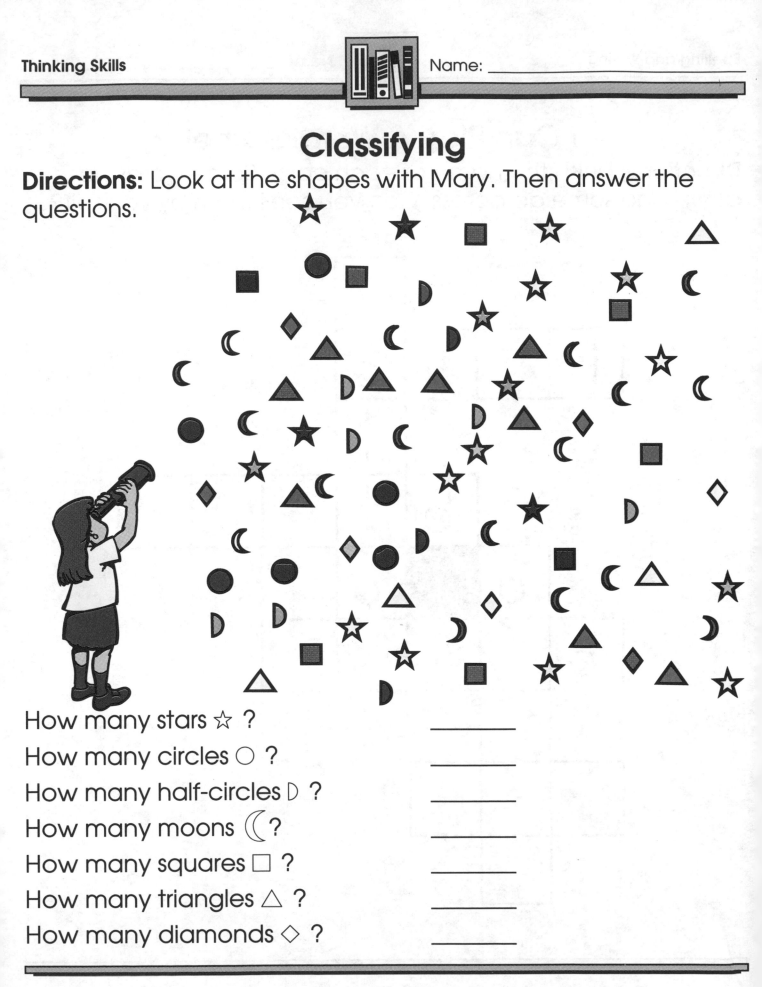

How many stars ☆ ? _____

How many circles ○ ? _____

How many half-circles ◗ ? _____

How many moons ☾ ? _____

How many squares □ ? _____

How many triangles △ ? _____

How many diamonds ◇ ? _____

Name: _____

Skills Review: Sequencing, Classifying

Directions: 1) Write numbers by the sentences to show the order they belong in. 2) Write each word from the word box in its correct place.

Kim picks out food.

_____

Kim pays the man.

_____

Kim goes to the store.

_____

apple	ice cream	cookie	banana	orange	cake

Fruits   Sweets

_____   _____

_____   _____

_____   _____

_____   _____

_____   _____

_____   _____

Name: _____

Review

Directions: Read about cookies. Then answer the questions.

Cookies are made with many things. All cookies are made with flour. Some cookies have nuts in them. Some cookies do not. Some cookies have chips. Some cookies do not. Cookbooks give directions on how to make cookies. First turn on the oven. Then get all the things out that go in the cookies. Mix them together. Roll out, then cut the cookies. Bake the cookies. Now eat them!

1. Tell 1 way all cookies are the same.

_____

_____

_____

2. Name 2 different things in cookies.

_____   _____

_____   _____

_____   _____

3. Where do you find directions for making cookies?

_____

_____

_____

Name: _____

Review

Directions: Color the shapes in the picture as shown.

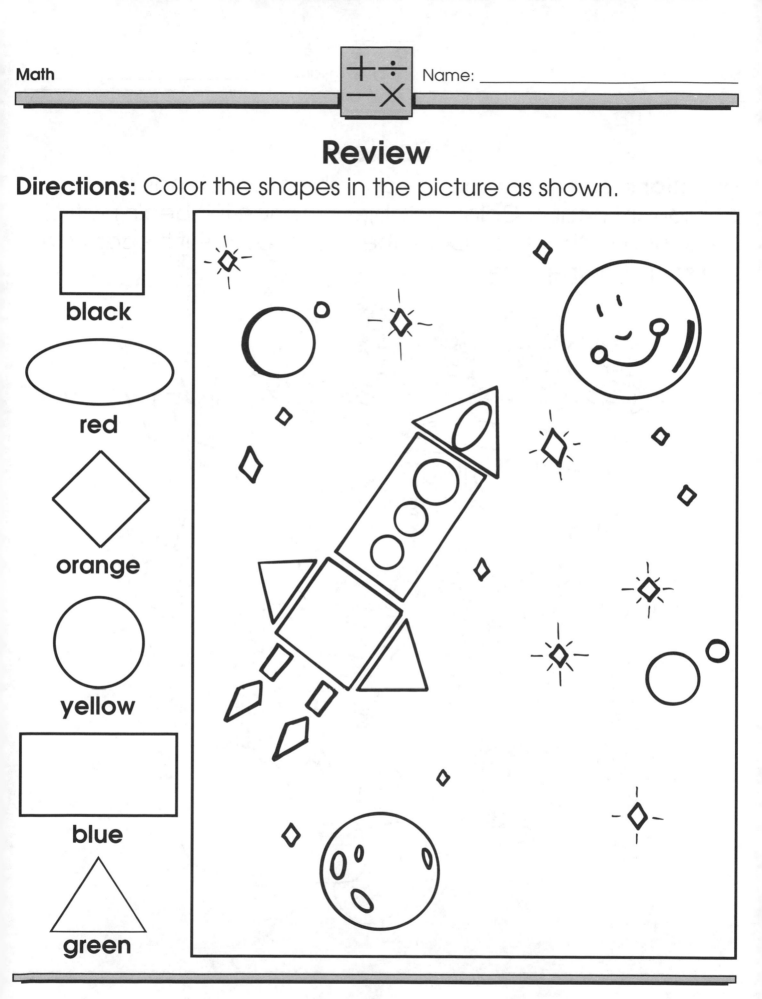

black

red

orange

yellow

blue

green

Review

Directions: Say the name of each object which has a consonant near it. Color the object orange if it begins with the sound of the letter. Color the object purple if it ends with the sound of the letter.

Review

Directions: 1. Write three sentences that tell about this picture. Use a color word in each one. Can you write the names of the colors and the pets by yourself now? 2. Remember to begin each sentence with a capital letter and end with a period.

Here are some more words you could use: **walks, sees, runs, flies, grows, eats, looks, jumps, sits.**

1. _____

_____

2. _____

_____

3. _____

_____

Review

Directions: Color the stars ☆ blue.

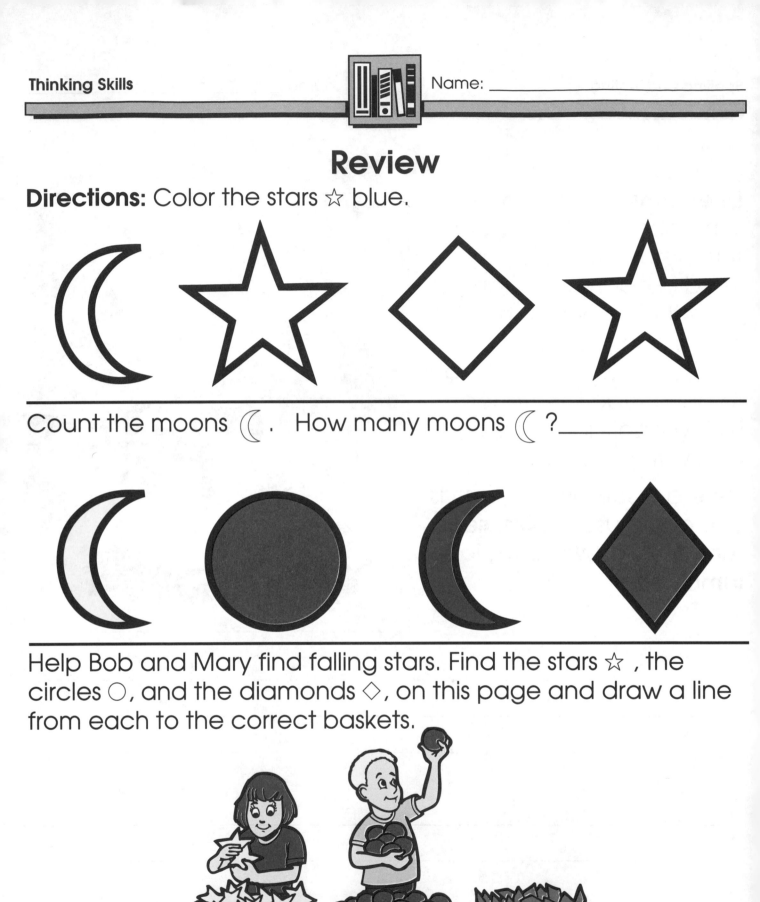

Count the moons ☾. How many moons ☾ ?_____

Help Bob and Mary find falling stars. Find the stars ☆ , the circles ○, and the diamonds ◇, on this page and draw a line from each to the correct baskets.

Name: _____

Rhyming Trains: Words with a

Directions: Each train has a group of pictures. Write the word that names the pictures. Read your rhyming words.

The short **a** sounds like the **a** in cat.

The long **a** sounds like the **a** in lake.

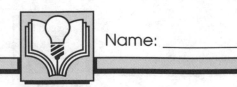

Name: _____

Find The Fruit

Directions: Fruit tastes good. It is sweet! Look at the pictures. Find the fruit. Then copy the name of each fruit in the blanks below.

banana

potato

carrot

apple

orange

grapes

broccoli

1. _____   3. _____

_____   _____

_____   _____

2. _____   4. _____

_____   _____

Name: _____

Addition 1, 2

Addition means "putting together" or adding two or more numbers to find the sum.

Directions: Count the cats and tell how many.

Short Vowel Sounds

The short vowel sounds used in this book are found in the following words: ant, egg, igloo, on, up.

Directions: Say the name of each picture. The short vowel sound may be in the front of the word or in the middle of the word. Color the pictures in each row that have the correct short vowel sound.

 a

 e

i

o

u

I Can Write The Names Of Food!

Directions: 1. Follow the lines to write the names of food.
2. Write the names by yourself. 3. Color the pictures. 4. Read the words to someone.

Like this:

bread   bread

cookie

apple

cake

milk

egg

Name: _____

Duplicating

Directions: Look at the colored shape. Color the one beside it the same. Then draw the shape.

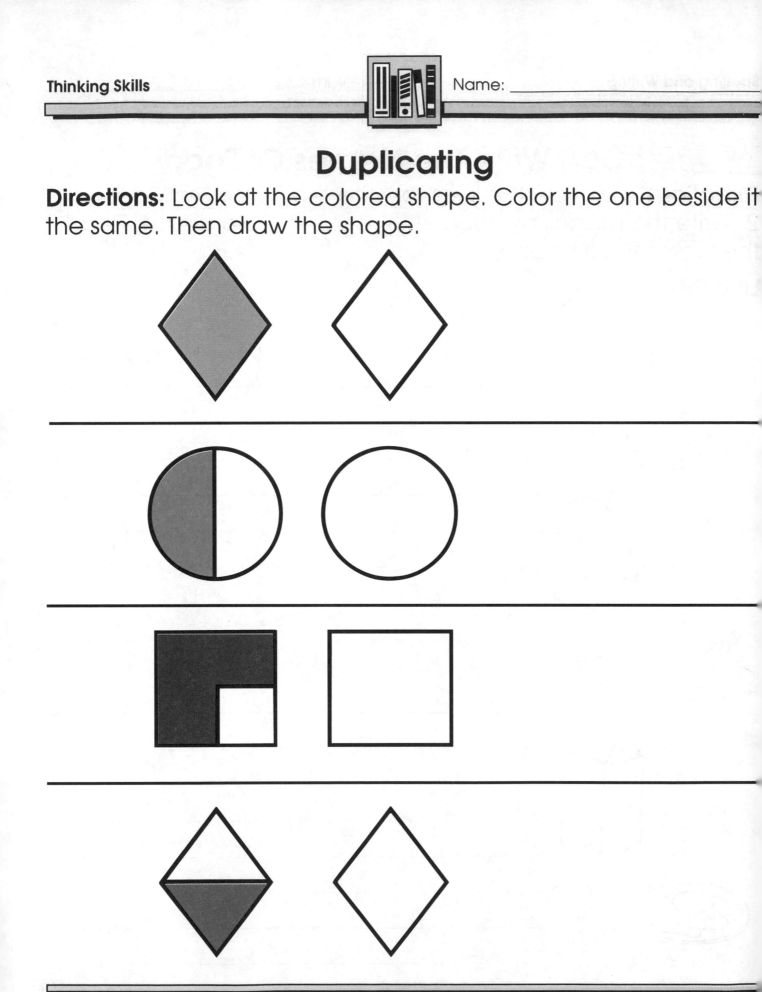

Words With e

Directions: Short **e** sounds like the **e** in hen. Long **e** sounds like the **e** in bee. 1) Look at the pictures. 2) If the word has a short **e** sound, draw a line to the hen. 3) If the word has a long **e** sound, draw a line to the bee.

hen

bee

Name: _____

An Animal Party

Directions: Look at the picture.
Look at the word list.
Then answer the questions.

bear	cat
dog	elephant
giraffe	hippo
pig	tiger

1. Which animals have on bow ties?

_____ _____

_____ _____

_____

2. Which animal has on a hat?

_____

_____

3. Which animal has on a striped shirt? _____

_____

Math

Name: _____

Addition 3, 4, 5, 6

Directions: Practice writing the numbers and then add.

3

4

5

6

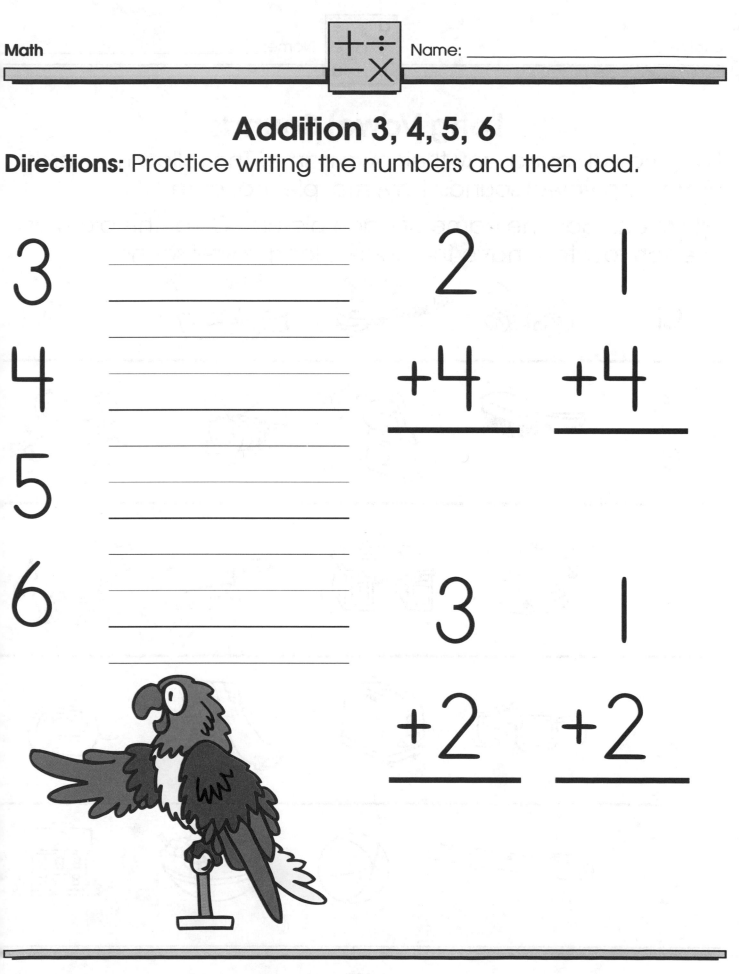

$$\begin{array}{r} 2 \\ +4 \\ \hline \end{array} \qquad \begin{array}{r} 1 \\ +4 \\ \hline \end{array}$$

$$\begin{array}{r} 3 \\ +2 \\ \hline \end{array} \qquad \begin{array}{r} 1 \\ +2 \\ \hline \end{array}$$

Name: _____

Long Vowel Sounds

Long vowel sounds say their own name. The following words have long vowel sounds: hay, me, pie, no, cute.

Directions: Say the name of each picture. Color the pictures in each row that have the correct long vowel sound.

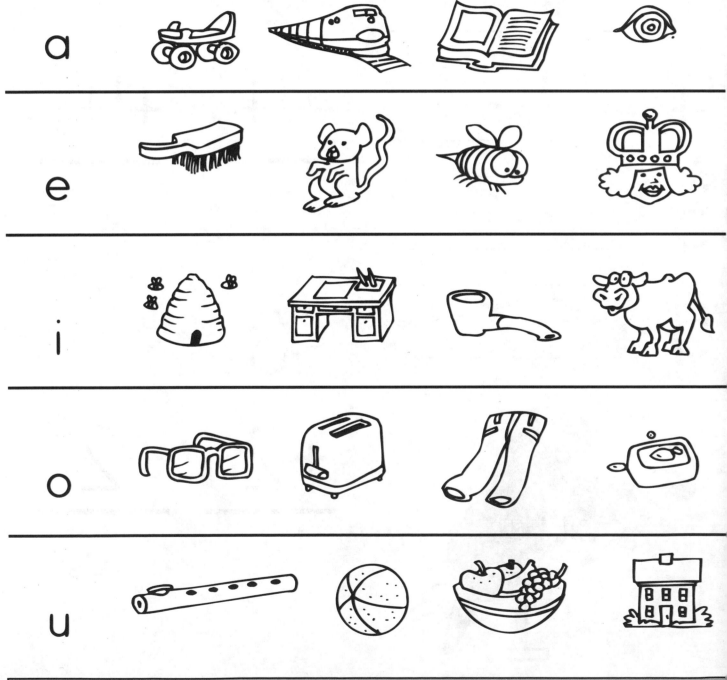

Name: _____

I Know Which Ones Are Questions!

A question is a sentence that asks something.

Directions: 1. Write each sentence on the line. 2. Start all the sentences with capital letters. 3. Put a period at the end of the telling sentences. 4. Put a question mark at the end of the asking sentences.

Like this: do you like ice cream

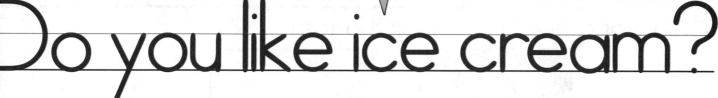

Do you like ice cream?

1. milk comes from cows

2. is that cookie good

3. did you eat your apple

Name: _____

Duplicating

Directions: Color your circle ○ to look the same.

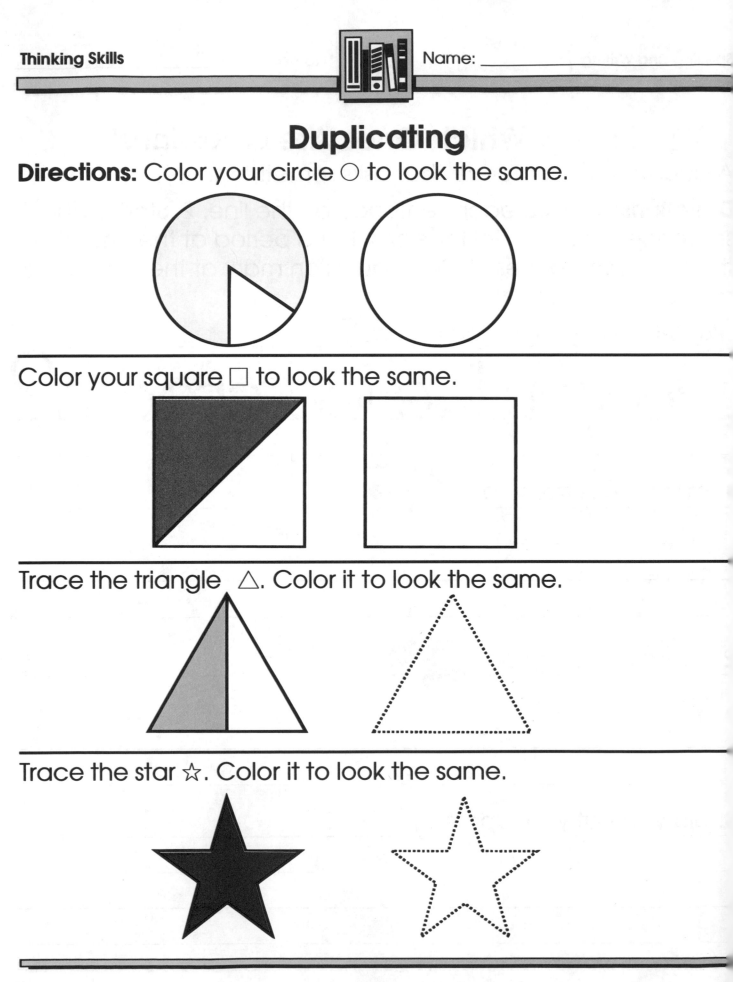

Color your square □ to look the same.

Trace the triangle △. Color it to look the same.

Trace the star ☆. Color it to look the same.

LESSON 5

The White House

We often hear about the White House in the news. The White House is where the President of the United States and his family live. The White House has 132 rooms. It has an indoor pool, a theater, a gym and a library.

Would you like to live in the White House? Why or why not?

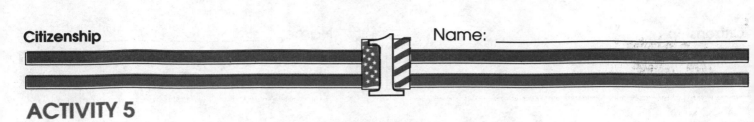

ACTIVITY 5

The White House

Directions: Pretend you have been asked to design a living room at the White House. What kinds of furniture, rugs, curtains, and lamps will your room have? What things will you include to show that the President and his family like to have fun together?

Start To Recycle

You know that trash pollutes the earth.
So people need to make less trash.
One way to make less trash is to recycle things.
Recycle means to save things and use them over and over.

Recycling is a way to help stop pollution.

People can recycle glass.

They can recycle paper.

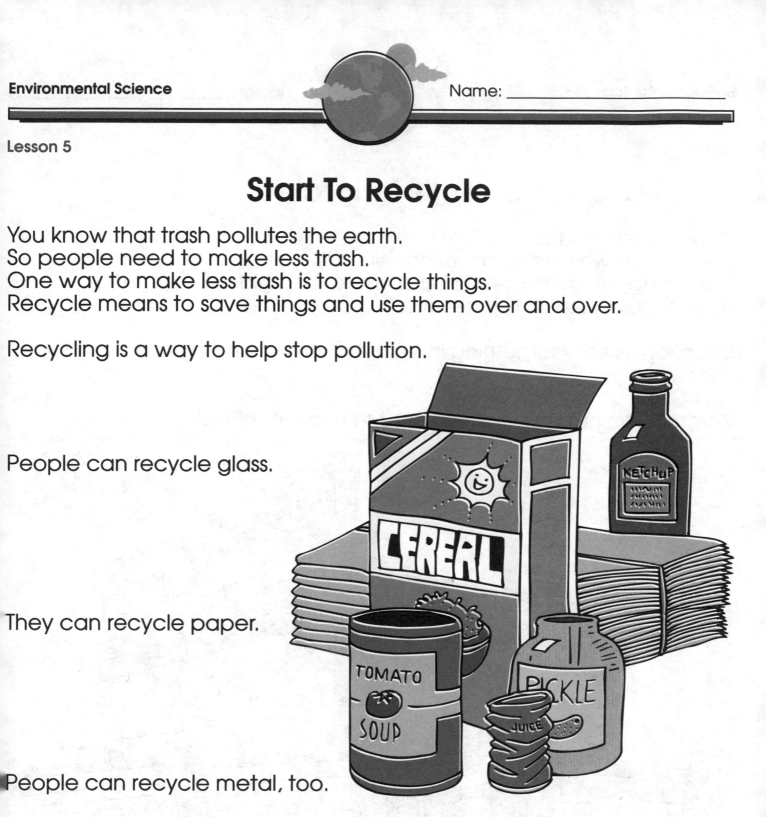

People can recycle metal, too.

What is the best thing to do with your empty lunch bag?

Activity 5

Let's Recycle

Look at the picture.
It is a place where people bring things to recycle.
They bring things made of paper, metal and glass.
What would you bring to recycle?

Directions: Draw something in each box that can be used over and over.

Where is the nearest place for you to recycle things?

Name: _____

Words With i

Directions: Short **i** sounds like the **i** in pig. Long **i** sounds like the in kite. 1) Draw a circle around the words with the short **i** sound. 2) Draw an X on the words with the long **i** sound.

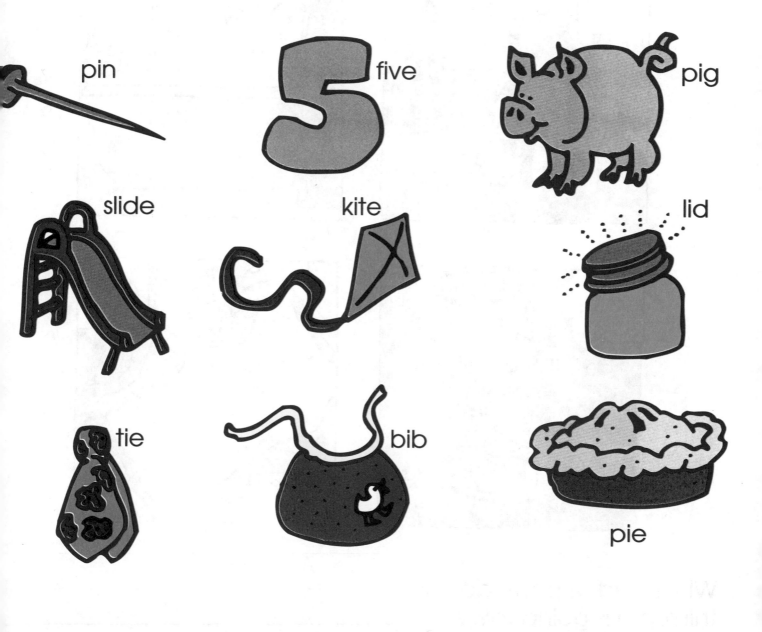

pin

five

pig

slide

kite

lid

tie

bib

pie

Name: _____

Pig Gets Ready

Directions: Look at the pictures of pig getting ready for the party. Then put them in 1-2-3-4 order.

What kind of party do you think pig is going to?

_____

_____

_____

Name: _____

Addition 4, 5, 6, 7

Directions: Practice writing the numbers and then add.

4 _____

5 _____

6 _____

7 _____

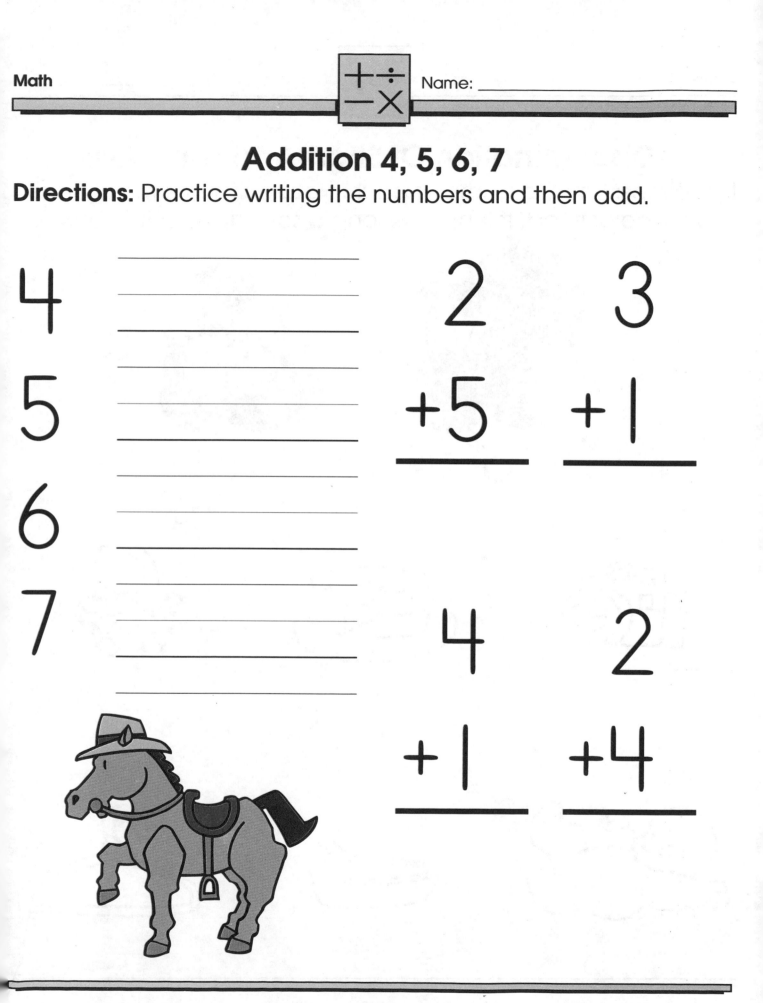

$$\begin{array}{r} 2 \\ +5 \\ \hline \end{array}$$

$$\begin{array}{r} 3 \\ +1 \\ \hline \end{array}$$

$$\begin{array}{r} 4 \\ +1 \\ \hline \end{array}$$

$$\begin{array}{r} 2 \\ +4 \\ \hline \end{array}$$

Discrimination Of Short And Long Aa

Directions: Say the name of each picture. If it has the short ă sound, color it red. If it has the long ā sound, color it yellow.

ă   ā

I Know Which Words Sound The Same!

Directions: Write the food words that answer the questions.

egg	milk	ice cream	apple	cookie	cake

1. Which food words start with the same sounds as the pictures?

_____ _____

_____ _____

_____

_____

2. Which food word ends with the same sound as the picture?

_____

_____

_____

_____

3. Which food words have two letters together that are the same?

_____ _____ _____

_____ _____ _____

Name: _____

Duplicating

Directions: Draw the triangle in the grid.

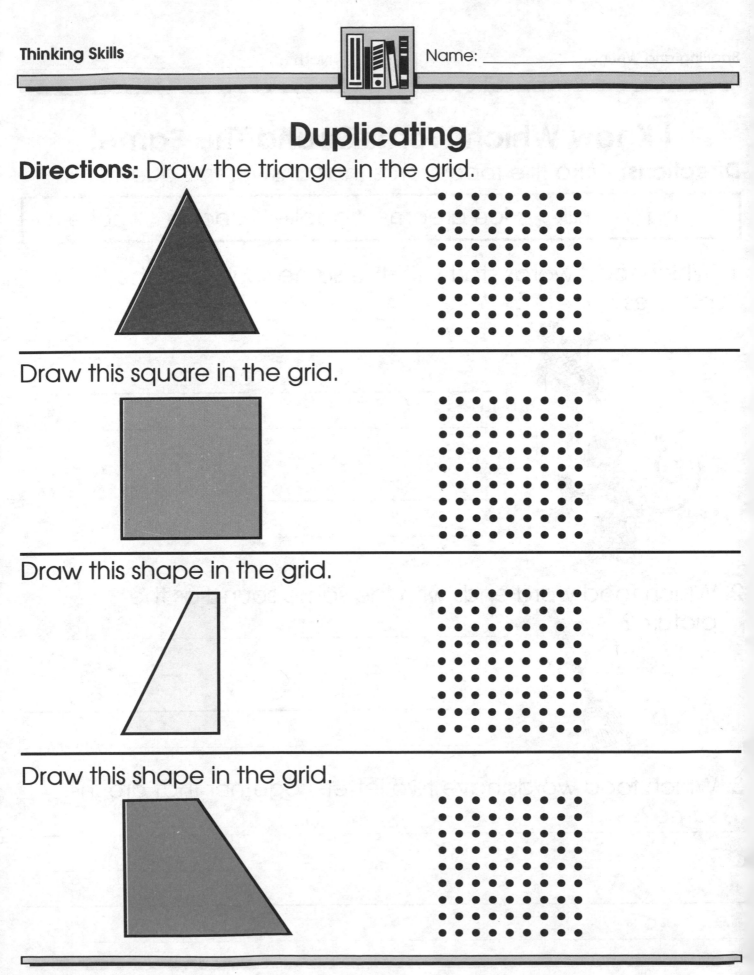

Draw this square in the grid.

Draw this shape in the grid.

Draw this shape in the grid.

Name: _____

Words With o

Directions: The short **o** sounds like the **o** in dog. Long **o** sounds like the **o** in rope. 1) Draw a line from the picture to the word that names it. 2) Draw a circle around the word if it has a short **o** sound.

hot dog

fox

blocks

rose

boat

Teddy Bear, Teddy Bear

Directions: Read the teddy bear song. Then answer the questions.

Do you know this song? It is very old!

Teddy bear, teddy bear Turn around.
Teddy bear, teddy bear Touch the ground.
Teddy bear, teddy bear Climb upstairs.
Teddy bear, teddy bear Say your prayers.
Teddy bear, teddy bear Turn out the light.
Teddy bear, teddy bear Say "good night!"

1. What is the first thing the teddy bear does?
_____
_____
_____

2. What is the last thing the teddy bear does?
_____
_____
_____
_____

3. What would you name _____
   a teddy bear? _____

Name: _____

Addition 6, 7, 8

Directions: Practice writing the numbers and then add.

6 _____

7 _____

8 _____

3
+4
___

5
+1
___

2
+6
___

4
+4
___

Name: _____

Discrimination Of Short And Long Ee

Directions: Say the name of each picture. Draw a circle around the pictures which have the short **ĕ** sound. Draw a triangle around the pictures which have the long **ē** sound.

ĕ   ē

Name: _____

I Can Ask Questions!

Directions: Change each telling sentence into a question by moving the words around. Remember to put a question mark at the end of your question.

Like this: The girl is eating ice cream.

Is the girl eating ice cream?

1.   The boy is giving a cookie.

_____

_____

2.   He is drinking milk.

_____

_____

3.   She is making a cake.

_____

_____

Duplicating

Directions: Draw this shape in the grid.

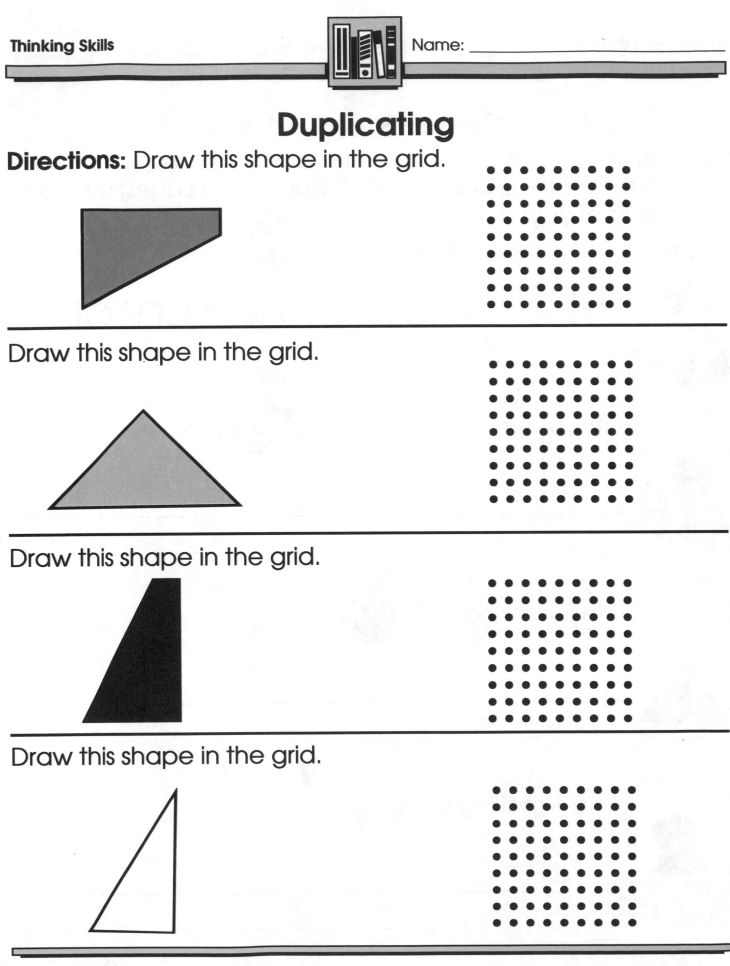

Draw this shape in the grid.

Draw this shape in the grid.

Draw this shape in the grid.

Name: _____

Words With u

Directions: The short **u** sounds like the **u** in bug. The long **u** sounds like the **u** in blue. 1) Draw a circle around the words with short **u**. 2) Draw an X on the words with long **u**.

rug

cup

music

tub

suit

glue

bug

puppy

gum

Put Teddy Bear To Bed

Directions: Re-read the story about the teddy bear. Look at the pictures. Number them in 1-2-3-4 order.

Name: _____

Addition 7, 8, 9

Directions: Practice writing the numbers and then add.

7

8

9

_____
_____
_____
_____
_____
_____

$$\begin{array}{r} 8 \\ +1 \\ \hline \end{array}$$

$$\begin{array}{r} 3 \\ +5 \\ \hline \end{array}$$

$$\begin{array}{r} 2 \\ +7 \\ \hline \end{array}$$

$$\begin{array}{r} 6 \\ +1 \\ \hline \end{array}$$

Discrimination Of Short And Long Ii.

Directions: Say the name of each picture. Color it yellow if it has the short **i** sound. Color it red if it has the long **ī** sound.

ī

ĭ

I Know The Answers!

Directions: Use the food words to answer each question. The first letter is done for you. Can you write the other letters by yourself?

1. Which one can you drink?

m_____

2. Which one do you have to keep very cold?

i_____

3. Which one grows on trees?

a_____

4. Which one do you put birthday candles on?

c_____

5. Which one do people sometimes eat in the mornings?

e_____

6. Which one do you like best?

_____

Name: _____

Duplicating

Directions: Go outside. Look at your house. Now draw a picture of the shapes that make up your house. Name the shapes you see.

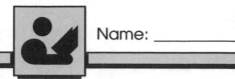

Name: _____

Short Vowel Sounds

Directions: In each box are three pictures. The words that name the pictures have missing letters. Write **a, e, i, o,** or **u** to finish the words.

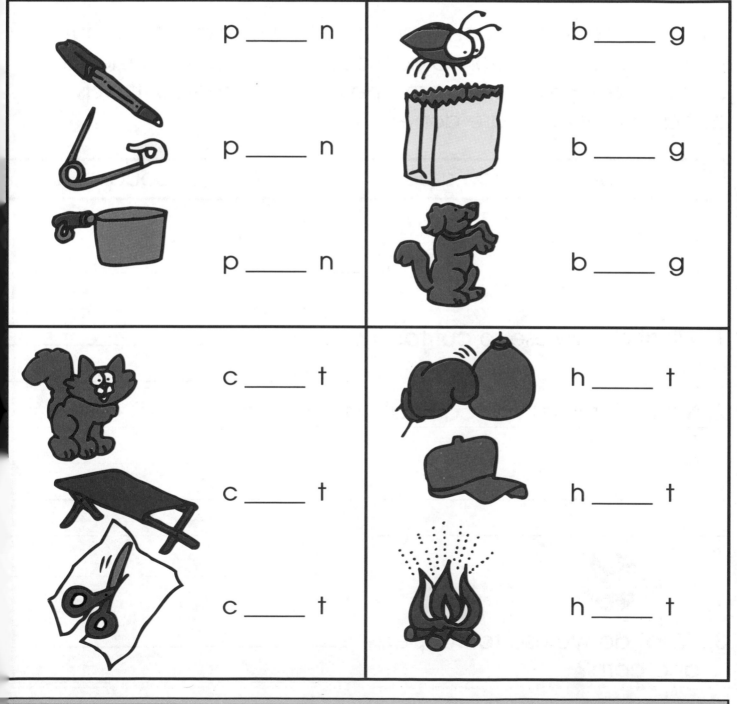

p ____ n

p ____ n

p ____ n

b ____ g

b ____ g

b ____ g

c ____ t

c ____ t

c ____ t

h ____ t

h ____ t

h ____ t

How We Eat

Directions: Read about meals. Look at the word list. Then answer the questions.

Big kids eat with spoons and forks. They use a knife to cut their food. They use a spoon to eat soup and ice cream. They use a fork to eat peas and corn. They say "Thank you. It was good!" when they are done.

fork	ice cream	knife	soup

_____

1. What do we use to cut food? _____

_____

2. Name 2 things you can eat with a spoon.

_____   _____

_____   _____

_____

3. What do we use to eat peas _____
   and corn?

_____

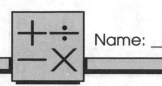

Subtraction 1, 2, 3

Subtraction means "taking away" or subtracting one number from another.

Directions: Practice writing the numbers and then subtract.

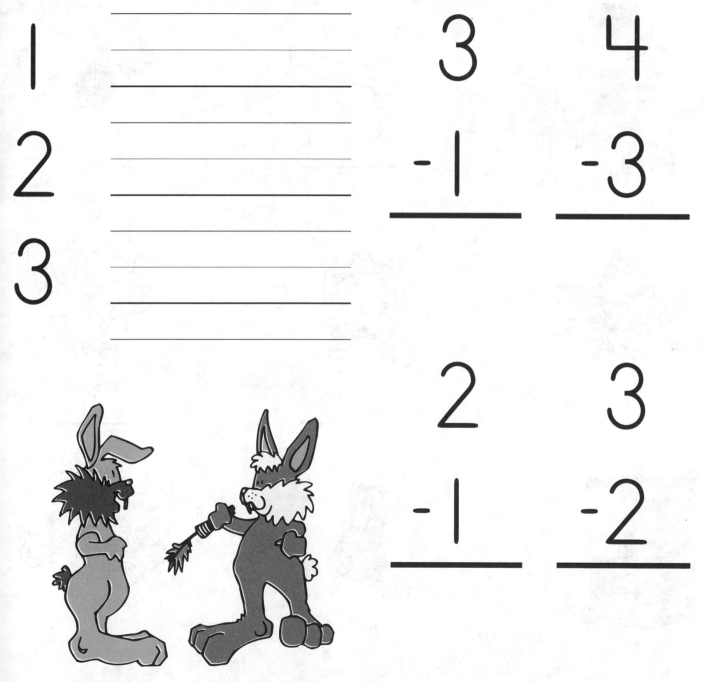

1

2

3

$$3$$
$$-1$$

$$4$$
$$-3$$

$$2$$
$$-1$$

$$3$$
$$-2$$

Name: _____

Discrimination Of Short And Long Oo

Directions: Say the name of each picture. If the picture has a long **o** sound, write a green **L** in the space. If the picture has a short **o** sound, write a red **S** in the space.

_____   _____

_____   _____   _____

_____   _____   _____

Name: _____

I Can Write My Own Sentences!

Directions: 1. For each sentence, write a word in the first space to tell who is doing something. Here are some words you could use: boy, girl, mother, father, baby. 2. Write one of the food words in the second space. 3. Draw a picture to show what is happening in your sentence.

Like this:

The _____ **mother** _____ is making _____ **a cake** _____ .

1. The _____ is eating _____ .

2. The _____ is buying _____ .

Name: _____

Finding Patterns

Directions: Find the hidden shape. Then color it.

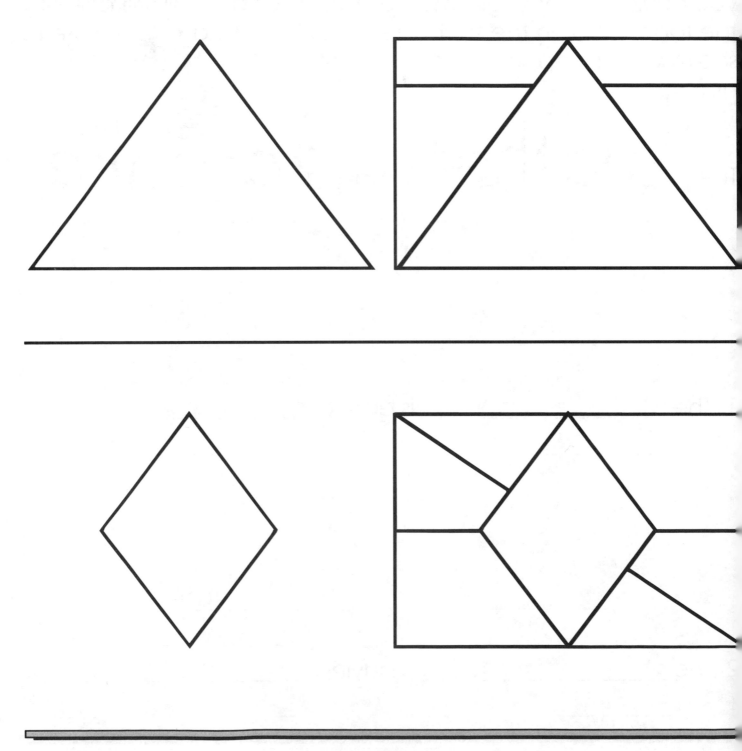

Name: _____

Christopher Columbus

In 1492, Christopher Columbus and his sailors bravely set sail across the Atlantic Ocean from Europe. His three ships were called the *Niña*, the *Pinta*, and the *Santa Maria*.

Columbus knew that the winds would carry his three ships westward. But he did not know that after many weeks, his ships would reach a land that would later be named America.

How do you think Columbus and the sailors felt on their long trip across the ocean?

Name: _____

ACTIVITY 6

Christopher Columbus

Directions: Ask someone to help you make a sailing ship. You will need a toothpick, a piece of flat, recycled plastic foam, scissors, a shallow pan, and water.

1. Cut out the boat shape. 2. Trace the boat shape on plastic foam. Cut it out. 3. Cut out the square of paper (sail). 4. Insert a toothpick (mast) through the sail at the marked dots. 5. Insert the mast and sail on your ship at the marked dot. 6. Fill the pan with water. Put your ship in the pan. 7. Gently blow on the sail like the wind.

Watch your ship sail across the water just like the *Niña*, the *Pinta*, and the *Santa Maria* !

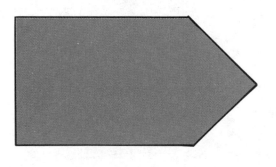 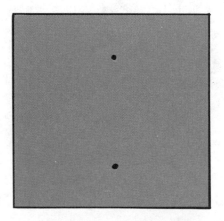

Name: _____

Summary

Directions: Read the sentences on this page and on page 166.

Draw a picture to go with each sentence.

Cut the pages on the dotted lines.

Put the page numbers in order.

Make a book.

Share your book with a friend.

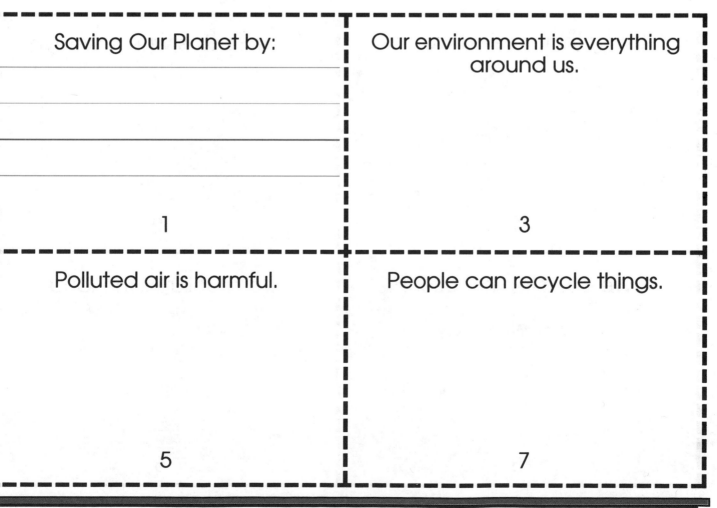

Saving Our Planet by:

_____

_____

_____

_____

1

Our environment is everything around us.

3

Polluted air is harmful.

5

People can recycle things.

7

Name: _____

Review

Follow the directions on page 165 and complete your book.

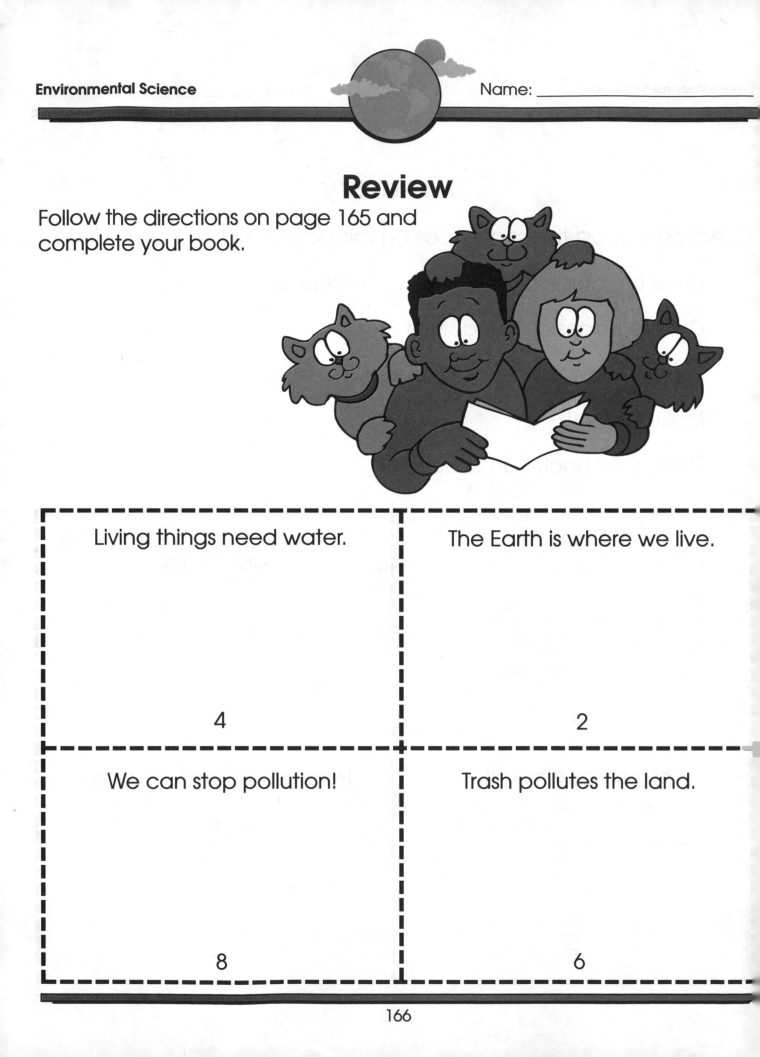

Living things need water.	The Earth is where we live.
4	2
We can stop pollution!	Trash pollutes the land.
8	6

Name: _____

Long Vowel Sounds

Directions: Write **a, e, i, o,** or **u** in each blank to finish the word. Draw a line from the word to its picture.

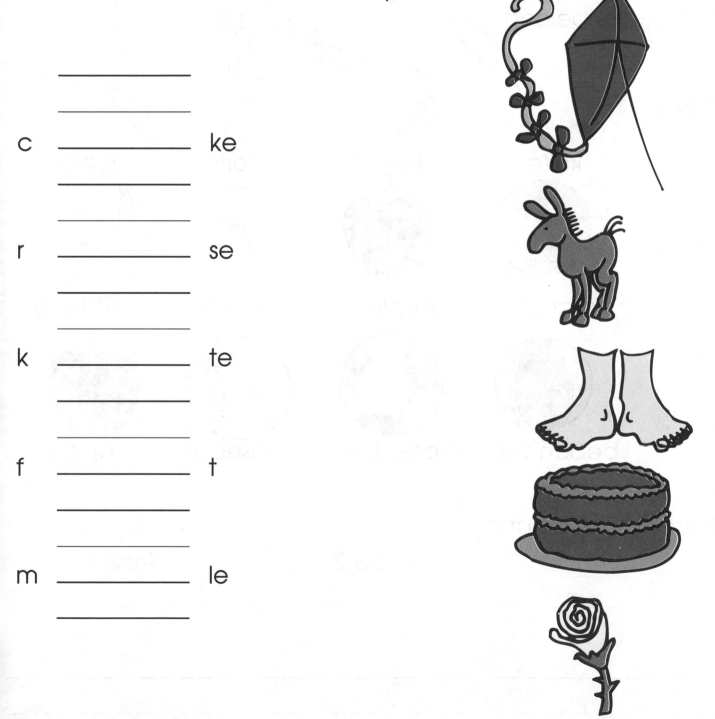

_____

c _____ ke

r _____ se

k _____ te

f _____ t

m _____ le

Name: _____

Things That Belong

Directions: Look at the pictures in each row across. Circle the ones in each row that belong. Write the names of the pictures that do not belong.

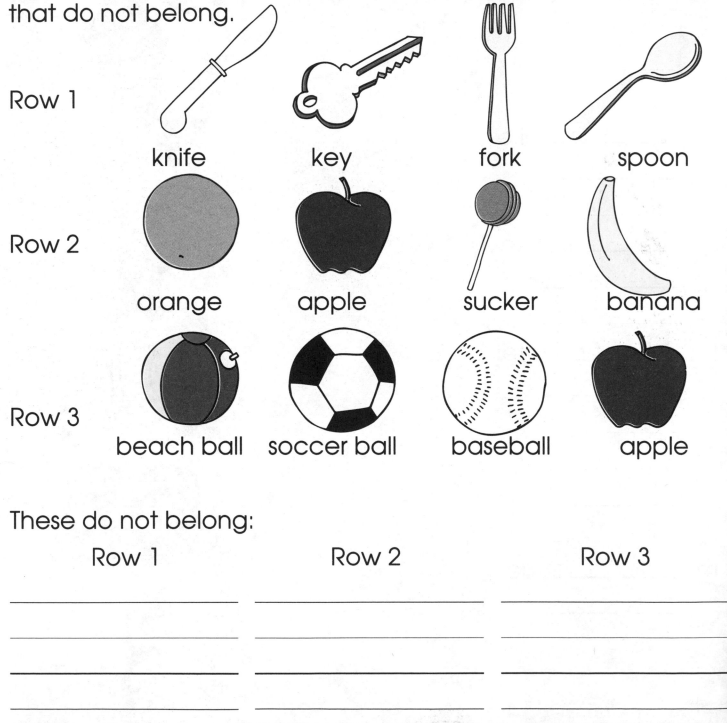

Row 1

knife   key   fork   spoon

Row 2

orange   apple   sucker   banana

Row 3

beach ball   soccer ball   baseball   apple

These do not belong:

Row 1   Row 2   Row 3

_____   _____   _____

_____   _____   _____

_____   _____   _____

_____   _____   _____

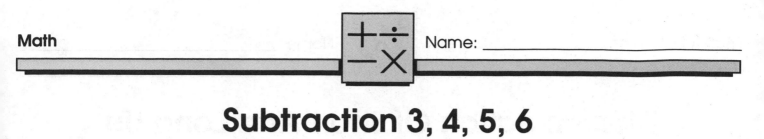

Name: _____

Subtraction 3, 4, 5, 6

Directions: Practice writing the numbers and then subtract.

3

4

5

6

_____
_____
_____
_____
_____
_____
_____

$$\begin{array}{r} 5 \\ -2 \\ \hline \end{array}$$

$$\begin{array}{r} 6 \\ -1 \\ \hline \end{array}$$

$$\begin{array}{r} 6 \\ -3 \\ \hline \end{array}$$

$$\begin{array}{r} 5 \\ -1 \\ \hline \end{array}$$

Discrimination Of Short And Long Uu

Directions: Say the name of the picture. If it has the long **u** sound, write a **u** in the unicorn column. If it has a short **u** sound, write a **u** in the umbrella column.

I Can Finish A Story!

Directions: Write the words in the story. Then read your story to someone.

Kim got up in the morning.

"Do you want an _____ ?" her mother asked.

"Yes, please," Kim said.

    "May I have some _____ , too?"

"OK," her mother said.

"How about some _____ ?" Kim asked with a smile.

Her mother laughed. "Not now," she said.

She put an _____ in Kim's lunch.

"Do you want a _____ or some

_____ today?"

"Both!" Kim said.

Name: _____

Finding Patterns

Directions: Find the hidden letter in each box. Trace it with a crayon.

1. Hidden letter: T

2. Hidden letter: E

Name: _____

Skills Review: Vowel Sounds

Directions: Draw a circle around the word if it has a long vowel sound. Remember: a long vowel says its name.

feet

snake

cup

hose

tie

hat

dog

rake

bug

bone

bib

net

Name: _____

Review

Directions: Read about how to ski. Answer the questions. Then put the skiing pictures in 1-2-3-4 order.

Skiing is Fun
You need to dress warmly to ski. Two skis will fit on your boots. You wear the skis to a chair. The chair is called a ski lift. It takes you up in the air to a hill. When you get off, ski down the hill.
Be careful!
Sometimes you will fall.

1. How many skis do you need?   _____

2. Skiing is classified as an   indoor sport.
                                 outdoor sport.

Name: _____

Review

Directions: Trace the numbers. Work the problems.

1 2 3 4 5 6 7 8 9 10

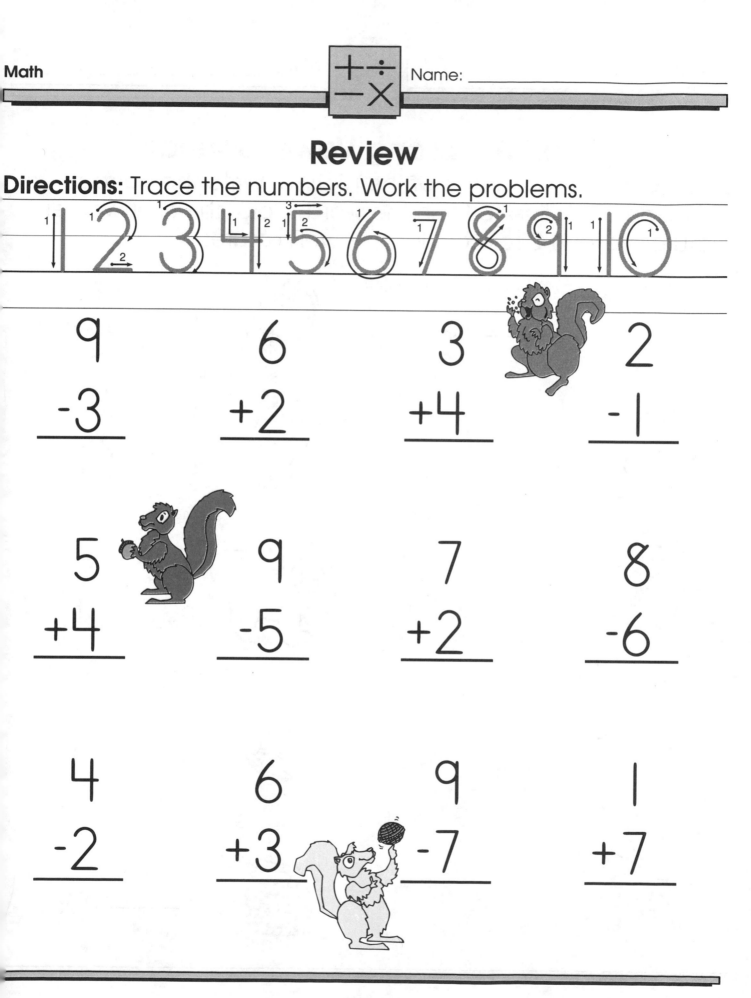

9	6	3	2
-3	+2	+4	-1

5	9	7	8
+4	-5	+2	-6

4	6	9	1
-2	+3	-7	+7

Short And Long Vowel Sounds

Directions: Say the name of the picture. Write the correct vowel on each line to finish the word. Color the short vowel pictures yellow. Circle the long vowel pictures.

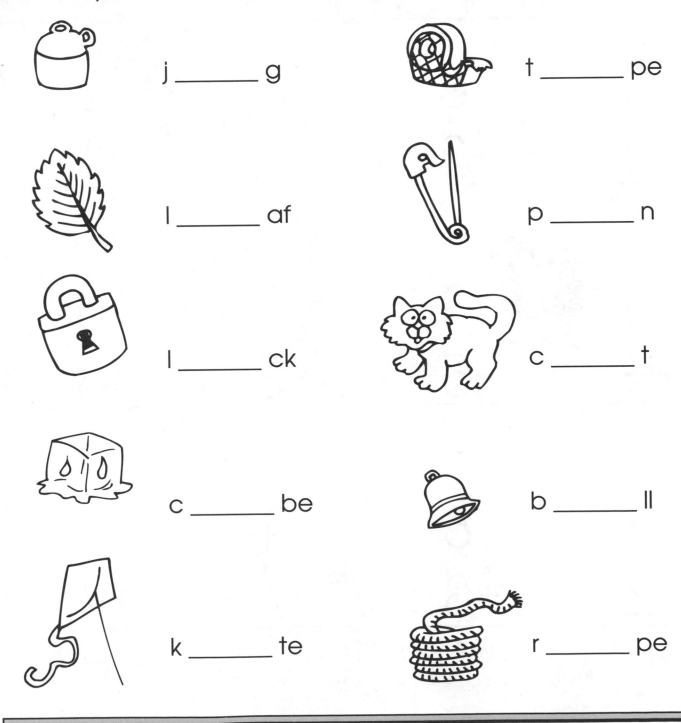

j _____ g

t _____ pe

l _____ af

p _____ n

l _____ ck

c _____ t

c _____ be

b _____ ll

k _____ te

r _____ pe

176

Review

Directions: Write two telling sentences and one question about this picture. Be sure to use the food words you know — and the color and pet words.

Here are some more words you could use: **boy, girl, water, table, candles, finds, birthday, out, eats, jumps, helps, sees, looks, stops, falls**.

Two telling sentences:

_____

1. _____

_____

2. _____

_____

One question: _____

_____

_____

_____

Name: _____

Review

Directions: Color your shape to look the same.

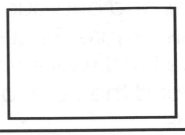

Draw the triangle in the grid. Color it to match.

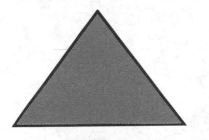
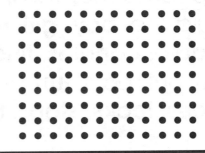

Find the shape in the squares. Color it.

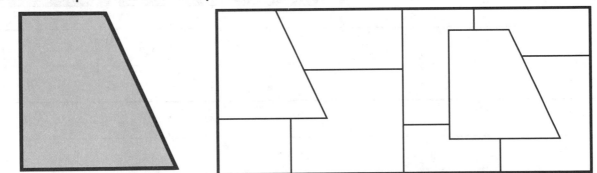

Find the letter **M** in each square. Trace it with a crayon.

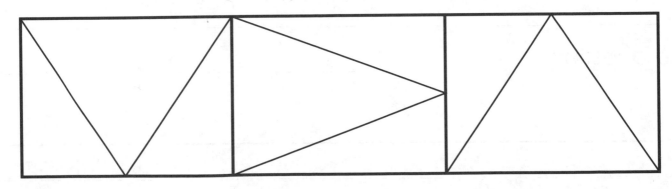

Name: _____

Consonant Blends: bl, cl, fl, gl, pl, sl

Directions: The name of each picture begins with a **blend**. Draw a circle around the beginning blend for each picture.

bl fl cl

cl fl gl

fl bl pl

fl cl gl

pl gl cl

sl fl gl

gl fl cl

fl sl cl

cl gl sl

Name: _____

Clowns

Directions: Color the clowns. Then answer the questions. Use your crayons this way: 1 = red, 2 = blue, 3 = orange, 4 = pink.

_____

_____

1. What color is the clowns' hair?   _____

_____

_____

2. What color are the clowns' noses?   _____

_____

3. What color are the clowns' hats?   _____

_____

4. What color are the clowns' clothes?   _____

_____

Name: _____

Zero

Directions: Write the number.

Example:

How many monkeys?

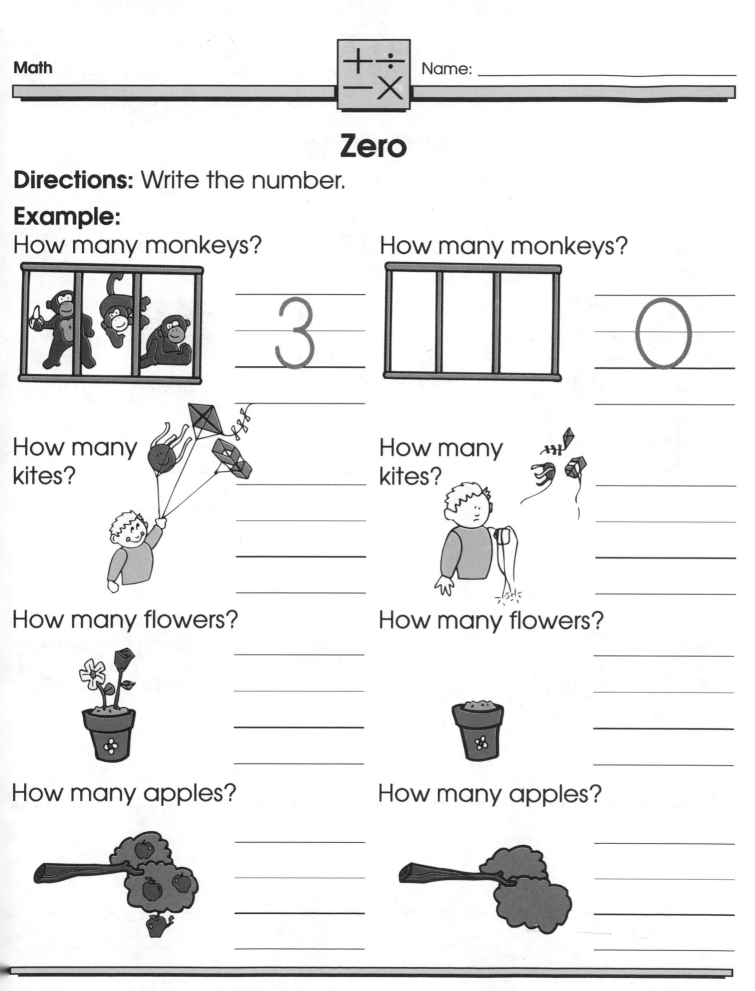

How many monkeys?

How many kites?

How many kites?

How many flowers?

How many flowers?

How many apples?

How many apples?

Name: _____

ABC Order

Use the first letter of each word to put the words in alphabetical order.

Directions: Draw a circle around the first letter of each word. Then, put the words in **ABC** order.

ⓒar ⓑird   moon   two   nest   fan

bird

car

card   dog   pig   bike   sun   pie

Name: _____

I Can Write "Doing" Words!

"Doing" words tell things we can do.

Directions: 1. Follow the lines to write the words. 2. Then write the words by yourself. 3. Read the words to someone.

Like this:

sleep   **sleep**

run

make

ride

play

stop

Finding Patterns

Directions: Draw a line from the shape on the left to the box of shapes on the right that has the same pattern.

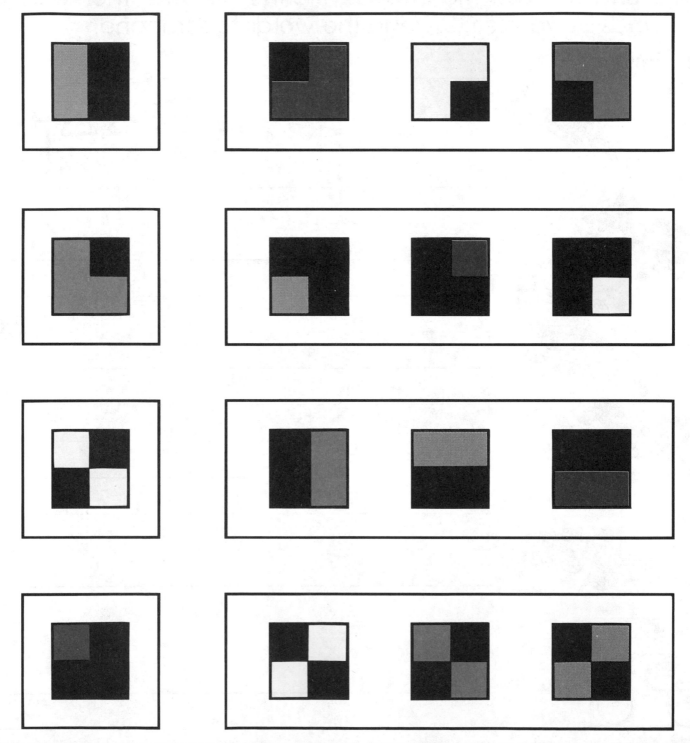

Name: _____

Consonant Blends: br, cr, dr, fr, pr, tr

Directions: The beginning blend for each word is missing. Using the list, fill in the correct blend to finish the word. Draw a line from the word to its picture.

_____

_____ ain

_____ og

_____ ab

_____ um

_____ ush

_____ esent

Name: _____

Simon Says

Directions: Read about how to play Simon Says. Then answer the questions.

SIMON SAYS, CLAP YOUR HANDS!

Simon Says

Here is how to play "Simon Says." One kid is Simon. Simon is the leader. Everyone must do what Simon says and does, but only if the leader says "Simon says" first. Let's try it. "Simon says pat your head." "Simon says pat your nose." "Pat your toes." Oops. You patted your toes! I did not say "Simon says" first. You are out!

_____
_____
_____

1. Who is the leader in this game? _____
_____
_____

2. What must the leader say first each time? _____
_____
_____

3. What happens if you do something and the leader did not say "Simon says?" _____
_____

Name: _____

Zero

Directions: Write the number that tells how many.

How many sailboats?

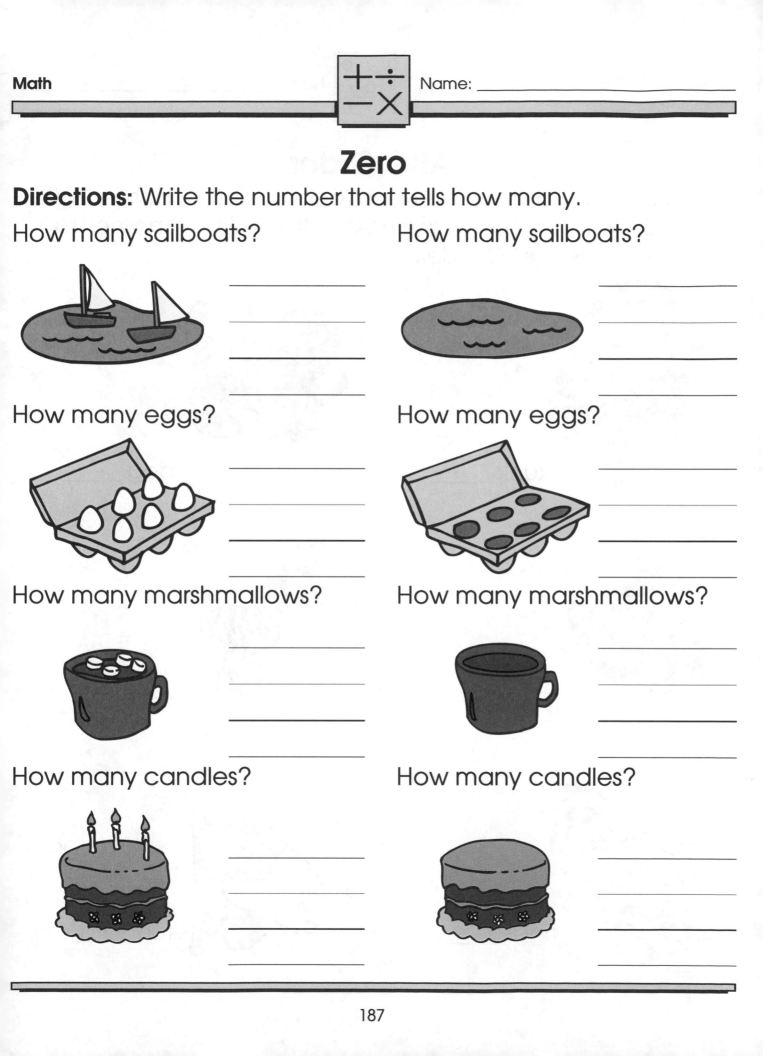

_____

How many sailboats?

_____

How many eggs?

_____

How many eggs?

_____

How many marshmallows?

_____

How many marshmallows?

_____

How many candles?

_____

How many candles?

_____

ABC Order

Directions: Circle the first letter of each animal's name. Write a 1, 2, 3, 4, 5, or 6 on the line next to the animals' names to put the words in **ABC** order.

skunk _____

dog _____

butterfly _____

zebra _____

tiger _____

fish _____

Name: _____

I Know Which Word To Write!

Directions: Read each sentence and write the words in the correct spaces.

Like this:

go
sleep   I will _go_ to bed and _sleep_ all night.

1.

see
jump   The girls _____ the frogs _____ .

2.

sit
run   After the boys _____ , they _____ and rest.

3.

stop
play   They _____ at the park so they can _____ .

4.

ride
make   They will _____ a car to _____ in.

Finding Patterns

Directions: Draw a line from the letter on the left to the group of squares with the same hidden letter.

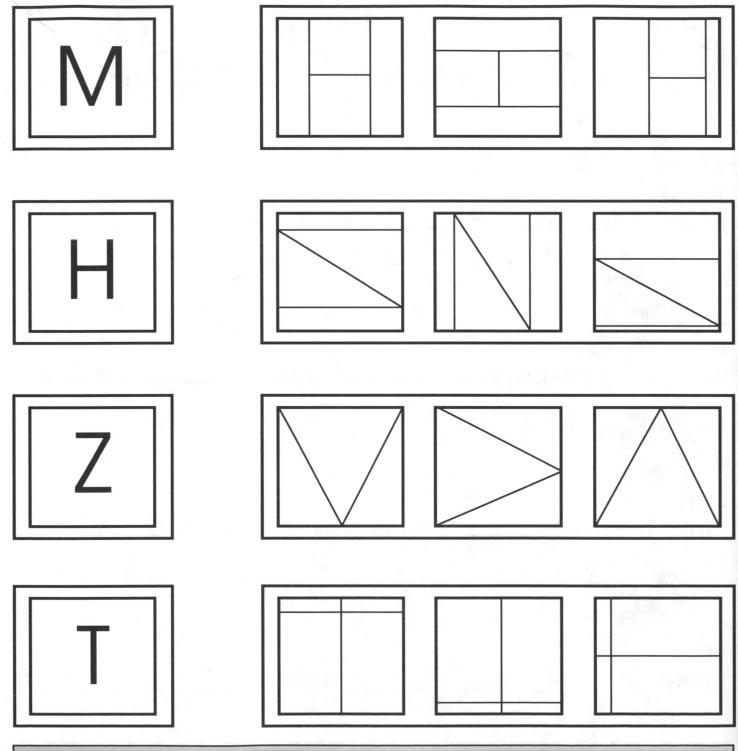

LESSON 7

The Statue of Liberty

The Statue of Liberty stands on an island in New York Harbor. Over the years, millions of people came to the United States on ships from other countries. As their ships passed the Statue of Liberty, the people cheered and waved. The Statue of Liberty became a symbol of hope and freedom for these people who dreamed of becoming United States citizens.

Why do you think millions of people would leave their countries to come to the United States?

ACTIVITY 7

The Statue of Liberty

What do you think the people on the ships said as they saw the Statue of Liberty in the Harbor? Write their words in the balloons.

Energy To Heat Our Homes

Most of our homes use electricity to make heat.
Most electricity is made by burning gas, oil, or coal.
Gas, oil, and coal are sources of energy.
Now new kinds of houses are being built.
These homes use solar energy, or energy from the sun.
They are called solar homes.

A solar home has glass sheets on its roof.
There are black plates under the glass sheets.
The glass sheets and black plates collect sunlight.
On sunny days, the plates and sheets help turn sunlight into heat.

Solar homes do not cost much to heat because sunlight is free.
They do not use up gas, oil, or coal.
They do not make the air dirty.
Solar homes do not pollute the environment.

How is your home heated?

Activity 6

Would You Build A Solar Home?

Directions: Think about what you
know about solar homes.
Read each question.
Write your answer on the
lines.

1. Why might a person build a solar home?

_____

_____

2. Why would people not build solar homes in some places?

_____

_____

3. Would you like to live in a solar home? Tell why you think as you do.

_____

_____

_____

_____

_____

Name: _____

Consonant Blends: sk, sl, sm, sp, st, sw

Directions: Draw a line from the picture to the blend that begins its word.

sk

sl

sm

sn

sp

st

sw

Name: _____

Same/Different: Look At Simon

Directions: Look at both pictures. Find 4 things in picture #2 that are not in picture #1. Look at the word list to see how to spell the word. Write your answers in the numbered spaces.

hat	head	socks	bare feet
feather	watch	untied shoes	tied shoes

1. _____

2. _____

3. _____

4. _____

Name: _____

Addition 1, 2, 3, 4, 5

Directions: Add the numbers. Put your answers in the nests.

Example: 2 + 3 = 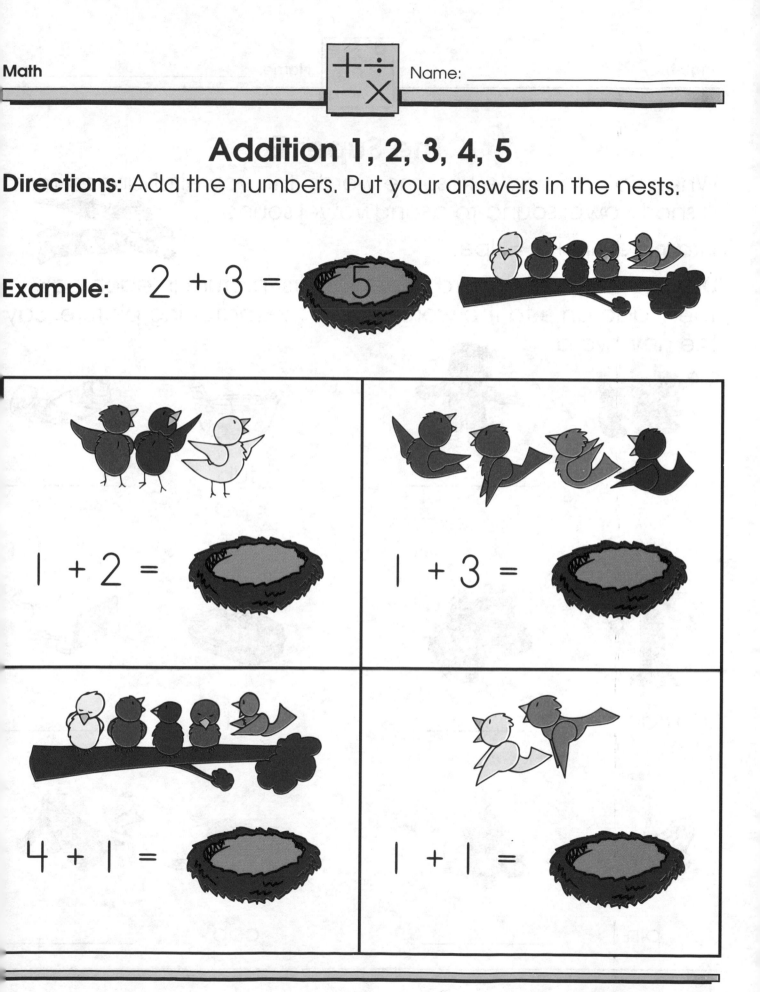 5

1 + 2 =

1 + 3 =

4 + 1 =

1 + 1 =

The Super E

When you add an **e** to some words, the vowel changes from a short vowel sound to a long vowel sound.

Example: rip + **e** = ripe.

Directions: Say the word under the first picture in each pair. Then, add an **e** to the word under the matching picture. Say the new word.

pet _____

tub _____

man _____

kit _____

pin _____

cap _____

I Know Which Words Sound The Same!

Directions: Write the "doing" words that answer the questions.

| sit   run   make   see   jump   stop   play   ride |

1. Which three words start the same as 🌞 ?

_____ _____ _____

_____ _____ _____

2. Which two words start the same as

_____ _____

_____ _____

3. Which words start the same as each of these words?

_____ _____ _____

_____ _____ _____

4. Which words end the same as these?

_____ _____ _____

_____ _____ _____

199

Name: _____

Tracking

Directions: Trace the lines to connect the shapes. Then color the matching shapes the same color.

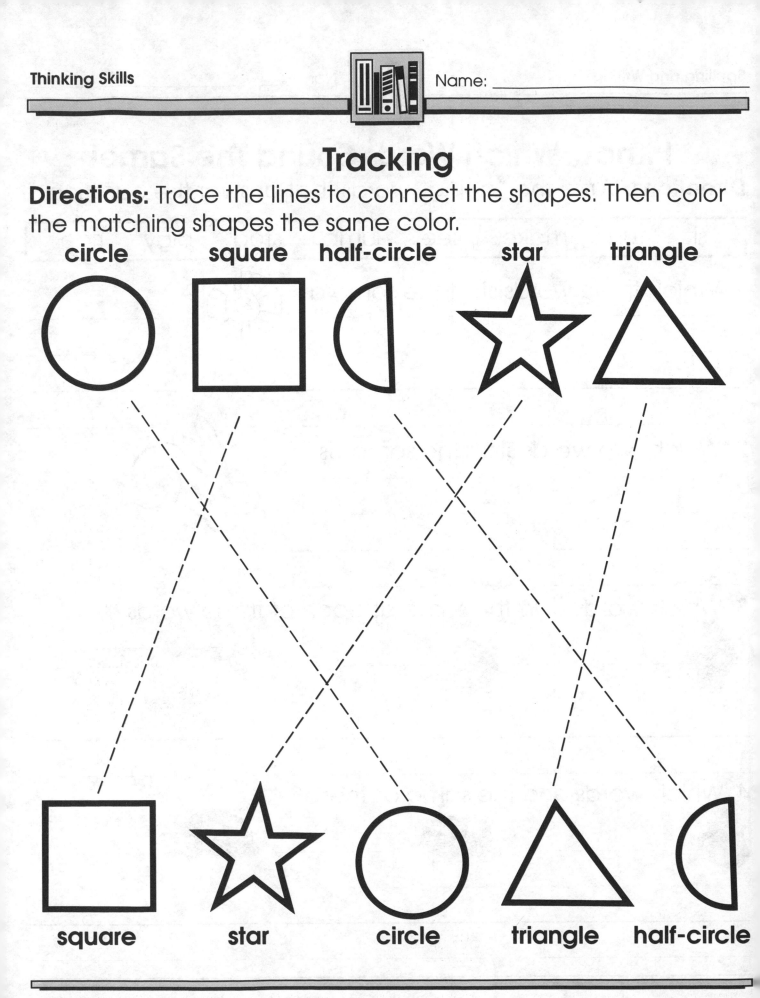

circle   square   half-circle   star   triangle

square   star   circle   triangle   half-circle

Name: _____

Consonant Digraphs: ch, sh, th, wh

Directions: Look at the first picture in each row. Circle the pictures in the row that start with the same sound.

chair

shell

thumb

wheel

Name: _____

Comprehension: Do You Like Crayons?

Directions: Read about crayons. Then answer the questions.

There are many colors of crayons
Some crayons come in bright colors.
Some crayons come in light colors.
All crayons have wax in them.

_____

_____

1. Crayons come in _____ colors

_____

_____

and   _____ colors.

_____

2. How many colors of crayons are there?

     few   many

_____

_____

3. What do all crayons have in them?   _____

_____

Addition 6, 7, 8, 9, 10

Directions: Add the numbers. Put your answers in the doghouses.

Example: 4 + 2 =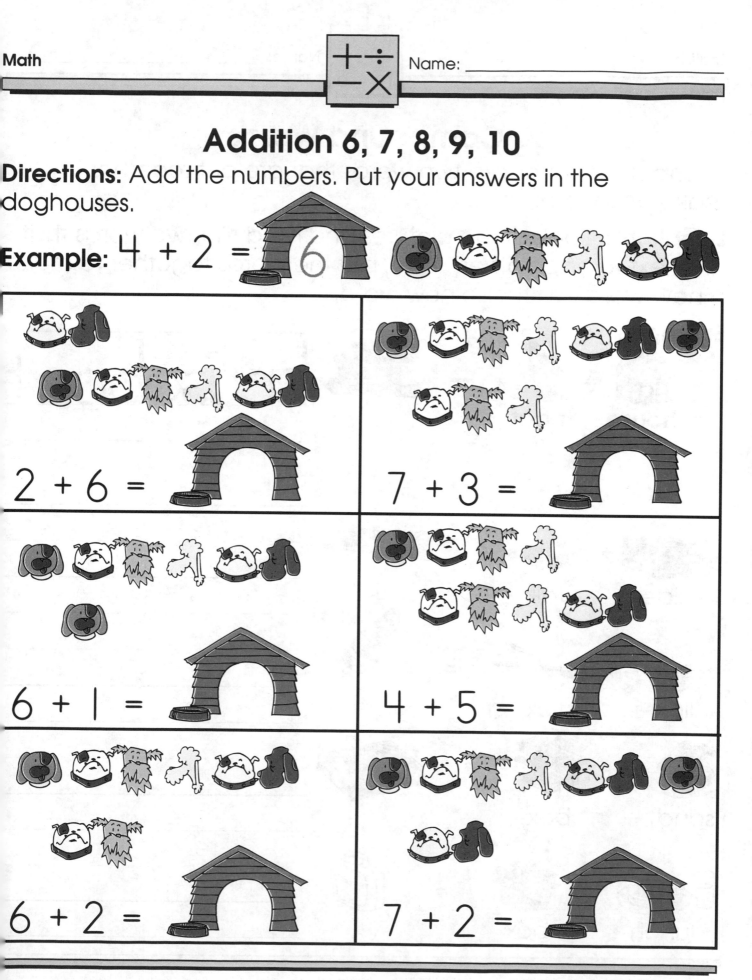

2 + 6 =

7 + 3 =

6 + 1 =

4 + 5 =

6 + 2 =

7 + 2 =

Name: _____

Compound Words

Compound words are two words that are put together to make one word.

Directions: Look at the pictures and read the two words that are next to each other. Now, put the words together to make a new word. Write the new word.

Example:

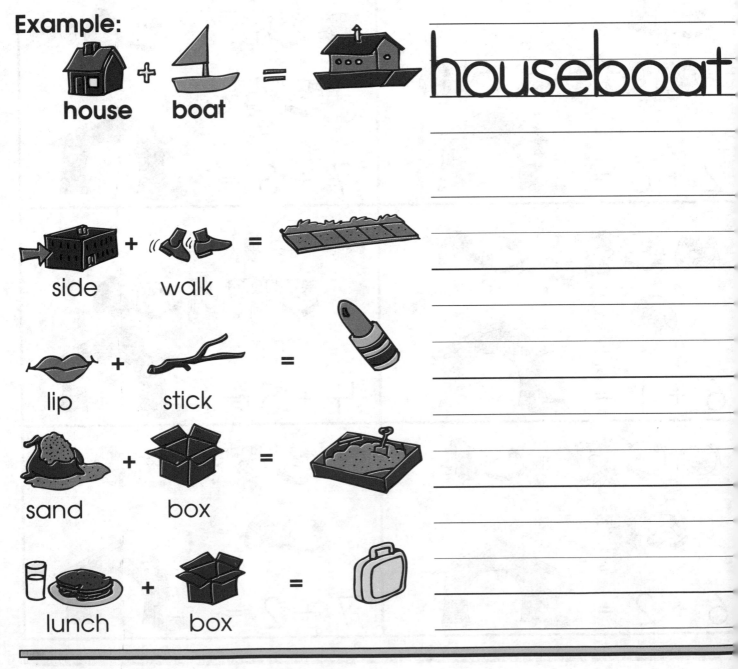

house + boat =

houseboat

side + walk =

lip + stick =

sand + box =

lunch + box =

I Can Show Two Of Something!

To show two or more of something, most of the time we add "s" to the end of the word.

Like this:

one cat    two cats

Directions: For each sentence, add "s" to show two or more. Then write in the "doing" word that finishes the sentence.

| sit | jump | stop | ride |

Like this:

The frog **S** **sleep** in the sun.

1. The boy _____ _____ on the fence.

2. The car _____ _____ at the sign.

3. The girl _____ _____ in the water.

4. The dog _____ _____ in the wagon.

Name: _____

Tracking

Directions: Connect the letter on the left with the same letter on the right. Use a different color crayon for each line.

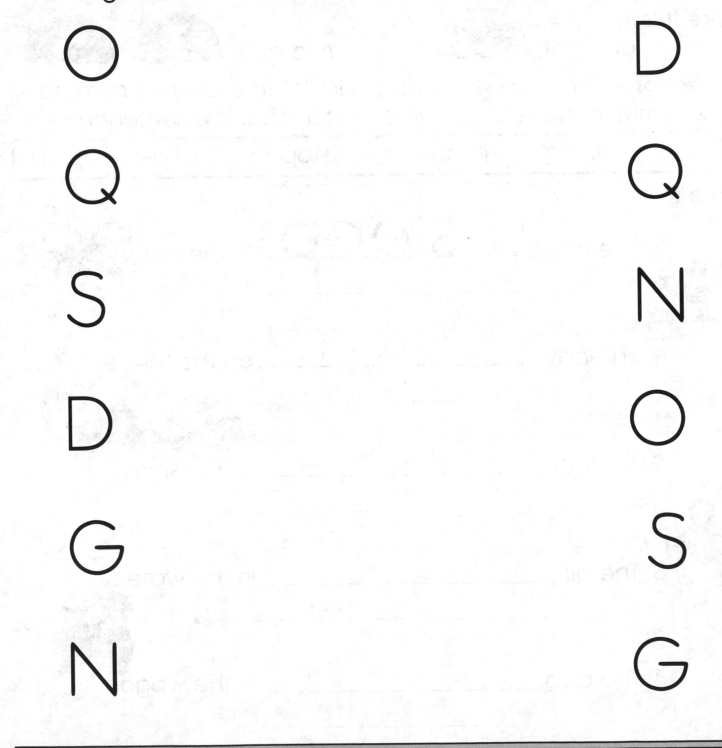

Name: _____

Consonant Blends: ft, lt

Directions: Write **lt** or **ft** to complete the words.

be _____

ra _____

sa _____

qui _____

ki _____

Can You Find Me?

Directions: To find the hidden picture, color only the shapes with a number inside. Do not color the shapes with a letter inside.

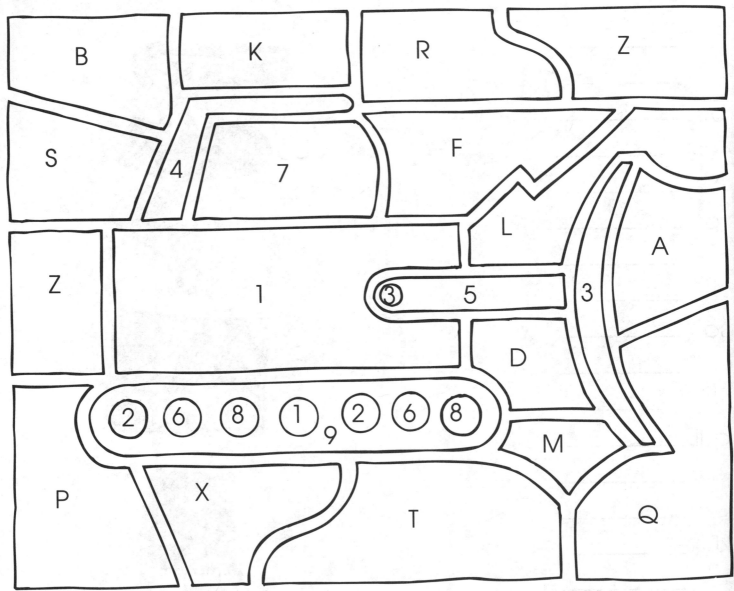

Name: _____

Subtraction 1, 2, 3, 4, 5

Directions: Count the fruit in each bowl. Write your answers on the blanks. Circle the problem that matches your answer.

4

5   4
-1 -2

___

3   4
-0 -2

___

5   4
-1 -3

___

3   5
-2 -0

Synonyms

Synonyms are words that mean the same thing. **Start** and **begin** are synonyms.

Directions: Find the two words that describe each picture. Write the words in the boxes below the picture.

small   funny   large   sad   silly   little   big   unhappy

Name: _____

I Know Which Spelling Is Right!

Directions: Circle the word that is spelled right. Then write the word the right way.

Like this:

seep
(sleep)
slep

sleep

paly
pay
play

seee
cee
see

rum
run
runn

jump
jumb
junp

mack
maek
make

Name: _____

Tracking

Directions: Draw a straight line from **A** to **B**. Use a different color crayon for each line.

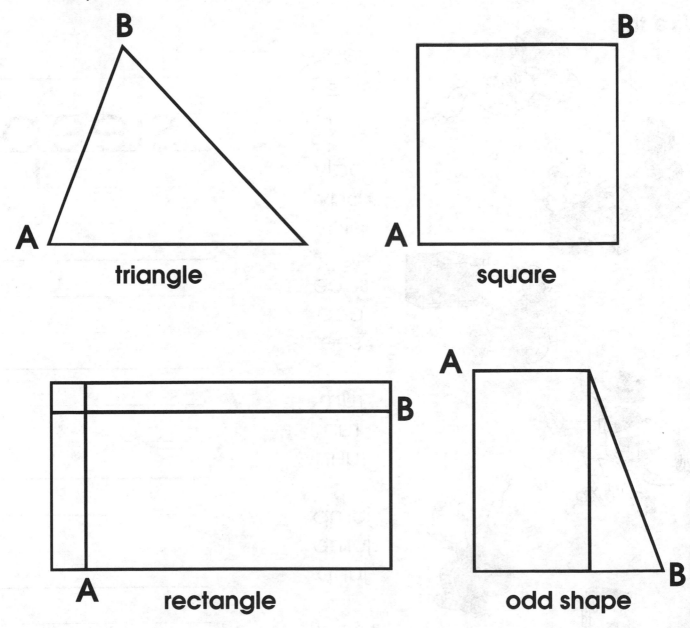

triangle

square

rectangle

odd shape

Name: _____

Consonant Blends: lf, lk, sk, sp, st

Directions: Draw a line from the picture to the blend that ends its word.

lf

lk

sk

sp

st

Name: _____

Rhyme Time

Directions: Read about words that rhyme. Then answer the questions.

Words that rhyme have the same end sounds. "Wing" and "sing" rhyme. "Boy" and "toy" rhyme. "Rhyme" and "time" rhyme. Can you think of other words that rhyme?

TREE, SEE
SHOE, BLUE
KITE, BITE
MAKE, TAKE
FLY, BUY

1. Words that rhyme have the same _____   end sounds
                                                                            end letters

2. Tell the words that rhyme with these words.

Wing	Boy	Rhyme

3. Can you think of a word on your _____
   own that rhymes with "pink?" _____

Name: _____

Subtraction 6, 7, 8, 9, 10

Directions: Count the flowers. Write your answers on the blanks. Circle the problems with the same answer.

Antonyms

Antonyms are words that are opposites. **Hot** and **cold** are antonyms.

Directions: Draw a line between the words that are opposites. Can you think of other words that are opposites?

closed

below

full

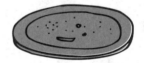

empty

above

old

new

open

I Can Ask Questions!

Directions: Write a question about each picture. Start with "can." Add a "doing" word. Remember that a question starts with a capital letter and ends with a question mark.

Like this:

I with you can _____

Can I sit with you?

cookies she can _____

_____

_____

with you can I _____

_____

_____

can in the box _____

_____

_____

Name: _____

Tracking

Directions: Trace 3 paths from **A** to **B**.

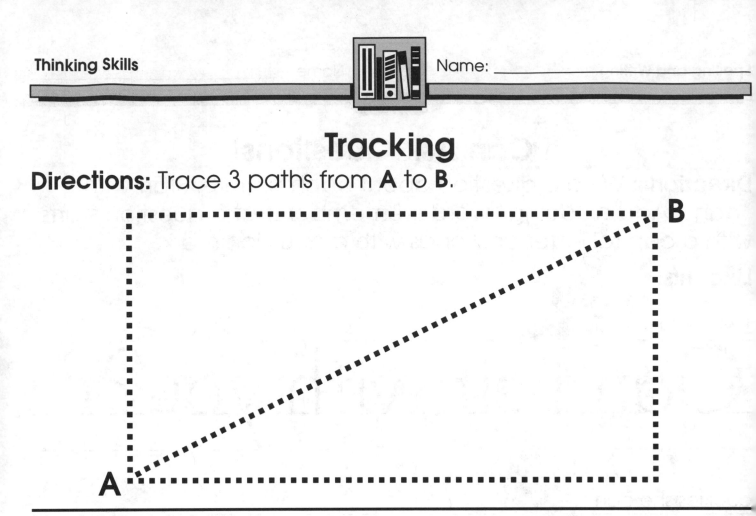

Trace the path from **A** to **B**.

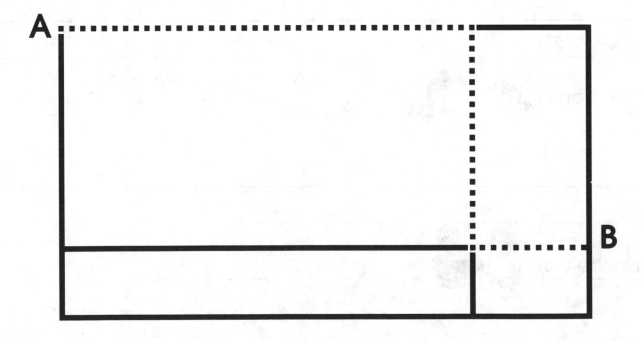

How many corners did you turn? _____

LESSON 8

The Liberty Bell

The Liberty Bell is a symbol of our country. It stands for America's independence.

On July 8, 1776, the Liberty Bell rang out to announce that the United States had become a new country. Later, the Liberty Bell cracked, so it could no longer be rung.

Today, people can see the Liberty Bell in Philadelphia. Visitors can look at the bell and think about when it rang to declare freedom.

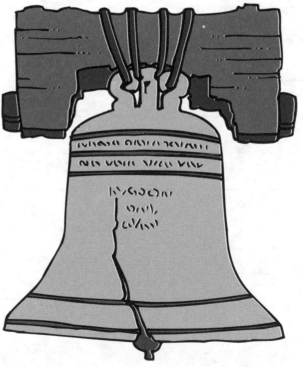

Suppose you heard the Liberty Bell ringing on July 8, 1776. What might you say? How would you feel?

ACTIVITY 8

The Liberty Bell

Directions: A newspaper headline tells about something important. Think about the day the Liberty Bell rang to tell people that the United States had become a new country. What would the newspaper headline say about the new country? What would it say about the bell? Write the headline on the lines.

Rain Forests

Trees need a lot of water and warm weather to grow.
It is always hot in a rain forest.
There is always plenty of rain.
Trees grow and grow in a rain forest.

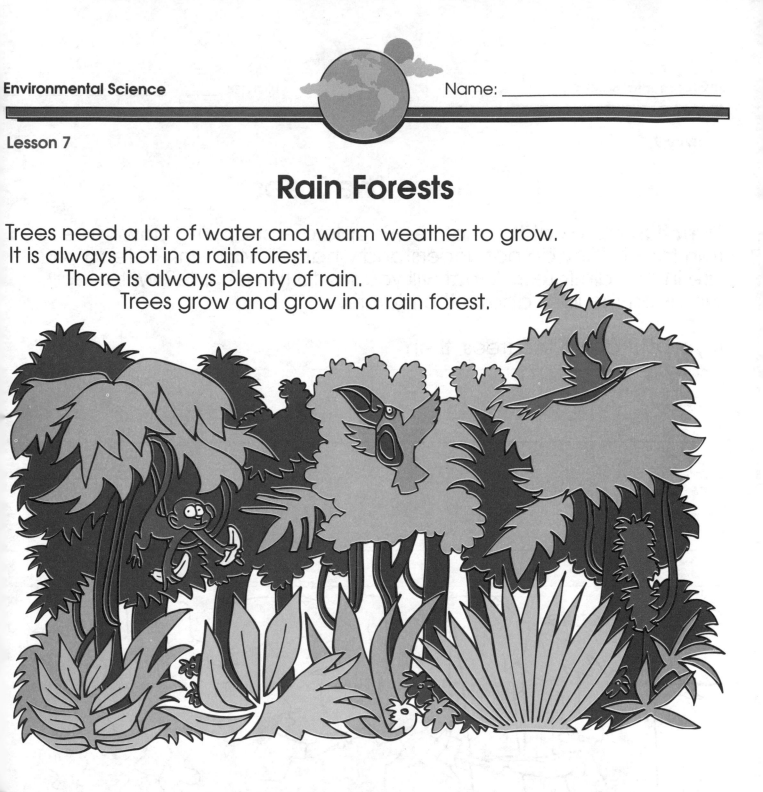

Now people have started to chop down trees in rain forests.
This chopping harms the environment.
It hurts the many animals that live in rain forests.
It may change the weather all around the world.
It may even change the air we breathe.
People must stop cutting down the trees in rain forests.

How does cutting down the trees in rain forests hurt animals?

Activity 7

Save The Trees

Directions: Look at the picture. People are chopping down trees in a rain forest. They do not understand what will happen. Pretend you are in this rain forest. What will you say to the people? Write your words on the lines above the picture.

If you cut down the trees, then

_____

_____

_____

_____

_____

Color the picture.

Get some drawing paper.

Draw what will happen after you talk to the people.

Consonant Blends: mp, nd, nk, ng

Directions: In every box is a word ending and a list of letters. Add each of the letters to the word ending to make rhyming words.

_____ and
b _____
h _____
l _____
s _____

_____ ent
b _____
d _____
t _____
w _____

_____ ump
b _____
d _____
j _____
p _____

_____ ink
p _____
s _____
l _____
th _____

_____ ing
r _____
s _____
st _____
k _____

_____ ank
b _____
r _____
s _____
t _____

Name: _____

I Can Find A Rhyme

Directions: Look at the pictures in each row across. Circle the ones that rhyme. Then write the names of the ones that do not rhyme in the blanks below.

Row 1

Row 2

Row 3

These words do not rhyme with the others in the row.

Row 1	Row 2	Row 3
_____	_____	_____
_____	_____	_____
_____	_____	_____
_____	_____	_____

ANSWER KEY

COMPREHENSIVE CURRICULUM

OF BASIC SKILLS

1

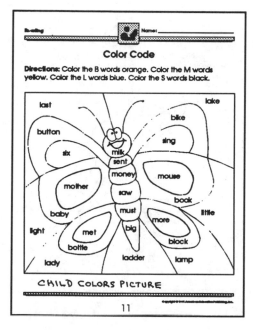

I Can Write The Names Of Pets!

Directions: 1. Follow the lines to write the name of each pet.
2. Write each name again by yourself. 3. Color the pictures.
4. Read the words to someone.
Like this:

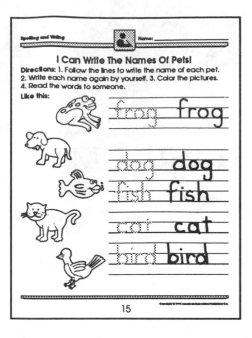

frog frog

dog dog

fish fish

cat cat

bird bird

15

Snow Is Cold!

Directions: Read about snow. Then answer the questions.

When you play in snow, dress warmly. Wear a coat. Wear a hat. Wear gloves. Do you wear these when you play in snow?

1. Snow is   warm / **cold**

2. When you play in snow, dress   **warmly** / quickly

3. List 3 things to wear when you play in snow.

coat hat gloves

18

Following Directions

Directions: Put a box around the circle ○.

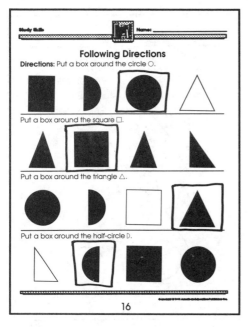

Put a box around the square □.

Put a box around the triangle △.

Put a box around the half-circle D.

16

Number Recognition 1, 2, 3, 4, 5

Directions: Use the color code to color the parrot.

Color:
1's red
2's blue
3's yellow
4's green
5's orange

Copyright © 1991 American Education Publishing Co.

19

Building A Snowman

Directions: Read the sentences. Do what they tell you to do.

Bob is making a snowman. He needs your help. Draw a black hat on the snowman. Draw red buttons. Now, draw a green scarf. Draw a happy face on the snowman.

CHILD ADDS ELEMENTS TO COMPLETE PICTURE

17

abc order

Directions: Draw a line to connect the dots. Follow the letters in abc order.

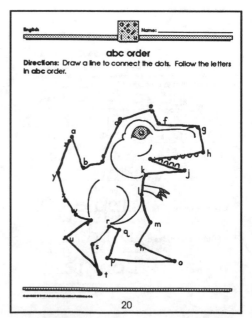

20

226

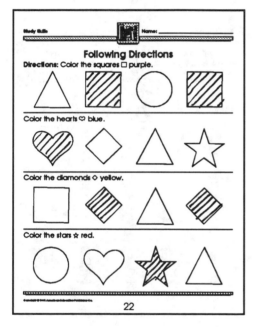

Citizenship

Children Are
Citizens Now Activity

Refer to page **261**
for Answer Key

Environmental Science

Your Environment

Refer to page **268**
for Answer Key

Citizenship

Children Are
Citizens Now

Refer to page **261**
for Answer Key

Environmental Science

Your Environment
Activity

Refer to page **268**
for Answer Key

Color The Eggs

Directions: Read the words. Color the picture.

CHILD COLORS PICTURE

27

Look And See

Directions: 1. Look at both pictures. 2. Find five things in picture # 1 that are not in picture # 2. 3. Say your answers aloud. 4. Draw a circle around them.

#1

#2

28

Number Recognition 6, 7, 8, 9, 10

Directions: Use the code to color the carousel horse.

Color:
6's purple
7's yellow
8's black
9's pink
10's brown

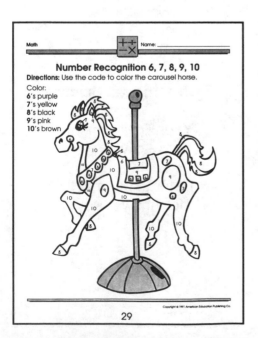

29

Beginning Consonants Bb, Cc, Dd, Ff

Beginning consonants make the sounds that come at the beginning of words. Consonants are the letters b, c, d, f, g, h, j, k, l, m, n, p, q, r, s, t, v, w, x, y, z.

Directions: Say the name of each letter. Say the sound each letter makes. Draw a circle around the letters that make the beginning sound for each picture. Say the name of someone you know whose name begins with each letter.

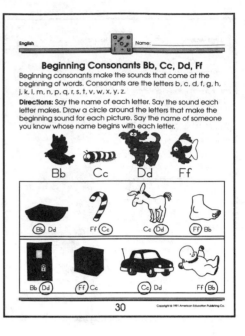

30

I Know Which Words Begin The Same!

Directions: 1. Say the name of the pet and write the first letter under the name. 2. Find the two pictures in each row that begin the same as the pet. 3. Write the same first letter under them.

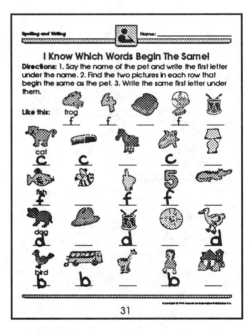

31

Following Directions

Directions: Color the picture.
red crayon for □.
blue crayon for ○.
purple crayon for △.

green crayon for D.
yellow crayon for ☆.
black crayon for ♡.
pink crayon for ◇.

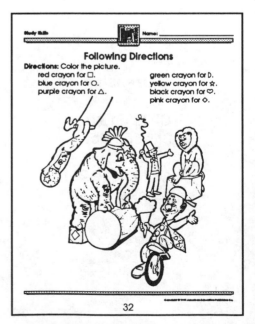

32

Color The Pictures

Directions: Color each picture the correct colors. Draw and color another picture like the first one.

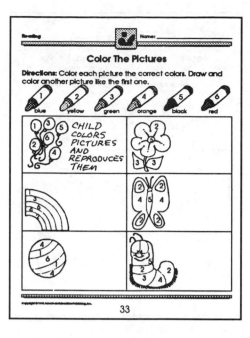

1 blue 2 yellow 4 green 5 orange 8 black 6 red

CHILD COLORS PICTURES AND REPRODUCES THEM

Beginning Consonants Gg, Hh, Jj, Kk

Directions: Say the name of each letter. Say the sound that each letter makes. Then, trace the letter that makes the beginning sound in the picture. After you finish, look around the room. Name the things that start with the letters Gg, Hh, Jj, and Kk.

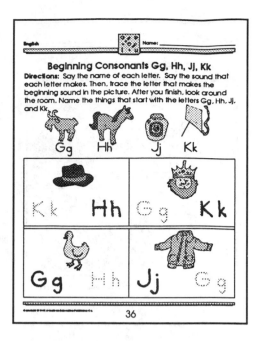

Gg   Hh   Jj   Kk

Kk   Hh   Gg   Kk

Gg   Hh   Jj   Gg

I Like Apples

Directions: Read about apples. Then answer the questions.

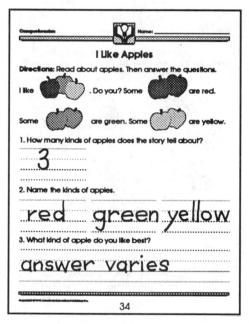

I like [apples]. Do you? Some [apples] are red.

Some [apples] are green. Some [apples] are yellow.

1. How many kinds of apples does the story tell about?

   3

2. Name the kinds of apples.

   red   green   yellow

3. What kind of apple do you like best?

   answer varies

I Can Write A Whole Sentence!

A telling sentence ends with a period.

Directions: 1. Write the name of the pet on the line with the same number. 2. Find a picture that shows the pet doing something. 3. Write that word on the line to make a whole sentence. 4. Put a period at the end of each sentence.

Like this:

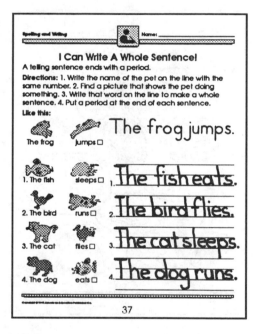

The frog   jumps □   The frog jumps.

1. The fish   sleeps □   1. The fish eats.

2. The bird   runs □   2. The bird flies.

3. The cat   flies □   3. The cat sleeps.

4. The dog   eats □   4. The dog runs.

Number Recognition

Directions: Count the number of objects in each group. Draw a line to the correct number.

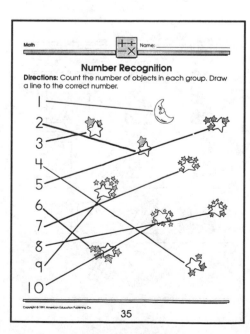

1
2
3
4
5
6
7
8
9
10

Following Directions

Directions: Trace a circle O, a square □, a triangle △, and a half-circle D. Color each one. Draw other shapes. Color them.

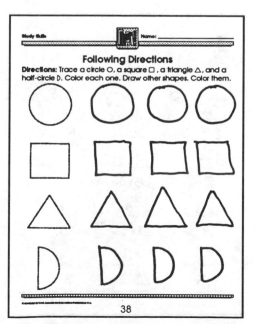

Following Directions

Directions: Look at the pictures. Follow the directions in each box.

Draw a circle around the caterpillar. Draw a line under the stick.

Put an X on the mother bird. Draw a triangle around the baby birds.

Put a box around the rabbit.

Color the flowers. Count the bees.

39

Beginning Consonants Ll, Mm, Nn, Pp

Directions: Say the name of each letter. Say the sound each letter makes. Then, trace the letters. Now, draw a line from each letter to the picture which begins with the letter. After you finish, say the letters Ll, Mm, Nn, Pp again.

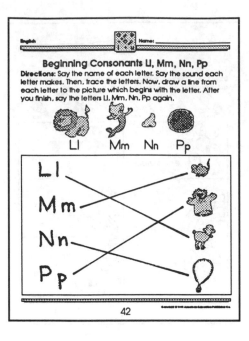

Ll   Mm   Nn   Pp

42

These Keep Me Warm

Directions: Look at the pictures. Color only the things that keep you warm.

40

I Know Which Letters Are Missing!

Directions: Fill in the missing letters for each word. Then write the word by yourself.

Like this:

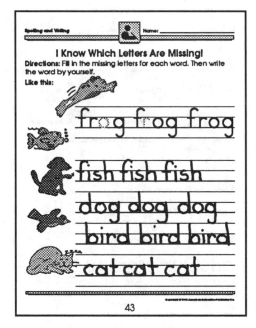

frog frog frog

fish fish fish

dog dog dog

bird bird bird

cat cat cat

43

Sequencing Numbers

Sequencing is putting numbers in the correct order.

Directions: Write the missing numbers.

Example: 4, __5__ , 6

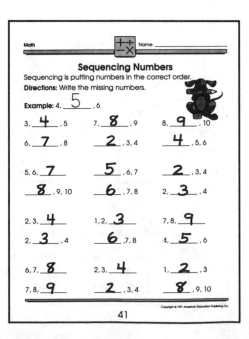

3, **4** , 5	7, **8** , 9	8, **9** , 10
6, **7** , 8	**2** , 3, 4	**4** , 5, 6
5, 6, **7**	**5** , 6, 7	**2** , 3, 4
8 , 9, 10	**6** , 7, 8	2, **3** , 4
2, 3, **4**	1, 2, **3**	7, 8, **9**
2, **3** , 4	**6** , 7, 8	4, **5** , 6
6, 7, **8**	2, 3, **4**	1, **2** , 3
7, 8, **9**	**2** , 3, 4	**8** , 9, 10

41

Same/Different

Directions: Color the shape next to it that looks the same as the first shape in each row.

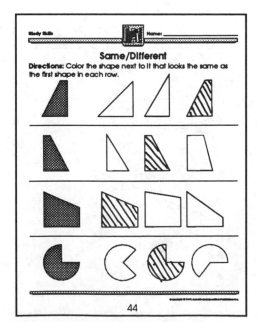

44

Finish The Pictures

Directions: Read the words. Finish the pictures.

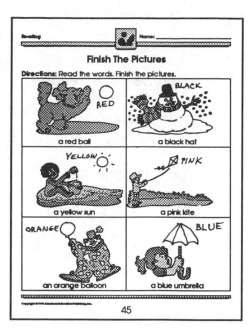

a red ball — a black hat
a yellow sun — a pink kite
an orange balloon — a blue umbrella

45

I Like To Rake Leaves

Directions: Read about raking leaves. Then answer the questions.

I like to rake leaves. Do you? Leaves die each year. They get brown and dry. They fall from the trees. Then we rake them up.

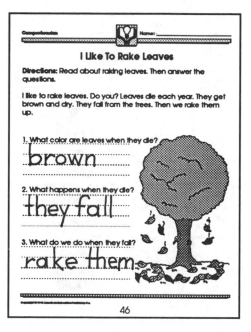

1. What color are leaves when they die?

brown

2. What happens when they die?

they fall

3. What do we do when they fall?

rake them

46

Counting

Directions: How many are there of each? Write the answers in the boxes. The first one is done for you.

| | 1 | | 7 | | 6 |
| | 10 | | 3 | | 2 |

47

Beginning Consonants Qq, Rr, Ss, Tt

Directions: Say the name of each letter. Say the sound that each letter makes. Then, trace each letter in the boxes. Color the picture which begins with the sound of the letter.

Qq   Rr   Ss   Tt

48

I Know Which Words Make A Sentence!

Directions: 1. Finish writing the names of the pets. 2. Draw a line from the pet's name to the end of the sentence. 3. Put a period at the end of each sentence. 4. Read your sentences to someone.

Like this:

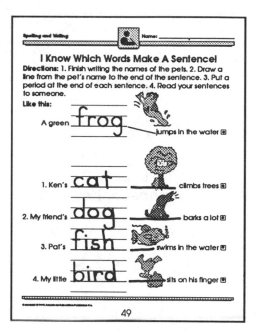

A green **frog** — jumps in the water

1. Ken's **cat** — climbs trees
2. My friend's **dog** — barks a lot
3. Pat's **fish** — swims in the water
4. My little **bird** — sits on his finger

49

Same/Different

Directions: Put an X on the shapes in each row that do not match the first shape.

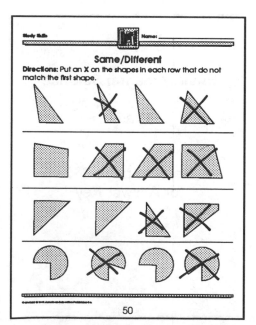

50

231

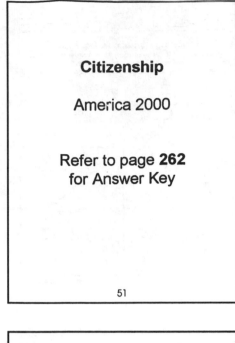

Citizenship

America 2000

Refer to page **262**
for Answer Key

51

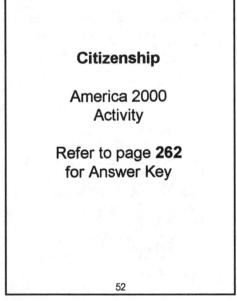

Citizenship

America 2000
Activity

Refer to page **262**
for Answer Key

52

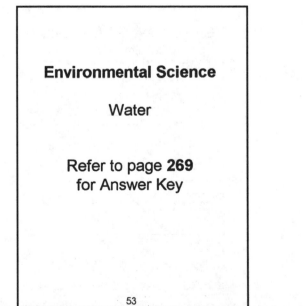

Environmental Science

Water

Refer to page **269**
for Answer Key

53

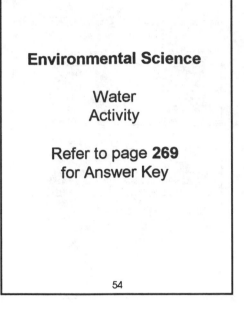

Environmental Science

Water
Activity

Refer to page **269**
for Answer Key

54

Counting

Directions: How many are there of each? Write the answers in the boxes. The first one is done for you.

cloud	7
frog	4
apple	10
leaf	5
bird	3

57

Same/Different

Directions: Color the shape that does not belong in each group.

Example:

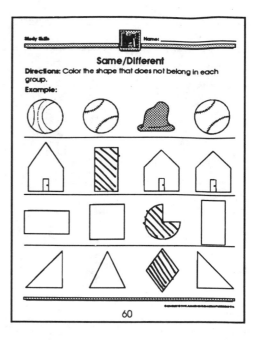

60

Beginning Consonants Vv, Ww, Xx, Yy, Zz

Directions: Say the name of each letter. Say the sound the letter makes. Then, trace the letters. Now, draw a line from the letters that match the beginning sound in each picture.

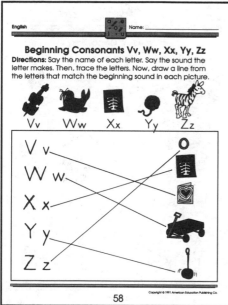

V v
W w
X x
Y y
Z z

58

Skills Review: Following Directions, Color Word Vocabulary

Directions: Read the sentences. Follow the directions.

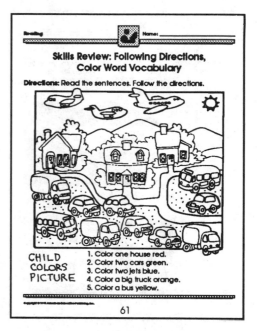

CHILD COLORS PICTURE

1. Color one house red.
2. Color two cars green.
3. Color two jets blue.
4. Color a big truck orange.
5. Color a bus yellow.

61

I Know How The Letters Go!

Directions: The letters in the name of each pet are mixed up. Write them the way they should be.

Like this:

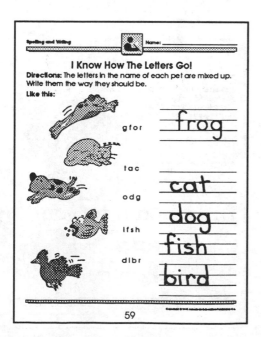

g f o r	frog
t a c	cat
o d g	dog
l f s h	fish
d i b r	bird

59

Do You Like To Bake?

Directions: Read the story. Then follow the instructions.

Some things used in baking are dry. Some things used in baking are wet. To bake a cake, first mix the salt, sugar and flour. Then add the egg. Now add the milk. Stir. Put the cake in the oven.

1. Circle the things that are wet.

2. Tell the order to mix things when you bake.

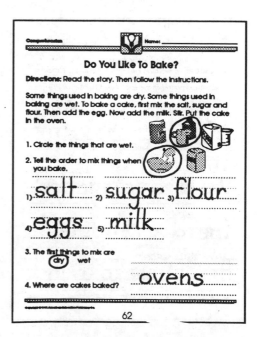

1) salt   2) sugar   3) flour

4) eggs   5) milk

3. The first things to mix are (dry)   wet

4. Where are cakes baked?   ovens

62

Review

Directions: Count the shapes and write the answers.

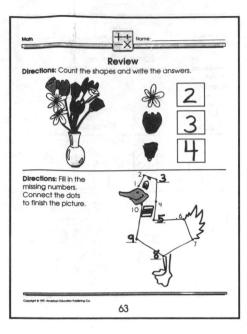

| 2 |
| 3 |
| 4 |

Directions: Fill in the missing numbers. Connect the dots to finish the picture.

63

Review

Directions: Color the circles O red.

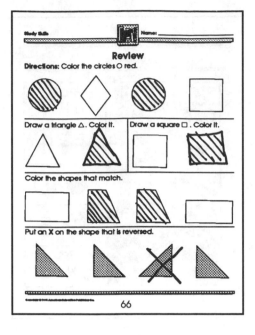

Draw a triangle △. Color it.

Draw a square ☐. Color it.

Color the shapes that match.

Put an X on the shape that is reversed.

66

Review

Directions: Help Meg and Kent and their dog, Sam, get to the magic castle. Trace all of the letters of the alphabet. Then, write the lower case consonant next to the matching upper case letter on the road to the magic castle. Make the sound for each consonant. After you finish, draw a picture on another paper of what you think Meg and Sam will find in the magic castle.

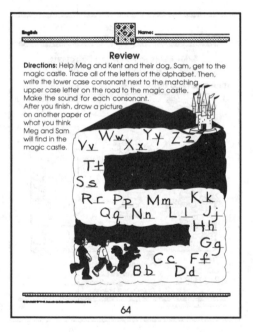

64

Which Are Opposites?

Directions: Draw a line between the opposites.

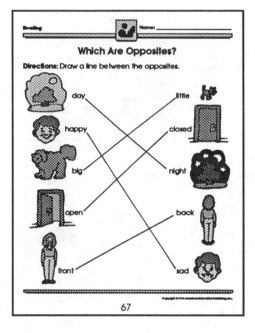

day — little
happy — closed
big — night
open — back
front — sad

67

Review

Directions: Use the words in the pictures to write a sentence about each pet. Can you spell the name of the pet by yourself? Put a period at the end of each sentence.

Like this:

The 🐸 eats bugs   The frog eats bugs.

The 🐱 drinks milk

The cat drinks milk.

The 🐦 eats an apple

The bird eats an apple.

The 🐶 jumps out

The dog jumps out.

The 🐟 sees a friend

The fish sees a friend.

65

I Like Cats

Directions: Read the story. Then answer the questions.

Do you like cats? I do. To pet a cat, move slowly. Hold out your hand. The cat will come to you. Then pet its head. Do not grab a cat! It will run away.

1. To pet a cat, move ~~fast~~ **slow.**

2. Give directions on how to pet a cat.

1) Hold out your   **hand** .

2) The cat will   **come to you** .

3) Pet the cat's   **head** .

3. Do not do this to a cat!   **grab it**

68

234

Number Words

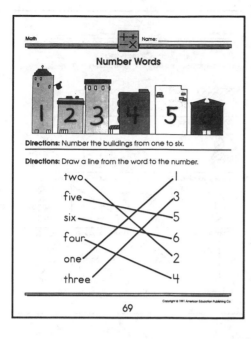

Directions: Number the buildings from one to six.

Directions: Draw a line from the word to the number.

two   1
five   3
six   5
four   6
one   2
three   4

69

Classifying

Directions: Bob is looking for stars. Help him find them. Color all the stars blue.

How many stars did Bob find? **10**

72

Ending Consonants b, d, f

Ending consonants are the sounds that come at the end of the words that are not the vowel sounds.

Directions: Say the name of each picture. Then, write b, d, or f to name the ending sound for each picture.

70

Game Of Opposites

Directions: Write each word from the word box under its opposite.

no	bad	hot	up	in	went	go	off

good	came
bad	went

yes	stop
no	go

down	on
up	off

out	cold
in	hot

73

I Can Write The Names Of Colors!

Directions: Follow the lines to print the name of each color. Then print the name again by yourself.

Like this:

orange   orange
blue   blue
green   green
yellow   yellow
red   red
brown   brown

71

Where Flowers Grow

Directions: Read about flowers. Then answer the questions.

Some flowers grow in pots. Many flowers grow in flower beds. Others grow beside the road. Some flowers begin from seeds. They grow into small buds. Then they open wide and bloom. Flowers are pretty!

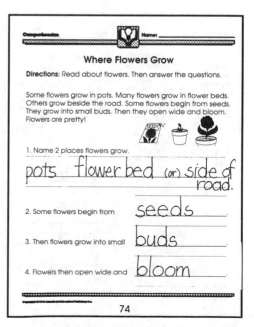

1. Name 2 places flowers grow.

pots   flower bed (or) side of road.

2. Some flowers begin from   seeds

3. Then flowers grow into small   buds

4. Flowers then open wide and   bloom

74

235

Number Words

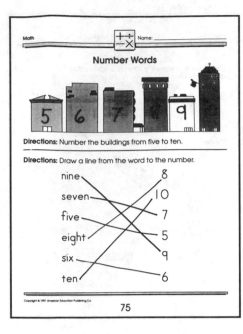

Directions: Number the buildings from five to ten.

Directions: Draw a line from the word to the number.

nine   8
seven   10
five   7
eight   5
six   9
ten   6

75

Ending Consonants g, m, n

Directions: Say the name of the picture. Draw a line from each letter to a picture which ends with the sound of that letter.

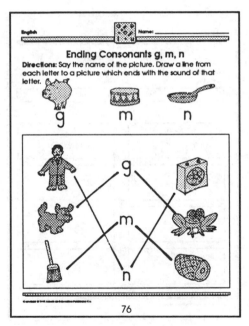

g   m   n

76

I Can Finish A Sentence!

Directions: Use the color words to finish these sentences. Then put a period at the end.

Like this: My new ___ are __orange__ .

green tree   blue bike   yellow chick   red ball

1. The baby ___ is __yellow__ .

2. This ___ is __green__ .

3. My ___ is big and __red__ .

4. My sister's ___ is __blue__ .

77

Classifying

Directions: Color the stars ☆.   How many stars? __2__

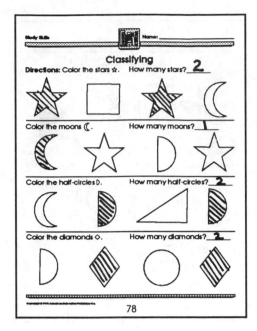

Color the moons ☾.   How many moons? __1__

Color the half-circles D.   How many half-circles? __2__

Color the diamonds ◇.   How many diamonds? __2__

78

Citizenship

The United States Flag

Refer to page **263** for Answer Key

79

Citizenship

The United States Flag Activity

Refer to page **263** for Answer Key

80

Environmental Science

Air

Refer to page **269**
for Answer Key

81

Environmental Science

Air
Activity

Refer to page **269**
for Answer Key

82

Classifying

Directions: Draw a circle around the correct pictures.

What Can Swim?

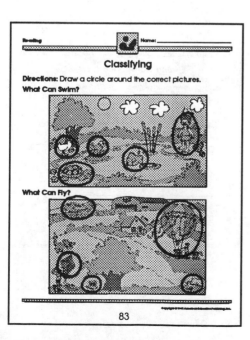

What Can Fly?

83

Flower Puzzle

Directions: Re-read the story about flowers on page 10. Then fill in the puzzle with the right answers about flowers.

Across
1. Flowers do this when they open wide.
2. Some flowers grow from these.

Down
1. Before it blooms, a flower grows a ___.
3. A flower can grow in a flower bed or a ___.

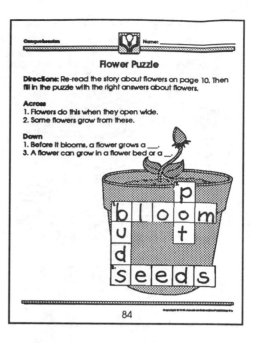

84

Shapes: Square

A square is a figure with four corners and four sides of the same length. This is a square □.

Directions: Find the squares and circle them.

Directions: Trace the word.   Write the word.

square   square

85

Ending Consonants k, l, p

Directions: Say the name of the pictures. Color the pictures in each row that end with the sound of the letter at the beginning of the row. Trace the letters.

86

I Know Which Words Sound The Same!

Directions: Circle the words that start with the same sound.
Like this:

red **blue** green **brown** **black** yellow

Directions: Circle each word that has two letters the same in it. Write the two letters under the word.
Like this: (happy) man (feet) boat

pp   ee

red   blue (green) brown black (yellow)
             ee   ll

Directions: This time, circle the words that end with the same sound.
Like this:

red   blue (green) (brown) black yellow

87

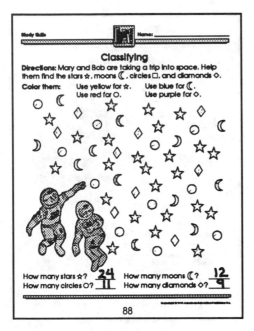

Classifying

Directions: Mary and Bob are taking a trip into space. Help them find the stars ☆, moons ☾, circles ○, and diamonds ◇.

Color them: Use yellow for ☆. Use blue for ☾.
Use red for ○. Use purple for ◇.

How many stars ☆? **24**   How many moons ☾? **12**
How many circles ○? **11**   How many diamonds ◇? **9**

88

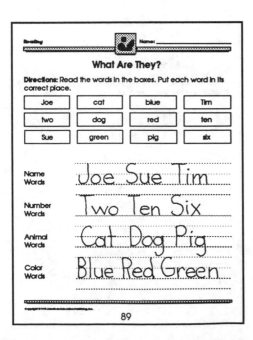

What Are They?

Directions: Read the words in the boxes. Put each word in its correct place.

Joe	cat	blue	Tim
two	dog	red	ten
Sue	green	pig	six

Name Words   Joe Sue Tim

Number Words   Two Ten Six

Animal Words   Cat Dog Pig

Color Words   Blue Red Green

89

Balloons

Directions: Read about balloons. Then answer the questions.

Some balloons float. They are filled with gas. Some balloons do not float. They are filled with air. Some clowns carry balloons. The balloons come in many colors. What color do you want?

1. What makes balloons float?   gas

2. What is in balloons that do not float?   air

3. What kind of balloons is the clown holding?   gas

90

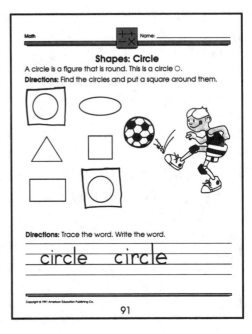

Shapes: Circle

A circle is a figure that is round. This is a circle ○.
Directions: Find the circles and put a square around them.

Directions: Trace the word. Write the word.

circle   circle

91

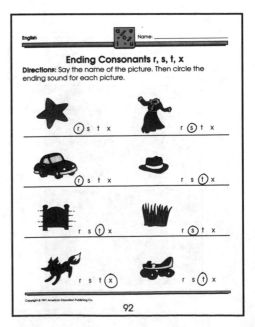

Ending Consonants r, s, t, x

Directions: Say the name of the picture. Then circle the ending sound for each picture.

r (s) t x   r (s) t x

(r) s t x   r s (t) x

r s (t) x   r s (t) x

r s t (x)   r s (t) x

92

238

I Know Which Ones Are Sentences!

Directions: Some of these sentences tell the whole idea. Others have something missing. If you think something is missing, draw a line to a word that would finish that sentence. Remember to put a period after the last word in the sentence.

1. He is holding up his
2. Ken has a new puppy.
3. I can read a
4. We like to play games.
5. Pat wants to eat some
6. I will color the
7. This is my birthday.

book.
hand.
tree.
cake.

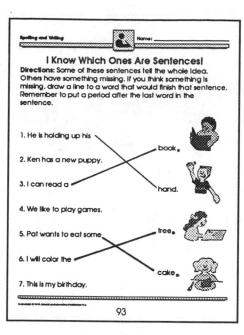

93

Clowning Around

Directions: Look at the pictures of the clowns. Find 4 things that are different in picture 2. Color the things that are different.

96

Classifying

Directions: Help Mary and Bob sort their shapes. Draw a line from each shape to the basket it should go in.

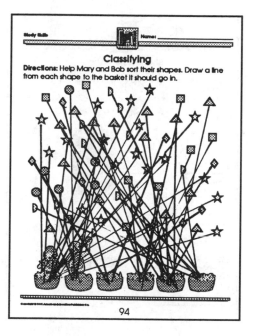

94

Shapes: Triangle

A triangle is a figure with three corners and three sides. This is a triangle △.

Directions: Find the triangles and put a circle around them.

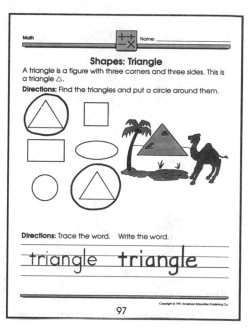

Directions: Trace the word.   Write the word.

triangle   triangle

97

Alphabetical Order

Directions: Look at the words in each box. Circle the word that comes first in a-b-c order.

A-B-C Order

(duck) four rock	chair (apple) yellow	(peach) this walk
game (boy) pink	light (come) one	(mouse) ten orange
(angel) table hair	zebra watch (five)	foot (boat) mine
look (blue) rope	who dog (black)	(book) tan six

95

Beginning and Ending Sounds Discrimination

Directions: Say the name of the picture. Draw a blue circle around the picture if it begins with the sound of the letter. Draw a green triangle around the picture if it ends with the sound of the letter.

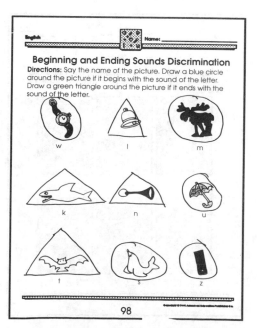

w   l   m

k   n   u

t   s   z

98

239

I Know Which Words Begin The Same!

Directions: Say the name of the color and the picture beside it. If they begin with the same sound, write an X in the box.
Like this:

red ✗   ✗ blue

yellow ☐   ✗ black

green ✗   ☐ brown

99

Classifying

Directions: Look at the shapes. Answer the questions.

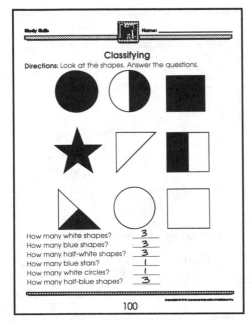

How many white shapes? __3__
How many blue shapes? __3__
How many half-white shapes? __3__
How many blue stars? __1__
How many white circles? __1__
How many half-blue shapes? __3__

100

Story Order

Directions: The pictures tell a story, but they are in the wrong order. Write a number under each box to show the order they belong in.

__1__   __3__   __2__

__3__   __1__   __2__

101

Tigers

Directions: Read about tigers. Then answer the questions.

Tigers sleep during the day. They hunt at night. Tigers eat meat. They hunt deer. They like to eat wild pigs. If they cannot find meat, tigers will eat fish.

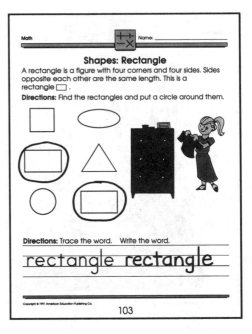

1. When do tigers sleep?
   night   (day)

2. Name 2 things tigers eat.

   deer   fish (or) wild pig

3. When do tigers hunt?
   day   (night)

102

Shapes: Rectangle

A rectangle is a figure with four corners and four sides. Sides opposite each other are the same length. This is a rectangle ☐ .

Directions: Find the rectangles and put a circle around them.

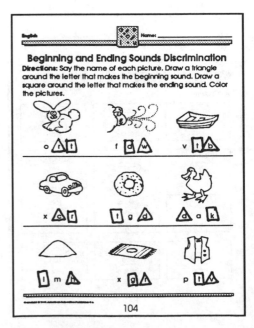

Directions: Trace the word.   Write the word.

rectangle rectangle

103

Beginning and Ending Sounds Discrimination

Directions: Say the name of each picture. Draw a triangle around the letter that makes the beginning sound. Draw a square around the letter that makes the ending sound. Color the pictures.

104

240

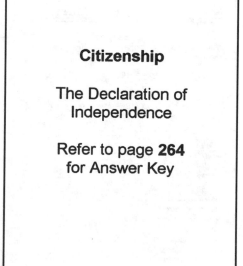

I Know How To Start A Sentence!
A sentence starts with a capital letter.

Directions: 1. Read the words by each picture. 2. Write them to make a sentence that tells about the picture. 3. Start each sentence with a capital letter—and end with a period.

Like this: the girl coat a red has

The girl has a red coat.

1. box sees he a blue

He sees a blue box.

2. picks the flower yellow she

She picks the yellow flower.

3. green house colors he the

He colors the house green.

Classifying
Directions: Look around your home or school. Find some pencils, pens, straws, toothpicks, paintbrushes, and crayons. Count them.

How many: answers vary

pencils ? ____ straws ? ____
paintbrushes ? ____ pens ? ____
toothpicks ? ____ crayons ? ____

Draw a picture of each thing you found.

pictures vary

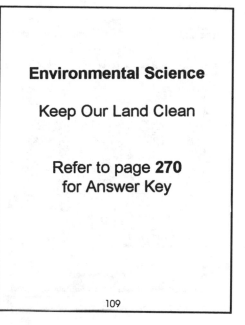

Citizenship

The Declaration of Independence Activity

Refer to page **264** for Answer Key

Environmental Science

Keep Our Land Clean

Refer to page **270** for Answer Key

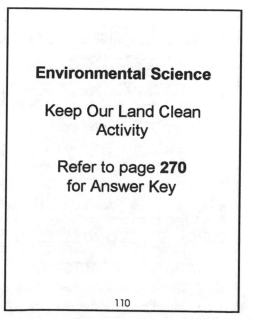

Citizenship

The Declaration of Independence

Refer to page **264** for Answer Key

Environmental Science

Keep Our Land Clean Activity

Refer to page **270** for Answer Key

Story Order

Directions: 1) Look at the picture story. 2) Read the sentences. 3) Write 1, 2, 3 or 4 by each sentence to show the order of the story.

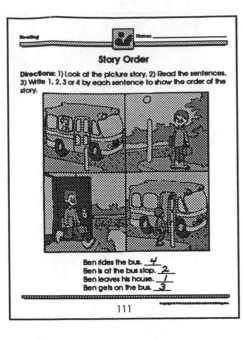

Ben rides the bus. __4__
Ben is at the bus stop. __2__
Ben leaves his house. __1__
Ben gets on the bus. __3__

Tiger Puzzle

Directions: Re-read the story about tigers on page 14. Then fill in the puzzle with the right answers about tigers.

Across
3. The food tigers like best.
4. Tigers like to eat this meat: wild ____ .

Down
1. Tigers do this during the day.
2. When tigers cannot get meat, they eat this.

Shapes: Oval And Diamond

An oval is an egg-shaped figure. A diamond is a figure with four sides of the same length. Its corners form points at the top, sides, and bottom. This is an oval ⬭. This is a diamond ◇.
Directions: Color the ovals red. Color the diamonds blue.

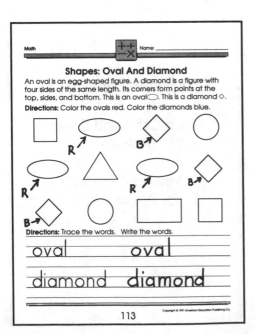

Directions: Trace the words. Write the words.

oval   oval

diamond   diamond

Beginning and Ending Sounds Discrimination

Directions: Look at the example. Say the beginning and ending sounds for the word pipe. Write the letter that makes the beginning and ending sound for each picture.

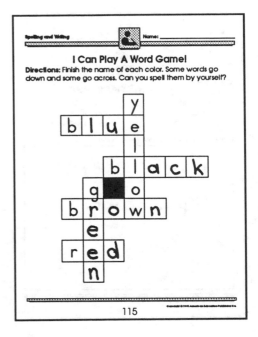

I Can Play A Word Game!

Directions: Finish the name of each color. Some words go down and some go across. Can you spell them by yourself?

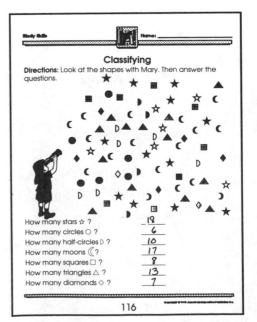

Classifying

Directions: Look at the shapes with Mary. Then answer the questions.

How many stars ☆ ? __18__
How many circles ○ ? __6__
How many half-circles D ? __10__
How many moons ☾ ? __17__
How many squares □ ? __8__
How many triangles △ ? __13__
How many diamonds ◇ ? __7__

Skills Review: Sequencing, Classifying

Directions: 1) Write numbers by the sentences to show the order they belong in. 2) Write each word from the word box in its correct place.

Kim picks out food. __2__

Kim pays the man. __3__

Kim goes to the store. __1__

| apple | ice cream | cookie | banana | orange | cake |

Fruits	Sweets
apple	ice cream
banana	cookie
orange	cake

117

Review

Directions: Say the name of each object which has a consonant near it. Color the object orange if it begins with the sound of the letter. Color the object purple if it ends with the sound of the letter.

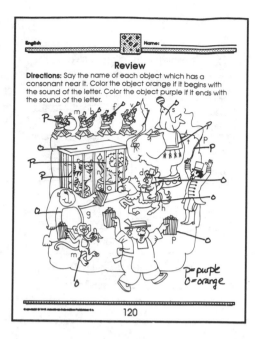

P = purple
O = orange

120

Cookies

Directions: Read about cookies. Then answer the questions.

Cookies are made with many things. All cookies are made with flour. Some cookies have nuts in them. Some cookies do not. Some cookies have chips. Some cookies do not. Cookbooks give directions on how to make cookies. First turn on the oven. Then get all the things that go in the cookies. Mix them together. Cut out or roll out the cookies. Bake the cookies. Now eat them!

1. Tell 1 way all cookies are the same.

made with flour

2. Name 2 different things in cookies.

chips   nuts

3. Where do you find directions for making cookies?

cookbooks

118

Review

Directions: 1. Write three sentences that tell about this picture. Use a color word in each one. Can you write the names of the colors and the pets by yourself now? 2. Remember to begin each sentence with a capital letter and end with a period.

Here are some more words you could use: walks, sees, runs, flies, grows, eats, looks, jumps, sits.

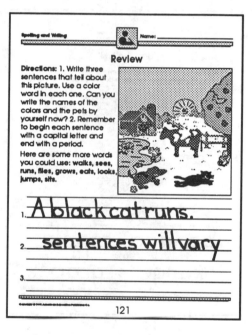

1. A black cat runs.

2. sentences will vary

3. _____

121

Review

Directions: Color the shapes in the picture as shown.

black

red

orange

yellow

blue

green

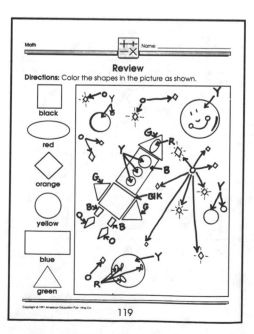

119

Review

Directions: Color the stars ☆ blue.

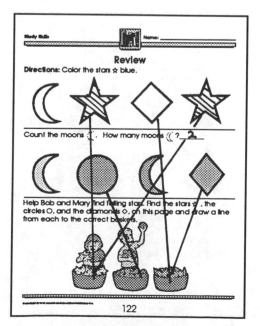

Count the moons ☾. How many moons ☾? __2__

Help Bob and Mary find falling stars. Find the stars ☆, the circles ○, and the diamonds ◇, on this page and draw a line from each to the correct baskets.

122

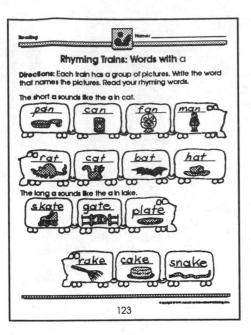

Rhyming Trains: Words with a

Directions: Each train has a group of pictures. Write the word that names the pictures. Read your rhyming words.

The short a sounds like the a in cat.

pan | can | fan | man

rat | cat | bat | hat

The long a sounds like the a in lake.

skate | gate | plate

rake | cake | snake

123

Short Vowel Sounds

The short vowel sounds used in this book are found in the following words: ant, egg, igloo, on, up.

Directions: Say the name of each picture. The short vowel sound may be in the front of the word or in the middle of the word. Color the pictures in each row that have the correct short vowel sound.

a

e

i   brick

o

u

126

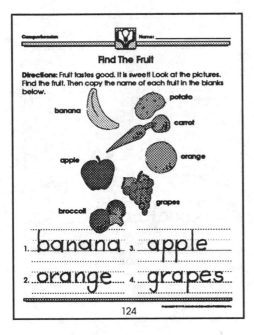

Find The Fruit

Directions: Fruit tastes good. It is sweet. Look at the pictures. Find the fruit. Then copy the name of each fruit in the blanks below.

banana
potato
carrot
apple
orange
broccoli
grapes

1. banana   3. apple

2. orange   4. grapes

124

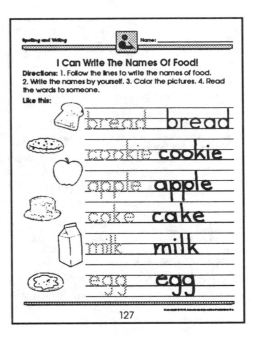

I Can Write The Names Of Food!

Directions: 1. Follow the lines to write the names of food.
2. Write the names by yourself. 3. Color the pictures. 4. Read the words to someone.

Like this:

bread   bread

cookie   cookie

apple   apple

cake   cake

milk   milk

egg   egg

127

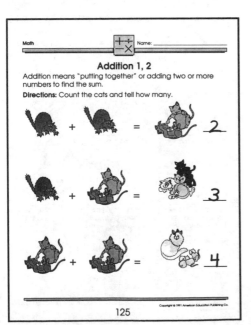

Addition 1, 2

Addition means "putting together" or adding two or more numbers to find the sum.

Directions: Count the cats and tell how many.

+ = 2

+ = 3

+ = 4

125

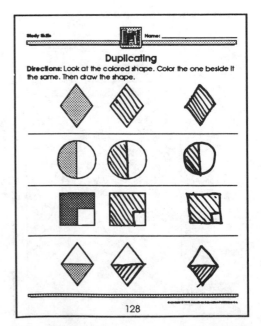

Duplicating

Directions: Look at the colored shape. Color the one beside it the same. Then draw the shape.

128

244

Words With e

Directions: Short e sounds like the e in hen. Long e sounds like the e in bee. 1) Look at the pictures. 2) If the word has a short e sound, draw a line to the hen. 3) If the word has a long e sound, draw a line to the bee.

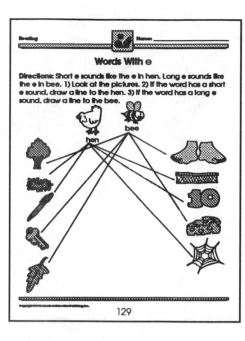

129

Long Vowel Sounds

Long vowel sounds say their own name. The following words have long vowel sounds: hay, me, pie, no, cute.

Directions: Say the name of each picture. Color the pictures in each row that have the correct long vowel sound.

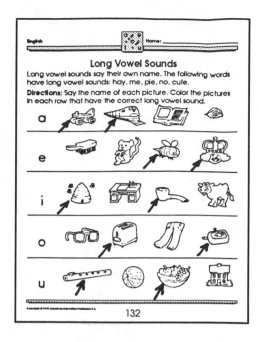

a

e

i

o

u

132

An Animal Party

Directions: Look at the picture. Look at the word list. Then answer the questions.

bear	cat
dog	elephant
giraffe	hippo
pig	tiger

1. Which animals have on bow ties?

cat   tiger

2. Which animal has on a hat?

bear

3. Which animal has on a striped shirt?

pig

130

I Know Which Ones Are Questions!

A question is a sentence that asks something.

Directions: 1. Write each sentence on the line. 2. Start all the sentences with capital letters. 3. Put a period at the end of the telling sentences. 4. Put a question mark at the end of the asking sentences.

Like this: do you like ice cream

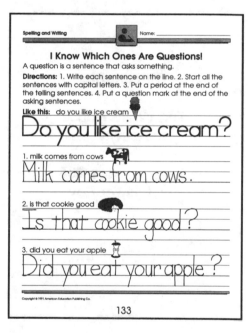

Do you like ice cream?

1. milk comes from cows

Milk comes from cows.

2. is that cookie good

Is that cookie good?

3. did you eat your apple

Did you eat your apple?

Copyright © 1991 American Education Publishing Co.

133

Addition 3, 4, 5, 6

Directions: Practice writing the numbers and then add.

$$3 \quad 3$$
$$4 \quad 4 \quad \frac{+4}{6} \quad \frac{+4}{5}$$
$$5 \quad 5$$
$$6 \quad 6 \quad \frac{+2}{5} \quad \frac{+2}{3}$$

Copyright © 1991 American Education Publishing Co.

131

Duplicating

Directions: Color your circle ◯ to look the same.

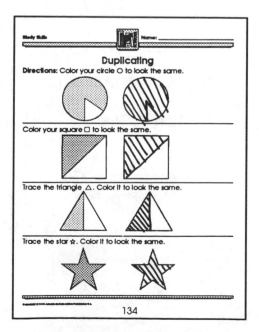

Color your square ▢ to look the same.

Trace the triangle △. Color it to look the same.

Trace the star ☆. Color it to look the same.

134

245

Citizenship

The White House

Refer to page **265**
for Answer Key

135

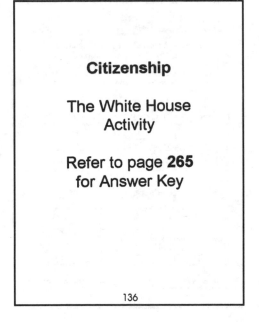

Citizenship

The White House
Activity

Refer to page **265**
for Answer Key

136

Environmental Science

Start To Recycle

Refer to page **270**
for Answer Key

137

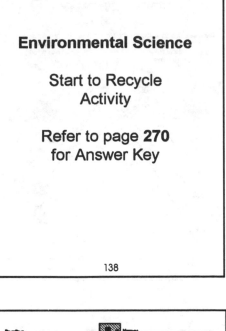

Environmental Science

Start to Recycle
Activity

Refer to page **270**
for Answer Key

138

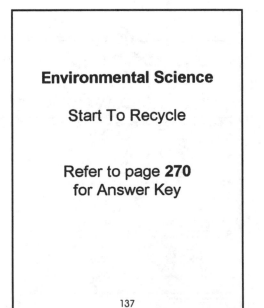

Addition 4, 5, 6, 7
Directions: Practice writing the numbers and then add.

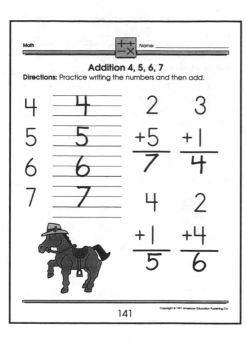

4	4		2	3
5	5		+5	+1
6	6		7	4
7	7			

$$+5 \atop 7$$ $$+1 \atop 4$$

$$4 \atop +1 \atop 5$$ $$2 \atop +4 \atop 6$$

141

Copyright © 1991 American Education Publishing Co.

Discrimination Of Short And Long Aa
Directions: Say the name of each picture. If it has the short ă sound, color it red. If it has the long ā sound, color it yellow.

ă   ā

red   yellow   red

yellow   red   red

142

I Know Which Words Sound The Same!
Directions: Write the food words that answer the questions.

egg	milk	ice cream	apple	cookie	cake

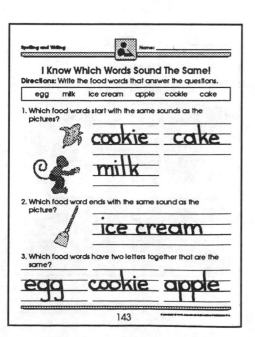

1. Which food words start with the same sounds as the pictures?

cookie   cake

milk

2. Which food word ends with the same sound as the picture?

ice cream

3. Which food words have two letters together that are the same?

egg   cookie   apple

143

Duplicating
Directions: Draw the triangle in the grid.

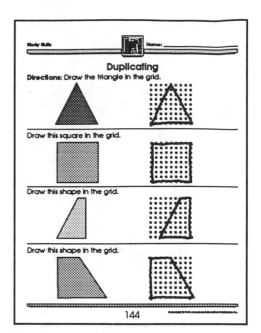

Draw this square in the grid.

Draw this shape in the grid.

Draw this shape in the grid.

144

Words With o
Directions: The short o sounds like the o in dog. Long o sounds like the o in rope. 1) Draw a line from the picture to the word that names it. 2) Draw a circle around the word if it has a short o sound.

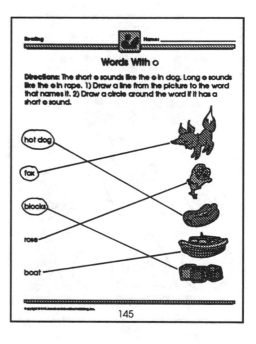

hot dog

fox

blocks

rose

boat

145

Teddy Bear, Teddy Bear
Directions: Read the teddy bear song. Then answer the questions.

Do you know this song? It is very old!

Teddy bear, teddy bear Turn around.
Teddy bear, teddy bear Touch the ground.
Teddy bear, teddy bear Climb upstairs.
Teddy bear, teddy bear Say your prayers.
Teddy bear, teddy bear Turn out the light.
Teddy bear, teddy bear Say "good night!"

1. What is the first thing the teddy bear does?

turns around

2. What is the last thing the teddy bear does?

says goodnight

3. What would you name a teddy bear?

answers vary

146

Addition 6, 7, 8

Directions: Practice writing the numbers and then add.

6   6   3   5

7   7   +4   +1
               7   6

8   8

              2   4
             +6   +4
              8   8

Duplicating

Directions: Draw this shape in the grid.

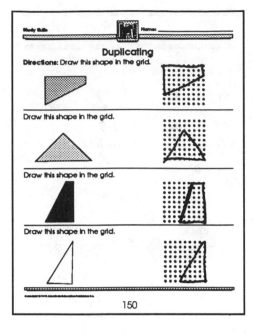

Draw this shape in the grid.

Draw this shape in the grid.

Draw this shape in the grid.

Discrimination Of Short And Long Ee

Directions: Say the name of each picture. Draw a circle around the pictures which have the short ĕ sound. Draw a triangle around the pictures which have the long ē sound.

ĕ   ē

Words With u

Directions: The short u sounds like the u in bug. The long u sounds like the u in blue. 1) Draw a circle around the words with short u. 2) Draw an X on the words with long u.

rug   cup   mice

tub   suit   glue

bug   puppy   gum

I Can Ask Question!

Directions: Change each telling sentence into a question by moving the words around. Remember to put a question mark at the end of your question.

Like this: The girl is eating ice cream.

Is the girl eating ice cream?

1.   The boy is giving a cookie.

Is the boy giving a cookie?

2.   He is drinking milk.

Is he drinking milk?

3.   She is making a cake.

Is she making a cake?

Put Teddy Bear to Bed

Directions: Re-read the story about the teddy bear. Look at the pictures. Number them in 1-2-3-4 order.

Addition 7, 8, 9
Directions: Practice writing the numbers and then add.

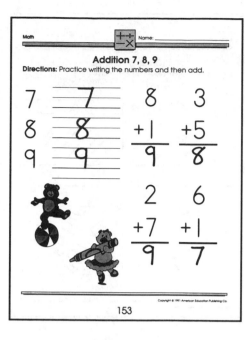

7   7   8   3
8   8   +1   +5
9   9   9   8

        2   6
       +7   +1
        9   7

153

Copyright © 1991 American Education Publishing Co.

Duplicating
Directions: Go outside. Look at your house. Now draw a picture of the shapes that make up your house. Name the shapes you see.

pictures vary

156

Discrimination Of Short And Long Ii.
Directions: Say the name of each picture. Color it yellow if it has the short i sound. Color it red if it has the long i sound.

RED   YELLOW   YELLOW   YELLOW

YELLOW   RED   RED   RED

154   Copyright © 1991 American Education Publishing Co.

Short Vowel Sounds
Directions: In each box are three pictures. The words that name the pictures have missing letters. Write a, e, i, o, or u to finish the words.

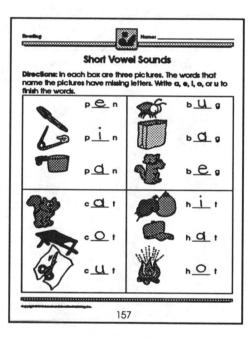

p e n   b u g
p i n   b a g
p a n   b e g

c a t   h i t
c o t   h a t
c u t   h o t

157

I Know The Answers!
Directions: Use the food words to answer each question. The first letter is done for you. Can you write the other letters by yourself?

1. Which one can you drink? milk

2. Which one do you have to keep very cold? ice cream

3. Which one grows on trees? apple

4. Which one do you put birthday candles on? cake

5. Which one do people sometimes eat in the mornings? egg

6. Which one do you like best? ans. vary

155

How We Eat
Directions: Read about meals. Look at the word list. Then answer the questions.

Big kids eat with spoons and forks. They use a knife to cut their food. They use a spoon to eat soup and ice cream. They use a fork to eat peas and corn. They say "Thank you. It was good!" when they are done.

| fork | ice cream | knife | soup |

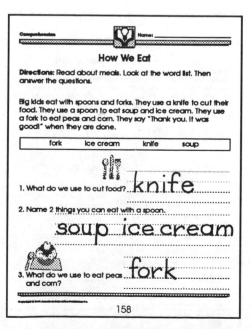

1. What do we use to cut food? knife

2. Name 2 things you can eat with a spoon.

soup ice cream

3. What do we use to eat peas and corn? fork

158

Subtraction

Subtraction means "taking away" or subtracting one number from another.

Directions: Practice writing the numbers and then subtract.

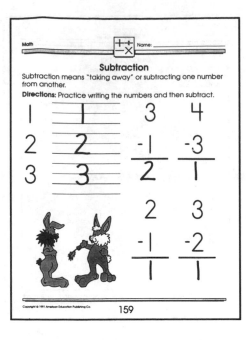

159

Discrimination Of Short And Long Oo

Directions: Say the name of each picture. If the picture has a long **o** sound, write a green **L** in the space. If the picture has a short **o** sound, write a red **S** in the space.

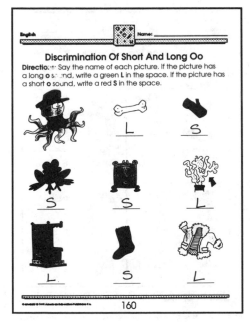

160

I Can Write My Own Sentences!

Directions: 1. For each sentence, write a word in the first space to tell who is doing something. Here are some words you could use: boy, girl, mother, father, baby. 2. Write one of the food words in the second space. 3. Draw a picture to show what is happening in your sentence.

Like this:

The ___mother___ is making ___a cake___.

answers will vary

1. The _____ is eating _____.

2. The _____ is buying _____.

161

Finding Patterns

Directions: Find the hidden shape. Then color it.

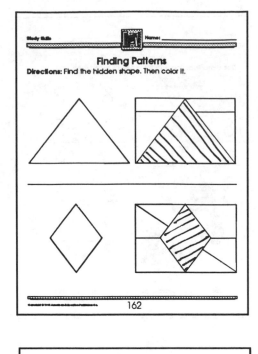

162

Citizenship

Christopher Columbus

Refer to page **266**
for Answer Key

163

Citizenship

Christopher Columbus
Activity

Refer to page **266**
for Answer Key

164

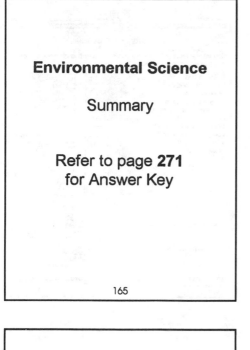

Long Vowel Sounds

Directions: Write a, e, i, o, or u in each blank to finish the word. Draw a line from the word to its picture.

c __a__ ke

r __o__ se

k __i__ te

f __ee__ t

m __u__ le

167

Things That Belong

Directions: Look at the pictures in each row across. Circle the ones in each row that belong. Write the names of the pictures that do not belong.

Row 1 — knife, key, fork, spoon

Row 2 — orange, apple, sucker, banana

Row 3 — beach ball, soccer ball, baseball, apple

These do not belong:

Row 1	Row 2	Row 3
key	sucker	apple

168

Subtraction 3, 4, 5, 6
Directions: Practice writing the numbers and then subtract.

3   3   5   6
4   4   -2   -1
5   5   ----   ----
6   6   3   5

6   6
     -3   -1
    ----   ----
      3   4

169

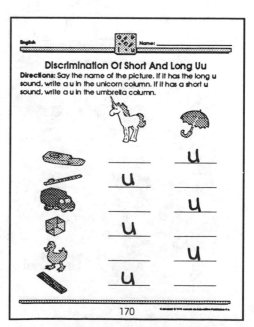

Discrimination Of Short And Long Uu
Directions: Say the name of the picture. If it has the long u sound, write a u in the unicorn column. If it has a short u sound, write a u in the umbrella column.

170

I Can Finish A Story!

Directions: Write the words in the story. Then read your story to someone.

Kim got up in the morning.

"Do you want an __egg__  ?" her mother asked.

"Yes, please," Kim said.

"May I have some __milk__ too?"

"OK," her mother said.

"How about some __ice cream__ ?" Kim asked with a smile.

Her mother laughed. "Not now," she said.

She put an __apple__ in Kim's lunch.

"Do you want a __cookie__ or some

__cake__ today?"

"Both!" Kim said.

171

Skiing Is Fun

Directions: Read about how to ski. Answer the questions. Then put the skiing pictures in 1-2-3-4 order.

Skiing Is Fun
You need to dress warmly to ski. Two skis will fit on your boots. You wear the skis to a chair. The chair is called a ski lift. It takes you up in the air to a hill. When you get off, ski down the hill. Be careful! Sometimes you will fall.

1. How many skis do you need? ___2___

2. Skiing is classified as an

indoor sport / (outdoor sport)

174

Finding Patterns

Directions: Find the hidden letter in each box. Trace it with a crayon.

1. Hidden letter: T

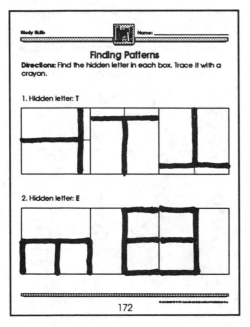

2. Hidden letter: E

172

Review

Directions: Trace the numbers. Work the problems.

1 2 3 4 5 6 7 8 9 10

$$\begin{array}{cccc} 9 & 6 & 3 & 2 \\ -3 & +2 & +4 & -1 \\ \hline 6 & 8 & 7 & 1 \end{array}$$

$$\begin{array}{cccc} 5 & 9 & 9 & 8 \\ +4 & -5 & +2 & -6 \\ \hline 9 & 4 & 9 & 2 \end{array}$$

$$\begin{array}{cccc} 4 & 6 & 9 & 1 \\ -2 & +3 & -7 & +7 \\ \hline 2 & 9 & 2 & 8 \end{array}$$

175

Skills Review: Vowel Sounds

Directions: Draw a circle around the word if it has a long vowel sound. Remember: a long vowel says its name.

feet   snake   cup

hose   tie   hat

dog   rake   bug

bone   bib   net

173

Short And Long Vowel Sounds

Directions: Say the name of the picture. Write the correct vowel on each line to finish the word. Color the short vowel pictures yellow. Circle the long vowel pictures.

Y j_u_g   B t_a_pe

B l_e_af   Y p_i_n

Y l_o_ck   Y c_a_t

B c_u_be   Y b_e_l

B k_i_te   B r_o_pe

176

252

Review

Directions: Write two telling sentences and one question about this picture. Be sure to use the food words you know — and the color and pet words.

Here are some more words you could use: boy, girl, water, table, candles, finds, birthday, out, eats, jumps, helps, sees, looks, stops, falls.

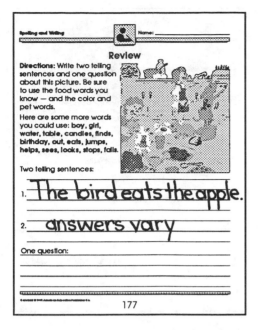

Two telling sentences:

1. The bird eats the apple.

2. answers vary

One question:

177

Clowns

Directions: Color the clowns. Then answer the questions. Use your crayons this way: 1 = red, 2 = blue, 3 = orange, 4 = pink.

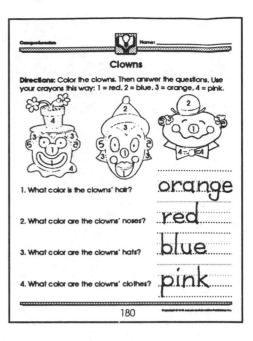

1. What color is the clowns' hair?   orange

2. What color are the clowns' noses?   red

3. What color are the clowns' hats?   blue

4. What color are the clowns' clothes?   pink

180

Review

Directions: Color your shape to look the same.

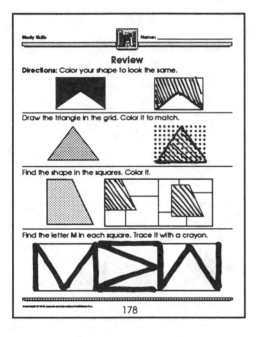

Draw the triangle in the grid. Color it to match.

Find the shape in the squares. Color it.

Find the letter M in each square. Trace it with a crayon.

178

Zero

Directions: Write the number.

Example:

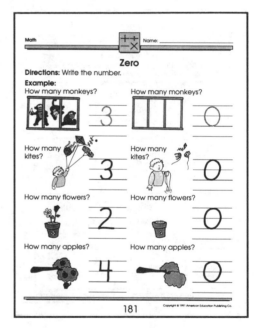

How many monkeys?   3

How many monkeys?   0

How many kites?   3

How many kites?   0

How many flowers?   2

How many flowers?   0

How many apples?   4

How many apples?   0

181

Consonant Blends: bl, cl, fl, gl, pl, sl

Directions: The name of each picture begins with a blend. Draw a circle around the beginning blend for each picture.

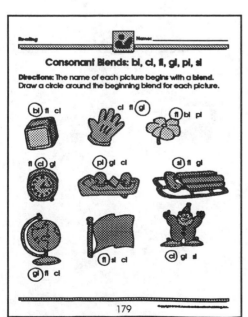

179

ABC Order

Use the first letter of each word to put the words in alphabetical order.

Directions: Draw a circle around the first letter of each word. Then, put the words in ABC order.

bird   moon   fan

car   two   nest

card   bike   pie

dog   pig   sun

182

253

I Can Write "Doing" Words!

"Doing" words tell things we can do.

Directions: 1. Follow the lines to write the words. 2. Then write the words by yourself. 3. Read the words to someone.

Like this:

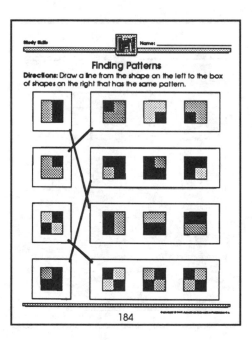

sleep   sleep

run   run

make   make

ride   ride

play   play

stop   stop

183

Finding Patterns

Directions: Draw a line from the shape on the left to the box of shapes on the right that has the same pattern.

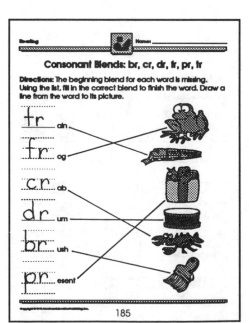

184

Consonant Blends: br, cr, dr, fr, pr, tr

Directions: The beginning blend for each word is missing. Using the list, fill in the correct blend to finish the word. Draw a line from the word to its picture.

tr ain

fr og

cr ab

dr um

br ush

pr esent

185

Simon Says

Directions: Read about how to play Simon Says. Then answer the questions.

Simon Says

SIMON SAYS CLAP YOUR HANDS!

Here is how to play "Simon Says." One kid is Simon. Simon is the leader. Everyone must do what Simon says and does. But only if the leader says "Simon says" first. Let's try it. "Simon says pat you head." "Simon says pat your nose." "Pat your toes." Oops. You patted your toes! I did not say "Simon says" first. You are out!

1. Who is the leader in this game?   Simon

2. What must the leader say first each time?   Simon says

3. What happens if you do something and the leader did not say "Simon says?"   you are out

186

Zero

Directions: Write the number that tells how many.

How many sailboats?   2

How many sailboats?   0

How many eggs?   6

How many eggs?   0

How many marshmallows?   4

How many marshmallows?   0

How many candles?   3

How many candles?   0

Copyright © 1991 American Education Publishing Co.

187

ABC Order

Directions: Circle the first letter of each animal's name. Write a 1, 2, 3, 4, 5, or 6 on the line next to the animals' names to put the words in **ABC** order.

skunk 4

dog 2

butterfly 1

zebra 6

tiger 5

fish 3

Copyright © 1991 American Education Publishing Co.

188

254

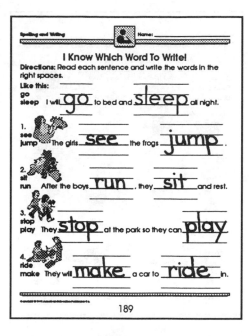

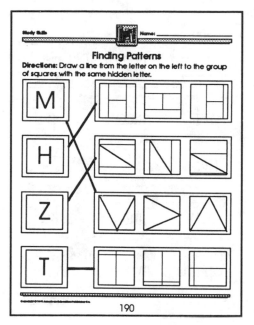

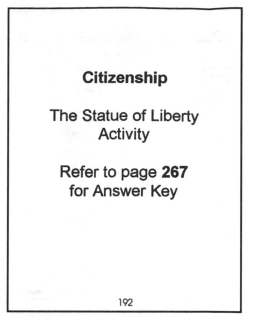

Citizenship

The Statue of Liberty
Activity

Refer to page **267**
for Answer Key

192

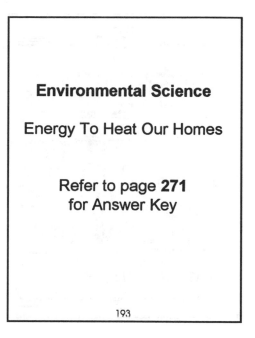

Environmental Science

Energy To Heat Our Homes

Refer to page **271**
for Answer Key

193

Citizenship

The Statue of Liberty

Refer to page **267**
for Answer Key

191

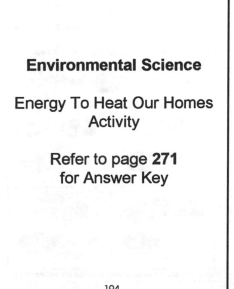

Environmental Science

Energy To Heat Our Homes
Activity

Refer to page **271**
for Answer Key

194

Consonant Blends: sk, sl, sm, sp, st, sw

Directions: Draw a line from the picture to the blend that begins its word.

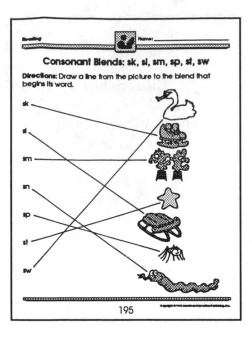

sk

sl

sm

sn

sp

st

sw

195

Look At Simon

Directions: Look at both pictures. Find 4 things in picture #2 that are not in picture #1. Look at the word list to see how to spell the word. Write your answers in the numbered spaces.

| hat | head | socks | bare | feet |
| feather | watch | untied shoes | tied shoes | |

1. watch

2. socks

3. feather

4. untied shoes

196

Addition 1, 2, 3, 4

Directions: Add the numbers. Put your answers in the nests.

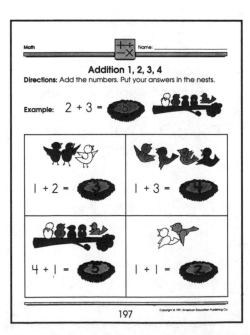

Example: 2 + 3 = 5

1 + 2 = 3

1 + 3 = 4

4 + 1 = 5

1 + 1 = 2

197

The Super E

When you add an **e** to some words, the vowel changes from a short vowel sound to a long vowel sound.

Example: rip + **e** = ripe.

Directions: Say the word under the first picture in each pair. Then, add an **e** to the word under the matching picture. Say the new word.

pet   Pete   tub   tube

man   mane   kit   kite

pin   pine   cap   cape

198

I Know Which Words Sound The Same!

Directions: Write the "doing" words that answer the questions.

| sit | run | make | see | jump | stop | play | ride |

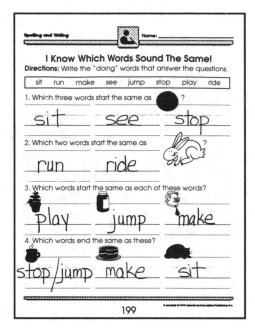

1. Which three words start the same as ⬤ ?

sit   see   stop

2. Which two words start the same as 🐰 ?

run   ride

3. Which words start the same as each of these words?

play   jump   make

4. Which words end the same as these?

stop/jump   make   sit

199

Tracking

Directions: Trace the lines to connect the shapes. Then color the matching shapes the same color.

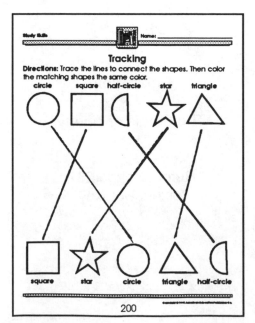

circle   square   half-circle   star   triangle

square   star   circle   triangle   half-circle

200

Consonant Digraphs: ch, sh, th, wh

Directions: Look at the first picture in each row. Circle the pictures in the row that start with the same sound.

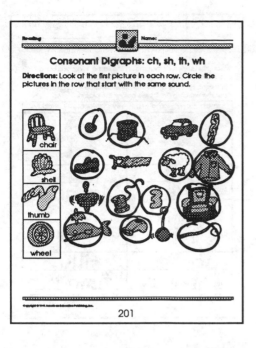

201

Do You Like Crayons?

Directions: Read about crayons. Then answer the questions.

Some crayons come in bright colors.
Some crayons come in light colors.
There are many colors of crayons.
All crayons have wax in them. Wax makes the crayon stick together.

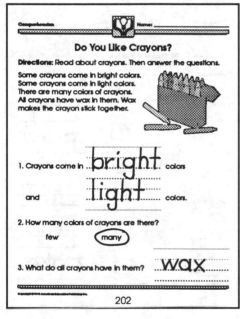

1. Crayons come in **bright** colors

   and **light** colors.

2. How many colors of crayons are there?

   few   (many)

3. What do all crayons have in them?   **wax**

202

Addition 6, 7, 8, 9, 10

Directions: Add the numbers. Put your answers in the doghouses.

Example: 4 + 2 = **6**

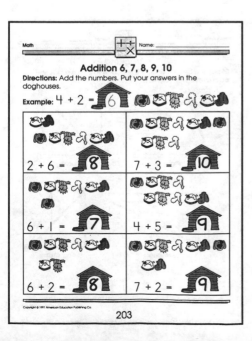

2 + 6 = **8**   7 + 3 = **10**

6 + 1 = **7**   4 + 5 = **9**

6 + 2 = **8**   7 + 2 = **9**

203

Compound Words

Compound words are two words that are put together to make one word.

Directions: Look at the pictures and read the two words that are next to each other. Now, put the words together to make a new word. Write the new word.

Example:

house + boat = **houseboat**

side walk = **sidewalk**

lip stick = **lipstick**

sand box = **sandbox**

lunch box = **lunchbox**

204

I Can Show Two Of Something!

To show two or more of something, most of the time we add "s" to the end of the word.

Like this: one cat   two cats

Directions: For each sentence, add "s" to show two or more. Then write in the "doing" word that finishes the sentence.

sit	jump	stop	ride

Like this:

The frog **s sleep** in the sun.

1. The boy **s sit** on the fence.

2. The car **s stop** at the sign.

3. The girl **s jump** in the water.

4. The dog **s ride** in the wagon.

205

Tracking

Directions: Connect the letter on the left with the same letter on the right. Use a different color crayon for each line.

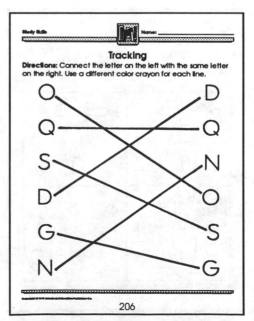

206

Consonant Blends: ft, lt

Directions: Write lt or ft to complete the words.

be | ft
ra | ft
sa | lt
qui | lt
ki | lt

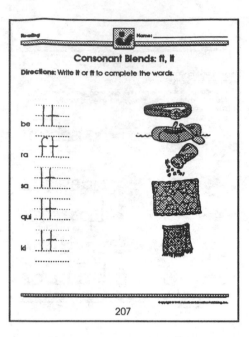

207

Synonyms

Synonyms are words that mean the same thing. Start and begin are synonyms.

Directions: Find the two words that describe each picture. Write the words in the boxes below the picture.

small	funny	large	sad	silly	little	big	unhappy

small
little

big
large

sad
unhappy

silly
funny

210

Can You Find Me?

Directions: To find the hidden picture, color only the shapes with a number inside. Do not color the shapes with a letter inside.

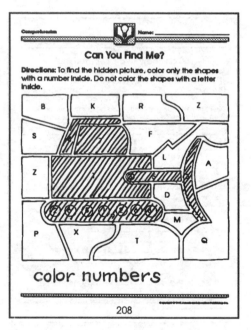

color numbers

208

I Know Which Spelling Is Right!

Directions: Circle the word that is spelled right. Then write the word the right way.

Like this:

seep
sleep
slep

sleep

paly
pay
play

play

seee
cee
see

see

rum
run
runn

run

jumm
jumb
junp

jump

mack
maek
make

make

211

Subtraction 1, 2, 3, 4, 5

Directions: Count the fruit in each bowl. Write your answers on the blanks. Circle the problem that matches your answer.

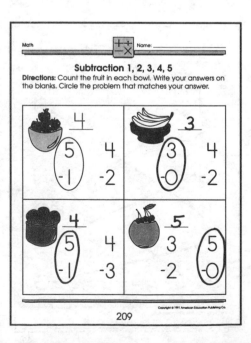

209

Tracking

Directions: Draw a straight line from A to B. Use a different color crayon for each line.

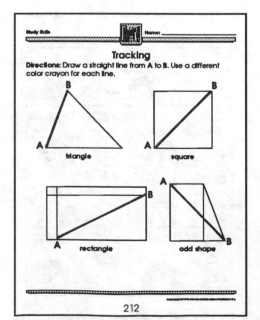

triangle

square

rectangle

odd shape

212

Consonant Blends: lf, lk, sk, sp, st

Directions: Draw a line from the picture to the blend that ends its word.

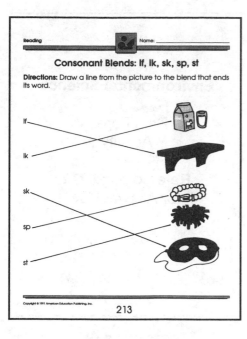

lf

lk

sk

sp

st

213

Rhyme Time

Directions: Read about words that rhyme. Then answer the questions.

Words that rhyme have the same end sounds. "Wing" and "sing" rhyme. "Boy" and "toy" rhyme. "Rhyme" and "time" rhyme. Can you think of other words that rhyme?

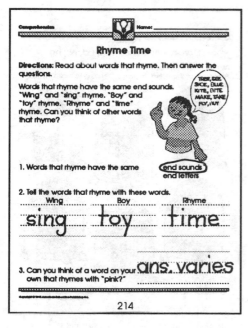

1. Words that rhyme have the same _____

2. Tell the words that rhyme with these words.

Wing	Boy	Rhyme
sing	toy	time

3. Can you think of a word on your own that rhymes with "pink"? _____ ans. varies

214

Subtraction 6, 7, 8, 9, 10

Directions: Count the flowers. Write your answers on the blanks. Circle the problems with the same answer.

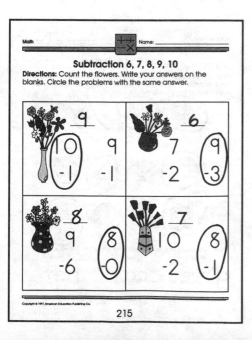

215

Antonyms

Antonyms are words that are opposites. **Hot** and **cold** are antonyms.

Directions: Draw a line between the words that are opposites. Can you think of other words that are opposites?

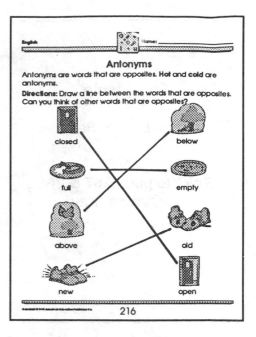

closed   below

full   empty

above   old

new   open

216

I Can Ask Questions!

Directions: Write a question about each picture. Start with "can." Add a "doing" word. Remember that a question starts with a capital letter and ends with a question mark.

Like this:

I with you can

Can I sit with you?

cookies she can

Can she make cookies?

with you can I

Can I play with you?

I can in the box

Can I see in the box?

217

Tracking

Directions: Trace 3 paths from A to B.

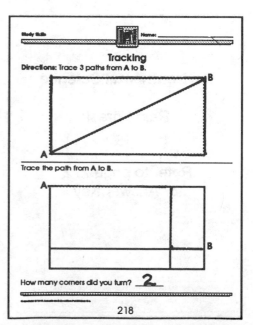

Trace the path from A to B.

How many corners did you turn? __2__

218

Citizenship

The Liberty Bell

Refer to page **267 & 268**
for Answer Key

219

Environmental Science

Rain Forest
Activity

Refer to page **272**
for Answer Key

222

Citizenship

The Liberty Bell
Activity

Refer to page **267 & 268**
for Answer Key

220

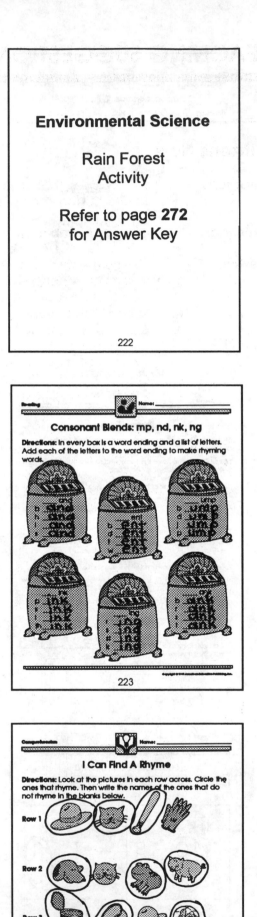

223

Environmental Science

Rain Forest

Refer to page **272**
for Answer Key

221

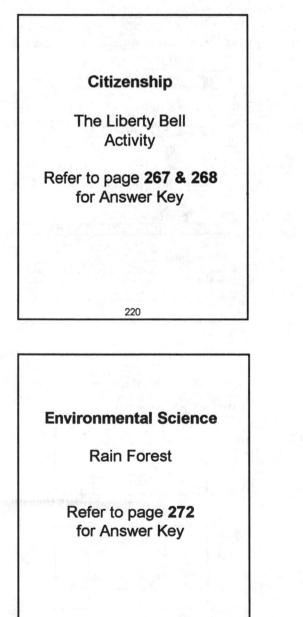

224

TEACHING SUGGESTIONS

Citizens Now
Lesson 1

Purposes:
To recognize that children are citizens
To identify the United States on a map

Materials:
classroom map, crayons, paste, large sheet(s) of paper

Prework:
Locate the United States on the Classroom map. Then read page 23 together. Point out that most people become citizens of the United States just by being born in this country. If the situation warrants, you may want to discuss circumstances in which children may not be United States citizens.

Instructions:
On chart paper draw a large outline shape of the United States. Make a collage of the children's faces on the map outline and title it **Citizens Now**. Then make a comparison/contrast chart on the board. Invite children to tell how United States citizens are the same and how they are different. Lead children to conclude that although American citizens are all different, they all live and work together in the same country. You may wish to organize the collage to allow space for the Art and Family Extension activities.

Extensions:
• Reading: Place *People* by Peter Spier on the reading table. Challenge partners to talk about how the people in the book are alike and how they are different. When children are finished sharing the book, ask them what makes the United States different from other countries.

• Writing: Ask children to finish this sentence: I am proud to be a United States citizen because_____ . Compile the sentences on a Proud Citizens chart.

• Art: Encourage children to work cooperatively to cut out pictures of all kinds of people from old magazines. Make a new collage or add the pictures to the **Citizens Now** collage.

• Family: Invite children to bring in photographs of their families or family members. Add the photos to the classroom **Citizens Now** collage.

AMERICA 2000

Purpose: To recognize that reading is important

Materials: crayons, familiar books

Prework: Read and discuss page 51 together. Be aware of children's backgrounds when presenting the idea that not all adults can read. Ask children to predict what they can do now as citizens to make AMERICA 2000 work.

Instructions: Display several familiar books. Discuss the titles and cover designs. Then read the directions on page 52. Be sure children understand that they will be drawing a cover for a book that a first grader would like to read. Ask children to cut out the book jackets. Then invite them to draw pictures of their older selves reading to first graders. Place the book jackets and the drawings on a bulletin board titled "Make AMERICA 2000 Come True."

Extensions:
- Reading: Read and discuss *My Mom Can't Read* by Muriel Stanek. In this book, first grader Tina discovers that her mother can't read and asks her teacher for help, so that she and her mother can learn to read together.

- Writing: Describe a problem a person who could not read might have.

- Math: Help children to calculate their ages in the year 2000.

- Family: Invite children to ask family members about their favorite books when they were in first grade. Compile a list and compare it with the books children enjoy today. Ask children to infer why some stories never grow old.

TEACHING SUGGESTIONS

The United States Flag

Purposes:
To recognize that the United States flag is a symbol of our country and its people
To recall places where the flag is displayed
To recognize that Sally Ride studied hard to become the first American woman astronaut

Materials:
United States flag, a piece of cloth approximately the same size as the flag, crayons

Prework:
Display the United States flag. Then show children a piece of cloth approximately the same size as the flag. Invite children to feel both the flag and the cloth. Then ask them to tell how the flag and the cloth are alike and how they are different. Lead them to conclude that the United States flag is more than just a piece of cloth because it stands for our country and its people.

Instructions:
After children have colored and cut out the flag patch on page 80, pin the patches to their left shoulder sleeves. Invite children to tell people who ask about the patch what the flag stands for.

Extensions:

• Reading: Read and discuss *Sally Ride, Astronaut: An American First* by June Behrens. Emphasize the importance of education in Sally's life by focusing on pages 12–17.

• Speaking: Remind children that the United States flag always flies over American schools. Invite small groups to discuss ways working hard in school can help them to be good **Citizens** . Instruct each group to appoint a spokesperson to share the group's responses with the class.

• Math: Invite children to work with a partner to count the stars and stripes on the United States flag.

• Family: Encourage children to ask family members to think of as many nicknames as they can for the United States flag (Old Glory, The Red, White, and Blue, The Stars and Stripes). Ask them to share their families' responses with the class.

The Declaration of Independence

Purposes: To recognize that Thomas Jefferson wrote the Declaration of Independence
To realize that the Declaration of Independence says that people have the right to be free

Materials: United States map

Prework: Point out the colonies on a United States map. Explain that this was the size of the country when the people in America decided they no longer wanted to follow England's rules. Point out that American leaders wanted a paper to be written that told why the people wanted to be free. Invite children to read page 107 to find out who wrote this important paper.

Instructions: Invite children to work with a partner to complete page 108. Circulate and give spelling assistance when necessary. Allow time for pairs to read their documents to the class.

Extensions:
- Reading: Read and discuss *A Picture Book of Thomas Jefferson* by David Adler. Ask children how Thomas Jefferson might have felt after he finished writing the Declaration of Independence.

- Speaking: Invite children to pretend they are the American leaders who approved the Declaration of Independence. Challenge them to write some comments the men may have written on Jefferson's rough draft of the Declaration. Ask: Would they mark for capital letters and periods? What about spelling? Would they talk about Jefferson's ideas?

- Physical Education: After moving outdoors or to a large open area, encourage children to demonstrate motions that make them feel free (running, arms rotating, skipping, leaping).

- Family: Encourage children to discuss with their families other kinds of official papers or documents such as licenses and diplomas. Share responses with the class and list them on the board.

TEACHING SUGGESTIONS

The White House
Lesson 5

Purpose: To recognize that the White House is where the President of the United States and his family live

Materials: map of the United States, crayons

Prework: Point out Washington D.C. on the map of the United States. Tell children that this is the city where a famous house called the White House is located. Ask children to read page 135 to find out who lives in the White House.

Instructions: Encourage children to tell about times when they have visited or seen pictures of the White House. Record their descriptions on a semantic map around the words *White House*. Talk about what the President and his family might do in their home. After children complete the living room designs, challenge groups to role play situations that might happen in the living room of the White House.

Extensions:
- Reading: Read *Arthur Meets the President* by Marc Brown. Encourage children to talk about how they would feel if they had to give a speech for the President of the United States.

- Writing: Challenge groups to use reference books and books from the library to find out interesting facts about the White House. Record the facts on a poster titled: The President's House.

- Art: Invite children to use common art material and empty boxes to design a house for the President and his family. Encourage them to name their houses.

- Family: Encourage children to discuss this question with their families: If the President of the United States and his family did not live in the White House, where else might they live? Ask them to share their responses.

Christopher Columbus   Lesson 6

Purpose: To recognize that Columbus commanded three ships that reached a land unknown to Europeans

Materials: classroom map, a globe
For each child: a toothpick, a piece of flat, recycled plastic foam from the grocery store, scissors
For small groups: a shallow pan, water

Prework: Display pictures of Christopher Columbus. Tell children that Columbus made an ocean voyage in 1492 that opened up a whole new area of the world. Then use the classroom map to point out important places connected with Columbus's voyage: Europe, Spain, the Bahamas, North, South, and Central America.

Instructions: Use a globe to show why Columbus believed he could sail west from Spain to get to the East. Ask children to conclude why he did not reach India, as he had planned. Circulate and help children construct their boats. You may want groups of three to "sail" their boats in the same container of water. Encourage children to experiment with moving the sail to change the direction of the ship.

Extensions:
   • Reading: Read and discuss *Christopher Columbus: A Great Explorer* by Carol Greene. Encourage partners to sit together and look at the famous artworks included in this book.

   • Speaking: Explain that Columbus's crew members were afraid and wanted to return to Spain. Divide the class into Columbuses and sailors. Have the sailors make up excuses to turn around and go home. Allow the Columbuses to respond to the excuses, so the sailors will push on to try to complete the voyage successfully.

   • Music: Play music with a nautical theme, such as "Sailing" by Christopher Cross or "Columbus Sailed with Three Ships" by Margaret Dugard. As in sports stadiums, invite children to do the "wave" as the music plays.

   • Family: Invite children to take their sailing ships home. Encourage them to tell their families about Columbus's ships and his voyage across the ocean.

TEACHING SUGGESTIONS

The Statue of Liberty   Lesson 7

Purpose: To recognize that the Statue of Liberty was a symbol of hope and freedom for immigrants

Prework: Draw attention to the illustration on page 191. Tell children they will be learning why the statue is important to American citizens.

Instructions: After children complete the conversation balloons, invite them to share them with the class. Compile the pages into a book titled: *We Want to be Citizens!*

Extensions: • Reading: Encourage partners to read and discuss *The Long Way to a New Land* by Joan Sandin. After reading, ask partners to retell the story of the journey of the Swedish family to America during the famine of 1868.

• Writing: Ask children to pretend they are living in another country but would like to go to the United States to live. Encourage groups to make lists of questions they would like to know about the United States before leaving their own country. Invite children to share the questions and answer as many as possible.

• Language Arts: Challenge groups to role play this situation: A new student from another country has just come into the classroom. What will you do to make this new person feel welcome?

• Family: Encourage children to ask their family members what nationalities their ancestors were. When they share the responses with the class, tally the nationalities on the board. Challenge children to count the number of different countries that are represented.

The Liberty Bell   Lesson 8

Purpose: To identify the Liberty Bell To recognize that the Liberty Bell is a symbol of our country

Materials: United States map, newspapers

Prework: Ask children to look at the picture of the Liberty Bell on page 219. Explain that like the United States flag, the Liberty Bell is a symbol of our country. Then locate Philadelphia, Pennsylvania, on a map of the United States. Tell children that this is the city where the Liberty Bell is displayed. Invite children who have visited Philadelphia to share their experiences.

Instructions: Display several simple newspaper headlines. Point out that the important words in the headlines begin with capital letters. Then have children brainstorm for possible headlines. Examples: Bell Rings for New Country, Bell Rings for Freedom. Write children's responses on the board. Use the headlines as a handwriting lesson by asking each child to carefully copy one onto page 220.

The Liberty Bell (continued)

Lesson 8

Extensions:

- Reading: For a glimpse of colonial life, read and discuss *Yankee Doodle* by Steven Kellogg. You may wish to use one of the detailed illustrations as a story starter.

- Speaking: Explain that in the 1700s ringing bells was a way people knew there was news. Point out that a town crier would often walk the streets ringing a bell and calling out the news. Invite children to take turns being the town crier by walking around the room, ringing a bell, and announcing school news.

- Art: Ask partners to make clay models of the Liberty Bell. Invite each pair to talk about what they have learned about the Liberty Bell as they work. Display the bells beneath a sign that says "Let Freedom Ring."

- Family: Challenge children to ask family members two questions about the Liberty Bell. Remind them that they should be able to answer the questions if the family member has difficulty.

Grade 1

TEACHING SUGGESTIONS

PURPOSE:
To understand the meaning of the term environment
To identify things that comprise the local environment

PREWORK:
Take a walk and ask children to point out everything around them. Lead them to discover that some of the things were made by people and others by nature. Ask them to tell if each of the things named is living or nonliving.

INSTRUCTIONS:
Read the directions on page 26 together. Then help children name each picture. After children complete the page independently, discuss the pictures they drew.

EXTENSIONS:
Challenge children to classify the items on the chart as Living and Nonliving, Made by People and Made by Nature.

Read and discuss *The Little House* by Virginia Lee Burton. (Houghton Mifflin, 1978). This 1943 Caldecott winner shows environmental changes that take place around a little house over a long period of time.

ANSWER KEY   Activity 1

TEACHING SUGGESTIONS

PURPOSE:
To recognize that all living things need clean water
To predict how polluted water can harm living things

MATERIALS:
cups, bean seeds, soil, detergent, cooking oil

PREWORK:
Ask children to name ways they use water in their homes. Discuss how they would feel if they couldn't use the water in their homes because it was dirty and unsafe.

INSTRUCTIONS:
Safety: While children are planting, observe them closely. Caution them to place the seeds only in the cups. Have them wipe up spilled water. Ask children to observe the plants daily and water them when necessary. After a period of growing time, have them return to the drawings on page 54. Discuss whether the predictions were correct.

EXTENSIONS:
Place a large processed feather in oil, and have children observe what happens. Encourage them to predict how oil spills hurt birds that live around water.

Invite children to use waterpaints to create pictures of water scenes showing clean water. Compile paintings in a book titled: "Save Our Water".

Activity 2

Name: _____

Living Things Need Clean Water

Directions: You will need cups, two bean seeds, water, soap suds, and oil. Follow each step in order.

1. Fill two cups with soil.
2. Mark the cups 1 and 2.
3. Plant a bean seed in each cup.
4. Water cup 1 with clean water.
5. Water cup 2 with water that has some soap suds and oil mixed in it.
6. Watch your seeds each day.
7. Always water cup 1 with clean water.
8. Always water cup 2 with polluted water.

Draw what you think will happen to the seeds in each cup?

CUP 1   CUP 2

Picture should show cup 1 with a healthier plant

Copyright © 1992 American Education Publishing Co.

54

ANSWER KEY   Activity 2

PURPOSE:
To recognize that air pollution is harmful to living things
To identify ways people can help make air clean

MATERIALS:
petroleum jelly

PREWORK:
Spread a thin film of petroleum jelly on a piece of paper. Attach the paper to the outside window sill. After a few days, have children observe the paper. Encourage them to infer where the dirt came from.

INSTRUCTIONS:
Invite children to read the words in the bus. Do the first example together.

Lead children to conclude that one bus carrying 30 people gives off less pollution than 30 cars each carrying one person. You may want to mention car pooling as another way to stop air pollution.

EXTENSIONS:
Challenge children to use clay, blocks, paper and other readily available items to devise models of nonpolluting vehicles that people of the future may use. Display the inventions under the sign: "2092—No More Air Pollution!"

Activity 3

Name: _____

Stop Air Pollution

Directions: Read the words in the bus. Read the sentences. Use the words in the bus to complete the sentences.

| trash | burning | walk | cars | keep |

People can use ___cars___ less.

They can ___walk___ more.

Factories can ___keep___ dirt out of smoke.

People can stop burning ___trash___.

People can stop ___burning___ leaves.

Copyright © 1992 American Education Publishing Co.

82

ANSWER KEY   Activity 3

PURPOSE:
To identify ways of keeping the school environment clean. To formulate questions

PREWORK:
Ask children to look around the room, and point out examples of pollution (trash). As each item is named, ask that child to place it in the trash can. Review sentence structure by helping children to write questions about the trash they found in the room.

EXAMPLES:
Who put the paper on the floor?
Where is the other half of the pencil?
How did the crayon break?
Point out beginning capital letters and question marks.

INSTRUCTIONS:
Alternatives to the activity on page 110.
Present children's questions to the custodian, and ask him or her to provide written answers.
Speak informally with the custodian, and record his or her answers to the children's questions.

EXTENSIONS:
Ask children to write thank you notes to the custodian. Invite them to include drawings of how they followed his or her suggestions for keeping the school clean.

Read and discuss *The Wump World* by Bill Peet. (Houghton Mifflin, 1970). Various forms of pollution are shown as the Pollutians take over the crystal clean world of the Wumps.

ANSWER KEY   Activity 4

PURPOSES:
To understand the meaning of the term recycle
To categorize items which can be recycled

MATERIALS:
newspapers, an empty glass bottle, a used metal can, address of the nearest recycling center

PREWORK:
Display a newspaper, an empty bottle and a used metal can. Help children determine what material each item is made of. Using "Paper", "Metal" and "Glass" as headings, challenge children to think of other items which would fit in each column.

INSTRUCTIONS:
Discuss the drawings and reasons for placing items in each category. Explain that in areas that do recycling, people have to use separate containers for glass, paper and metal. Have children copy the address of the nearest recycling center on the lines on page 138. Be sure they understand the location (next to the post office, in front of the grocery store, in the mall).

EXTENSIONS:
Use the drawings on page 138 as a model for a bulletin board titled; "Over and Over". Ask children to cut out their drawings or enlarge them on separate sheets of construction paper. Encourage them to bring in the items which they drew to be placed on a display table near the bulletin board.

Read and discuss "New Ways of Handling Garbage" pages 30-33 from the series *A New True Book, Soil Erosion and Pollution* by Darlene R. Stille (Childrens Press, 1990).

ANSWER KEY   Activity 5

270

TEACHING SUGGESTIONS

PURPOSE:
To review and evaluate skill development for lessons on air, water, land and the environment

PREWORK:
Ask children to turn to the glossary. Explain that a glossary is a list of hard words from the book. Read and discuss the glossary explanations for earth, environment, polluted, pollution, school custodians, and recycle.

INSTRUCTIONS:
Point out the front cover of the booklet on page 165. Ask each child to print his or her name on the line. Then read the sentences on pages 165 and 166 together. When children are finished drawing, help them order the pages. Staple the pages for each child.

EXTENSIONS:
Invite students to share their booklets with another class.

ANSWER KEY   Review #1

PURPOSE:
To evaluate information about solar homes

PREWORK:
Ask children to close their eyes and visualize sitting at the pool or beach on a hot summer day. Ask them to describe what the sun feels like.

INSTRUCTIONS:
For children having difficulty drawing a conclusion for question 2, ask:
What do the plates and sheets on the roofs of solar homes collect? (sunlight)
What kind of weather is best for collecting sunlight? (sunny)
Besides sunny days, what are some other kinds of days? (cloudy, rainy)
Do all places have a lot of sunny days? (no)

EXTENSIONS:
Invite children to design newspaper ads for solar homes. Attach their ads to the pages of a local newspaper and place the newspaper on the reading table.

Read and discuss the poem "sun" from *small poems* by Valerie Worth. (Farrar, Straus, Giroux, 1972). Challenge children to write small poems about the sun's heat. Display their poems in a place where the sun shines in the room.

Ask children to record the number of sunny days on a calendar. After a month, form discussion groups to determine whether solar homes would be practical for the month in which they recorded the weather.

ANSWER KEY   Activity 6

PURPOSES:
To construct a simple if/then statement
To understand why rain forests should not be destroyed

MATERIALS:
crayons

PREWORK:
Ask children to describe what happens when they are sick. Record their responses in sentence form using the words if and then.

Examples:
If I am sick, then I will go to the doctor.
If I am sick, then I can't go to school.
Point out that the same event can have different outcomes.
Tell them it is important to think of all the different things that might happen.
Practice with other examples.

INSTRUCTIONS:
Ask children to recall what they read about the rain forest on page 221. Remind them that several different things might happen if the people chop down the trees. Ask them to choose just one thing to write on the line. Discuss the if/then statements and their drawings of what happened next.

EXTENSIONS:
Help children use research books to do oral reports on some of the strange plants and animals of a rain forest.

Read and discuss *The Great Kapok Tree* by Lynne Cherry (Harcourt, Brace, Jovanovich, 1990) In this beautifully illustrated book, animals who live in the branches of a Kapok tree in the Amazon rain forest beg a man with an ax not to destroy their home.

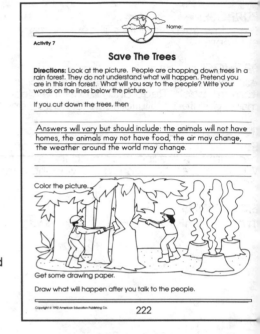

ANSWER KEY   Activity 7

PURPOSE:
To understand the purpose of wild animal refuges

PREWORK:
After reading page 249, draw children's attention to the illustrations. Explain that at one time only 21 whooping cranes were left in the world. Tell children that one way people have saved the whooping crane is by protecting them in refuges in Texas and Canada. Ask: What would a whooping crane need in its refuge? Point out that long ago thousands of elk died because people took over the places where they lived. Explain that refuges such as the National Elk Refuge in Wyoming have helped save the elk. Ask: What would a refuge for an elk be like?

INSTRUCTIONS:
Before reading page 250, ask children to think about books, movies and TV programs that showed the American bison, sometimes called the buffalo. Have them brainstorm for ideas about bison. Ask children to read page 250 to find out how the bison were saved. When the have completed the maze, invite them to

EXTENSIONS:
Invite children to devise mazes that help a lost elk or whooping crane find refuges. Compile their mazes in an Amazing Refuges book.

Read and discuss *Heron Street* by Ann Turner (Harper & Row, 1989). Invite children to repeat onomatopoeic words especially those of the animals as they are displaced from their marsh by the sea — "sqwonk-honk, chee-hiss, aroooo!".

ANSWER KEY   Activity 8